African American Cultural Theory and Heritage
Series Editor: William C. Banfield

The Jazz Trope: A Theory of African American Literary and Vernacular Culture, by Alfonso W. Hawkins Jr., 2008.

In the Heart of the Beat: The Poetry of Rap, by Alexs D. Pate, 2009.

George Russell: The Story of an American Composer, by Duncan Heining, 2010.

Cultural Codes: Makings of a Black Music Philosophy, by William C. Banfield, 2010.

Willie Dixon: Preacher of the Blues, by Mitsutoshi Inaba, 2011.

Representing Black Music Culture: Then, Now, and When Again?, by William C. Banfield, 2011.

The Black Church and Hip Hop Culture: Toward Bridging the Generational Divide, edited by Emmett G. Price III, 2012.

The Black Church and Hip Hop Culture

Toward Bridging the Generational Divide

Edited by
Emmett G. Price III

THE SCARECROW PRESS, INC.
Lanham • Toronto • Plymouth, UK
2012

Published by Scarecrow Press, Inc.
A wholly owned subsidiary of The Rowman & Littlefield Publishing Group, Inc.
4501 Forbes Boulevard, Suite 200, Lanham, Maryland 20706
http://www.scarecrowpress.com

Estover Road, Plymouth PL6 7PY, United Kingdom

British Library Cataloguing in Publication Information Available

Library of Congress Cataloging-in-Publication Data

The Black church and hip hop culture : toward bridging the generational divide / edited by Emmett G. Price III.
p. cm. — (African American cultural theory and heritage)
Includes bibliographical references (p.) and index.
ISBN 978-0-8108-8236-2 (cloth : alk. paper) — ISBN 978-0-8108-8237-9 (ebook)
1. African American churches. 2. African Americans—Religion. 3. Hip-hop. 4. Hip-hop—Religious aspects—Christianity. I. Price, Emmett George.
BR563.N4B5645 2012
277.3'08308996073—dc23
2011032607

♾™ The paper used in this publication meets the minimum requirements of American National Standard for Information Sciences Permanence of Paper for Printed Library Materials, ANSI/NISO Z39.48-1992.

Printed in the United States of America

This work is respectfully dedicated to my personal champions of faith who along with others gave (and prayed) so that I and those in my generation could have access and opportunities.

"Aunt Evelyn" Porché
"Auntie Lillian" Henry
"Auntie Shirley" R. Hurst
Commie Lee "Grandaddy" Armstead
Carrie Lee "Madea" Armstead
David "Papa Dave" Thompson
Emmett G. Price Sr.
Geraldine "Mom Mason"
"Grandma Mary" Thompson
Laura O. "Mama" Coco
Morris "Uncle Red" Porché Sr.
Olivia "Tee Tee" Porché French
Mattie B. "Mama Dear" Thompson
Moses L. "Grandpa" Gayle Sr.
Rev. Dr. Eliott J. Mason Sr.
"Uncle Andrew" Henry
"Uncle Oscar" A. Rollins

Contents

Acknowledgments   ix

Introduction   xi

Part I: From Civil Rights to Hip Hop   **1**

 1 From Civil Rights to Hip Hop: A Meditation   3
Alton B. Pollard III

 2 Dissed-Enfranchised: The Black Church under the Steeple   15
Joshua Hutchinson

 3 Chasing a Dream Deferred: From Movement to Culture   21
Emmett G. Price III

Part II: Hip Hop Culture and the Black Church in Dialogue   **31**

 4 Deep Calls to Deep: Beginning Explorations of the Dialogue
between the Black Church and Hip Hop   33
Charles L. Howard

 5 Rap Music as Prophetic Utterance   43
Cynthia B. Belt

 6 Binding the Straw Man: Hip Hop, African American Protestant
Religion, and the Dilemma of Dialogue   55
Lerone A. Martin

 7 Sermon: "Kick Your Delilah to the Curb"   63
Sherman A. Gordon

 8 Thou Shall Have No Other Gods before Me: Myths, Idols, and
Generational Healing   67
Shaundra Cunningham

 9 Hip Hop Children of a Lesser God   81
Paul Scott

10 Sermon: "Bling Bling"   85
Stephen C. Finley

11 Formality Meets Hip Hop: The Influence of Hip Hop Culture on
the Afro-European Church   95
Shana Mashego

Part III: Gospel Rap, Holy Hip Hop, and the Hip Hop Matrix   **105**

12 Beats, Rhymes and Bibles: An Introduction to Gospel Hip Hop   107
Josef Sorett

13 Isn't Loving God Enough? Debating Holy Hip Hop   115
Cassandra Thornton

14 Five Theses on the Globalization of Thug Life and 21st Century
Missions   131
Kenneth D. Johnson

15 Hip Hop, Theology, and the Future of the Black Church   153
Osagyefo Uhuru Sekou

16 Confessions of a Hip Hop Generation Minister   159
Patricia Lesesne

17 Spiritually Educating and Empowering a Generation: Growing
Up in a Hip Hop Matrix   165
René Rochester

18 An Invisible Institution: A Functional Approach to Religion in
Sports in Wounded African American Communities   173
Onaje X. Offley Woodbine

19 "To Serve the Present Age": A Benediction   189
Emmett G. Price III

Selected Bibliography   193

Index   ·197

About the Editor and Contributors   205

Acknowledgments

Praise God, from Whom all blessings flow;
Praise Him, all creatures here below;
Praise Him above, ye Heavenly Host;
Praise Father, Son, and Holy Ghost. Amen.
—Thomas Ken [1]

This book is the result of an intense journey that has taken many detours. From the initial concept in 2005 to its publication, numerous authors joined and departed the project for a host of valiant and legitimate reasons. I am grateful to all the contributors who not only made this project possible but provided thought-provoking, carefully constructed critiques and intellectually stimulating suggestions catalyzing generational healing. The authors could have completed their own manuscripts; instead, we agreed to participate in this dialogue to showcase the power of participation even when there is a difference in approach. I extend my gratitude to the expert and patient staff at Scarecrow Press. From the early interactions with Corinne O. Burton to the culminating conversations with Stephen Ryan, the Scarecrow staff has been diligent, detailed, and determined to move this project to fruition. I must express my most sincere gratitude to my dear friend and colleague Dr. William "Bill" C. Banfield for the initial invitation to publish with Scarecrow and, further, for the placement of this collection within the prestigious African American Cultural Theory and Heritage series.

I extend my gratitude to each of my teachers, mentors, and colleagues who have inspired, encouraged, and chastised me to stay true to what is shaping out to be my life's work. Further, I extend my gratitude to the many spiritual leaders who have impacted my life, my thoughts, and my beliefs. I would be remiss if I did not express my gratitude to my peers, contemporaries, and countless numbers of individuals who are part of the Hip Hop Generation both by choice and based on our dates of birth. We have the challenge of defining our own contributions to the rich legacy of our ancestors without minimizing the foundation that they laid for us. We have much work to do!

I extend my gratitude to my family for their patient endurance as I engaged in yet another one of my "projects." To my parents, Emmett G. Price Jr. and Carolyn J. Price, for their unyielding example of what it means to live, love, and lead; to Robert F. Gayle and Gloria T. Gayle for their exuberant encouragement and steady support; to my siblings, Melanie N. Price and Everett B. Price, and nephew, Elon Carruthers, for the courage and determination to navigate their own journeys of faith with all the obstacles that come with it.

Finally, I extend my gratitude to my wife, Nicole, for her beautiful strength and stunning brilliance. Thank you for "being you!" To my sons, Emmett George Price IV ("Bud") and Nicholas Robert Price ("Nick")—may you one day aspire to attain all of the things I once reached for but was not tall enough to grab. I am extremely proud of you both!

To God Be the Glory!

NOTE

1. Although "Praise God, from Whom all blessings flow" is most often referenced as a doxology in the Protestant church, it actually was introduced to the church by Thomas Ken (1637–1711), an Anglican Bishop who composed the hymns "Awake, My Soul, and with the Sun" and "Glory to thee, my God, this night." "Praise God, from Whom all blessings flow" served as the final verse of both hymns.

Introduction

If the Black Church were more vigilant toward the needs, concerns, and desires of its youth and young people during the late 1960s and early 1970s, there probably would be no Hip Hop Culture. Although a strikingly convicting statement, the sentiment is worth pondering. Throughout the 1950s and 1960s, the Black Church stood as the stronghold of the Black Community, fighting for equality and economic self-sufficiency and challenging its body to be self-determined and self-aware. The Black Church also served to offer large doses of spiritual centering to offset the rather racist aggression by unyielding provocateurs of hatred. From its very emergence during slavery, the Black Church was a response to the systematic and obstructive oppression at the hand of those with political power and economic means. An assemblage of small congregations emerged within the hush harbors under the cloak of invisibility, wherein these gatherings of saints emotionally and physically supported one another while spiritually uniting to petition, with a sense of urgency, for their own survival and the promise of hope for their offspring. The Black Church, as it would later emerge, has always been a collective of diverse clusters of disciples whose unity is based not on one liturgy but in the shared petition that God "would never leave nor forsake" them (Hebrews 13:5). Although it has been perceived as a homogeneous and monolithic institution, the Black Church has never been such. In fact, its early history is a poignant indicator of its present reality in ways that are revealed in this volume. As twenty-first-century scholars, homilecticians, pulpiteers, and even laypersons continue to debate whether the Black Church is alive or dead, the realization should be evident that as long as there is injustice, inequity, and imbalance in the Black Communities of the United States of America, the Black Church has a lifeline, a mission, and an opportunity to rise to the occasion.

From the days of the Free African Society and the first Black Baptist Churches (eighteenth century) through the rise of the African Methodist Episcopal Denomination, the African American Episcopal Zion, the Christian Methodist Episcopal, the National Baptist Convention, Inc. (USA), the National Baptist of America Inc. International, Progressive National Baptist Convention, Inc., the Church of God in Christ, the United House of

Prayer, the Church of Christ (Holiness), the Pentecostal Assemblies, the Apostolic Assemblies, the United Holy Church, National Black Catholic Congress, and numerous other organized clusters of peoples of faith, including the Nation of Islam and the Five Percent Nation of Gods and Earths, the Black Church, in its various manifestations and segments, has and remains relevant. The Black Church is alive, and, like any living organism, it has (individually and collectively) made some critical errors.

The Black Church has a fascinating, rich, and deep history—a history that has not only championed the survival, liberation, and equality of Black folks (and all folks) but struggled to delve into the internal chasms of generational difference. In many ways, the story of the Black Church is a narrative that puts so much focus on the future that limited time, energy, and resources were allocated to protecting the present. As the Black Church, through the various mantles of local congregations of various denominations, prayed for liberty and justice for all, a schism formed within the belly of the Black Community. Similar to the Black Church, the Black Community is an assemblage of numerous communities across the United States of America that find their common narrative as descendants of the African Diaspora in the United States, connected through the shared cultural characteristics passed down from generation to generation that both codify and code "Blackness." Although creative artists such as Paul Laurence Dunbar ("We Wear the Mask," circa 1896), Meta Warrick Fuller ("Ethiopia Awakening," circa 1910), Zora Neal Hurston (*Their Eyes Were Watching God*, 1937), Margaret Walker ("For My People," 1937), Jacob Lawrence ("Migration Series," 1941), and Duke Ellington (*Black, Brown and Beige*, 1943) captured the sounds, sentiments, and sensations of the Black experience in United States, it was award-winning filmmaker Marlon Riggs (*Black Is, Black Ain't*, 1995) who best pointed out that although we can describe what it is to be Black, it is extremely challenging to define, codify, and capture the holistic experience within a neatly constructed definition. Within the Black Community lie various strands of philosophical thought, theological belief, and very practical differences that have created difficult existences for many. It is clear that one can be a part of the Black Community and have a tremendously different experience than others. This reality is not limited to Black people, as no ethnic or racial enclave of people is as homogeneous or monolithic as stereotypical analysis might pose. Yet, among the diversity of expressions within the Black Community, there is no greater dilemma than that of the generational divide.

GENERATIONAL DIVIDE

From the days of Bishop Richard Allen and Bishop Absalom Jones, the difference in opinions on liturgy style and approach to worship created segmentation. During the late eighteenth century, both Allen and Jones were members of Philadelphia's interracial St. George's Methodist Church. After an altercation of blatant racism within the congregation, both departed to found the Free African Society. The two were challenged over decisions to associate with the Episcopal denomination or whether to establish a more innovative and progressive mantle of faith for Blacks. Jones founded the African Episcopal Church of St. Thomas and was later elevated to bishop. Allen would establish the Bethel African Methodist Episcopal and, subsequently, the African Methodist Episcopal denomination. Although it has not been exaggerated in previous scholarship, Jones and Allen were fourteen years apart, and it is possible that that fourteen-year gap may have aided in the determination of whether assimilation and accommodation were the best course of action, as opposed to creation and segmentation. It is clear that throughout the eighteenth, nineteenth, and twentieth centuries and even now into the twenty-first century, the challenge remains as to the question of segmentation and denominationalism within the church.

The Black Church is not the only prevalent ground for age-driven fractionalization. During the early years of the twentieth century, Booker T. Washington and W. E. B. DuBois would engage in a national debate over the best course of progress for the Negro. Washington, an exceptional educator, orator, and political leader, advocated that young people should focus attention on industrial education and the slow and steady accumulation of wealth. DuBois, an esteemed educator, pan-Africanist activist, and exemplary writer, articulated the investment of the community in the "exceptional," the "Talented Tenth." Note that Washington, considered conservative, was twelve years DuBois's senior.

During the 1960s, much attention was placed on polarizing the Reverend Dr. Martin Luther King Jr. and El-Hajj Malik El-Shabazz (aka Malcolm X) as diametrically opposed to each other. Yet, another reading through the reflective eyes of privilege reveals that there was actually an aged generation of elders who were opposed to both of them, due to their both rocking the boat of steady progress and potentially creating a frenzy that might take things backward instead of forward. It was the elders of the National Baptist Convention that would eventually create enough tension to create an exodus of relatively young pastors to establish the Progressive Baptist Conference. Likewise, it was a rather youthful cohort of former Nation of Islam devotees who would aid Brother Malcolm in establishing the Organization for African Unity. The generational divide is neither a unique consideration nor is its presence anything new.

From the historic debates on segregation versus integration to the debates over the prestige and power of Historically Black Colleges and Universities over the acceptance of Blacks into previously predominantly White institutions, these debates have continued to be evidence of eras of generational divide. A recent tipping point was captured during the 2007 frenzy launched by Bill Cosby's "Come on People" remark at the NAACP's Fiftieth Anniversary Celebration of the historic *Brown vs. Topeka Board of Education* Supreme Court case, which infuriated legions of folks on both sides of the generational aisle and ironically impacted the pulpits and pews of Black Churches across the nation as folks decided whether to agree and side with Cosby or join the prolific writer, orator, and philosphico-socio-politico Michael Eric Dyson, who responded loudly with *Is Bill Cosby Right? Or Has the Black Middle Class Lost Its Mind?* With twenty-two years of life experience separating the two, there was no splitting the fence; the Black Community had to take a side.

No previous generational divide has been as extreme, volatile, and destructive as the present divide between the Civil Rights Generation and the Hip Hop Generation. Hip Hop Culture grew from the soundscape, canvas, and battlegrounds of the concrete jungles of New York's well-known boroughs, inspired as a self-determined response by ostracized, disenfranchised urban youth who felt that they had no support system or resources. With no heroes in plain sight, these youth, passionate with the same urgent desires for survival and hope that their parents and grandparents carried, created their way from the bottom of America's belly one rhyme, piece, and step at a time. It was early Hip Hop Culture that courageously stood against gang warfare, guns, narcotics, and youth-on-youth violence. Rappers (and MCs), DJs (and turntablists), Breakers (and dancers), and Graffiti artists effectively and critically advocated for democracy through freedom of expression, social commentary, political debate, and economic critique. It was the next generation of this arising Hip Hop Community that begged for better schools, better health care, better playgrounds, better opportunities, and equal access for themselves and for their parents and grandparents. Cultural awareness became an early trademark of the multiethnic, multiracial, multifaith community of young people who desired to create the better existence that their parents, grandparents, godparents, aunts, and uncles (whether they were praying people or not) were not able to give them. For many young people during this early period, Hip Hop Culture was the supplement to the weekly dose of Sunday morning faith. Hip Hop Culture was "in addition to," as opposed to "instead of." The Hip Hop Generation proselytized and catechized through their innovative creations, allowing their intimate spirituality and articulated faith to bleed through their creative expressions. Trinitarian Protestant thought, as well as recitations of Islam, Five Percent Nations of Gods and Earth, Rastafarian, Judaism, Buddhism and beyond, permeated the lyrics, symbolisms, imagery, and fashion. The role of spirituality, faith, and religion in Hip Hop Culture has always been strong, even as we wrestle with the most current status of Gospel Hip Hop, Holy Hip Hop, or any of the other monikers. Rap/Hip Hop expressions have been inclusive of belief statements, faith tenets, and theological frameworks throughout the brief history of Hip Hop Culture, yet many in the Black Church have not felt comfortable with the new methods, modes, and manners of expressions.

On the first page of the opening chapter of *The Truth behind Hip-Hop*, Elder G. Craige Lewis posits that he will reveal "how hip-hop is destroying the lives of many, as they seek to be entertained by a supernatural influence that is beyond their natural control." Although I value Elder Lewis's commitment to truth and revelation, I would argue that we should be more concerned with the number of clergy and congregations who are turning their sanctified backs on the volatile youth who need to be loved (whether they are a part of the Hip Hop Community or not). Tirades of accusations of Hip Hop as being demonic, satanic, and essentially evil disregard the simple fact that in all human creative endeavors, there are some things that are widely appreciated and well received and others that are distasteful, not useful, and unpalatable. Yet, the presence of polar opposites does not negate the importance of the overall expression and the acknowledgment that the expressers availed themselves as vulnerable beings to share.

Although Hip Hop Culture in the twenty-first century is different from its infant state in the late 1960s and early 1970s, its urgent cries, moans, groans, and hollers remain consistently focused on the same survival, liberation, and equality that the Black Church has fought for over the generations. In fact, although the Hip Hop modus operandi is dramatically and drastically different, perhaps even polemic, Hip Hop and the Black Church are essentially fighting for the same thing and that is what makes this question of the dilemma of the generational divide and the initial and subsequent disengagement of the Black Church so intellectually perplexing.

This collection of writings from leading thinkers, preachers, scholars, and practitioners from around the country serves to give voice to a growing movement within the Black Church to deal with the dilemma of the generational divide and to consider new approaches to restoring health, vitality, and intergenerational dialogue between the Civil Rights Generation and the Hip Hop Generation and, subsequently, all generations. Conceived as an extension of previous conversations initiated by Anthony Pinn (*Noise and Spirit: The Religious Sensibilities of Rap Music*), Benjamin Stephens III and Ralph C. Watkins (*From Jay-Z to Jesus: Reaching and Teaching Young*

Adults in the Black Church), and Ralph C. Watkins, Jason A. Barr Jr., Jamal-Harrison Bryant, William H. Curtis, and Otis Moss III (*The Gospel Remix: Reaching the Hip Hop Generation*) and numerous others, the contributors in this volume have surpassed the simple goal of assessment to wrestle with the more challenging duties of providing timely commentary, critical analysis, and, in some cases, practical strategies toward forgiveness, healing, restoration, and reconciliation. This began in 2006 as an attempt to gather a few voices from within the fold to initiate a conversation (with a clear intent to have some of the voices be female); it has now turned into a rally call to challenge the generations to come back to the table to settle differences and move forward together. In many ways, this collection serves a greater community beyond the Black Church. Hip Hop Culture is an international phenomenon, and it has challenged the norms and traditions of numerous institutions beyond those conceived of faith. From the entertainment industry to the United (and Non-United) Nations to international commerce, Hip Hop Culture has had a dynamic influence. It has challenged traditional thought, and through the simultaneous rapid emergence of technology, it has challenged the ways that we communicate with one another, both in the United States and abroad. Many around the world are looking to the Black Church to take note on how we respond, react, and relate to the growing international dominance of Hip Hop Culture. So in many ways, this collection perhaps serves as a case study in acknowledging not only the issue but the prophetic role of the church to offer practical approaches to restoring health, vitality, and intergenerational dialogue where there is such lack.

Divided into three sections, this volume does not propose to be exhaustive; in fact, our sole aim is to be more effective in stimulating, inspiring, and encouraging dialogue. It is our collective goal to use this volume to challenge the Black Church and Hip Hop Culture to realize their shared responsibilities to each other and to the greater society.

Part I, "From Civil Rights to Hip Hop," explores the transition from one generation to another through the transmission of legacy and heritage or lack thereof. Each provocative piece examines the generational passing of the baton in unique fashion only to arise at the same conclusion: the Black Church must reengage in the lives of the youth and young adults who compose the Hip Hop Generation. It is mandatory, it is necessary, and it is urgent! In the opening piece of the section, Alton B. Pollard III offers "From Civil Rights to Hip Hop: A Meditation," based on a lecture delivered at Spelman College as part of its 2006 Distinguished Lecture Series. In this poignant diachronical examination of the legacy and heritage of the Black Freedom Struggle, the Howard University School of Divinity dean challenges the reader to position Hip Hop Culture as an extension of the struggle and an opportunity for ostracized communities to come together in the pursuit of a "just and inclusive world." Joshua Hutchinson follows with

"Dissed-Enfranchised: The Black Church under the Steeple," challenging the church to reclaim its traditional values and teachings, such as the importance of community and family. According to Hutchinson, the impact of the successes of previous generations has led to the demise of current and future generations due to a shift in values and priorities. This dynamic shift is explored in the closing piece, "Chasing a Dream Deferred: From Movement to Culture," where I use Lorraine Hansberry's *A Raisin in the Sun* to expose a broader realization of the generational divide while charging the church (and the Hip Hop Community) to reconnect, reconcile, and recommit to the collective pursuit of liberty, justice, and equality for all.

Part II, "Hip Hop Culture and the Black Church in Dialogue," explores the multitude of ways, shapes, and forms through which the conversation is already going on, with a prophetic gaze toward heightening and intensifying the dialogue. From sermons to theoretical examinations and spiritual ponderings, this part is riveted with stimulating discoveries, inspiring reflections, and empowering commentary. University of Pennsylvania chaplain Charles L. Howard leads the way with "Deep Calls to Deep: Beginning Explorations of the Dialogue between the Black Church and Hip Hop," by drawing attention to the numerous "contact points, intersections, and integrations" that the two share. Focused on moving the dialogue toward progressive results, Howard challenges both the church and the culture by offering strategies of success grounded in prophetic reflection. Pastor Cynthia B. Belt continues the challenge for fruitful dialogue with "Rap Music as Prophetic Utterance." Here she mixes practical experience and scriptural mandate to demand more accountability in the dialogue between the Black Church and Hip Hop Culture. Prof. Lerone A. Martin follows with "Binding the Straw Man: Hip Hop, African American Protestant Religion, and the Dilemma of Dialogue," a piece that offers his profound thinking around the central question "How can African American faith communities address and respond to Hip Hop Music and Culture in a manner that is faithful to the mission of Jesus Christ and correspondingly addresses the realities of African American life?" In the first of two sermons in the volume, Pastor Sherman A. Gordon offers another method and example of the ongoing dialogue that occurs during weekly worship experiences: "Kick Your Delilah to the Curb" reveals one of many ways in which this cross-generational dialogue occurs from the pulpit. Rising cultural critic and ordained minister Shaundra Cunningham penned "Thou Shall Have No Other Gods before Me: Myth, Idols, and Generational Healing," a piece that spotlights the reality of idol worship in both the Black Church and Hip Hop Culture. She boldly challenges us to relinquish the finger-pointing in exchange for much-needed transparency and confession with the desired goals of reconciliation and unity. With "Hip Hop Children of a Lesser God," prolific writer and esteemed activist "Truth Minista" Paul Scott offers a critical commentary of the ongoing dialogue, with the final assessment that both sides of the conversation are in desperate need of more TRUTH. In the second of two sermons, Prof. Stephen C. Finley offers "Bling Bling," a unique homiletical experience that presents yet another example of the cross-generational dialogue via the pulpit. Transcribed from a Youth Day service, this sermon offers one of many approaches of making biblical text and commentary practical and relevant to a multigenerational congregation. Closing is Prof. Shana Mashego's innovative exploration of the dialogue occurring within the forgotten Black Churches within predominately non-Black denominations (Catholic, Methodist, Lutheran, Episcopal, and Presbyterian). "Formality Meets Hip Hop: The Influence of Hip Hop Culture on the Afro-European Church" mixes personal reflection and scholarly analysis to reveal yet another layer of the ongoing dialogue.

Part III, "Gospel Rap, Holy Hip Hop, and the Hip Hop Matrix," introduces to some and emphasizes for others the perspectives and insights of practitioners, scholars, and activists from within the fold who are eager to share, with the hope that clarity would lead to engagement. Readers will explore the multitude of expressions of faith and the diversity of locations where these expressions take place. Prof. Josef Sorett's captivating "Beats, Rhymes and Bibles: An Introduction to Gospel Hip Hop" is the first of two pieces that are previously published. Reprinted from the winter 2006–2007 edition of *The African American Pulpit*, Sorett's work offers one of the first critical examinations of Gospel Hip Hop; it is a "must read" for all endeavoring to do ministry in the twenty-first century. Likewise, Cassandra Thornton's "Isn't Loving God Enough? Debating Holy Hip Hop" offers a provocative look at Holy Hip Hop from the inside out. Also known as DJ Lady Grace, Thornton offers insight into the ongoing debates concerning Holy Hip Hop using personal insight and scriptural backing. In the second of two reprinted contributions, scholar and consultant Kenneth D. Johnson offers "Five Theses on the Globalization of Thug Life and 21st Century Missions." Previously published in the *Antioch Agenda: Essays on the Restorative Church in Honor of Orlando E. Costas* (2007), this piece is effective in challenging the church to realize the global effect and impact of Hip Hop Culture. Esteemed activist and scholar Rev. Osagyefo Uhuru Sekou offers a theological read on Hip Hop Culture through personal reflection and by challenging the lens through which we see our young people. Rev. Patricia Lesesne, an administrator in the Broward County (Florida) Public School System, offers her personal struggle with attempting to empower and influence the next generation in "Confessions of a Hip Hop Generation Minister." Based on personal reflection and grounded in hope, Lesesne's prose grants us an eye-opening revelation of the urgency for generational bridging. Expert educational consultant Dr. René Rochester offers "Spiritually Educating and Empowering a Generation: Growing up in a Hip

Hop Matrix." This is an intriguing response to the central question "What do we do if a young person's existing knowledge of biblical truth is what they have learned in a song or from imitating the appearance of Holy Hip Hop?" and it is a clever description and examination of the Hip Hop Matrix. Rising African and African American religious thought scholar Onaje X. Offley Woodbine offers an important hypothesis of basketball as religion in "An Invisible Institution: A Functional Approach to Religion in Sports in Wounded African American Communities." He reveals basketball as a religious project that responds to suffering and can lead toward healing. As the book began with a meditation, it is fitting to close in the tradition with a benediction. "'To Serve the Present Age': A Benediction" is my attempt to close the volume with gratitude, in petition, and with the acknowledgment that our collective efforts are futile without the power of prayer.

I am grateful for each contributor to the project. Each has made himself or herself a vessel of ministry in one's own unique way, and it is our collective prayer that this work be beneficial in all the various ways that it may.

Part I

From Civil Rights to Hip Hop

Chapter One

From Civil Rights to Hip Hop: A Meditation

Alton B. Pollard III

When Spelman College asked me to address the subject "From Civil Rights to Hip Hop," to explore with a group of young African American women the profound connections that exist between our recent past and the present moment, I was very pleased and deeply honored.[1] I was also filled with no small amount of fear and trepidation. In the first and second place, I am not a member of the Hip Hop generation. I am a proud member of the "soul" generation that precedes it, offspring of those spirituals and blues and gospel and R&B and jazz children hewed out of hard living, who migrated from the "Black Belt" of the rural South to the cities and from there to all points North and West.

It was the work of scholar-activists such as Vincent Harding and his epic text *There Is a River: The Black Struggle for Freedom in America* that first led me into the cascading and darkly radiant depths of the Black-led freedom movement in this land. Upon reflection, I decided to share some words with those of you who may be very much like me, who need to rediscover or perhaps discover for the first time some of the resources that can serve to inspire and empower us as a people on the journey to self-understanding and sustained commitment in a very unsettled time. I hope you will allow me to share with you stories of hope and struggle from my life to yours, from my experiences to yours, from my faith to yours.

I invite you, as members of the Hip Hop generation, to remember and never to forget that there is something infinitely worthy about the Black freedom struggle, that even and especially now there is something that yields the clue that testifies to the fact that the visitations of the spirit to our ancestors in this land, whether four hundred years ago or forty, are far from over. In the post–September 11 world, there has been a veritable retreat from progress toward a radically inclusive society and a reactionary tendency to demonize, criminalize, and marginalize that magnificent Black-led movement of militancy, mass struggle, and hope a generation ago. Indeed, the nation appears ready to turn back the clock in many such respects. Fortunately, African Americans did not choose to respond in kind to such blatant racism and wanton disrespect. Instead, we have embraced our historic legacy—sometimes haltingly, at times falteringly—and experienced continual renewal. We receive our separate past as a wellspring, a touchstone, a fount, a present source of strength. This is our sacred calling and our moral responsibility.

I recount the story of that sacred struggle here in narrative form. The first story briefly calls to remembrance the horrific saga of the Black movement from enslavement to freedom. The second story attends with greater depth to the struggle for freedom at mid-twentieth-century America. The third and most expansive story turns to the contemporary struggle for Black freedom being led by young people. Through the lens of history and culture, I want to bear witness to that long and continuous, marvelous and unyielding belief that Black people have always had and continue to have in their own humanity.

THE *MAAFA*

The moment of our transfiguration as a people began with the transatlantic transport of Africans to the Western hemisphere, the mainlands of North America and South America, the New World. Before this time, modern notions of African unity and "race" were relatively unknown.[2] Deep in the bowels of foul and squalid European ships with names such as *Justice, Liberty, Grace, John the Baptist, Mary,* and *Jesus,* the children of Africa—Fula, Bambara, Ibo, Iboni, Fulani, Karamanti, Ashanti, Jolof, Fanti, Hausa, Mandingo, Yoruba, Dahomey, Bini, Efik, Congo, Moco, Mondongo, Sengale, Ga, Fon, Kru, and more—came to experience the height of human alienation and disorientation. They cried out their misery to God—Nyame, Yala, Olorun, Imana, Mawu, Olodumare, Meketa, Ondo—each in their native tongue. Forcibly removed from family, friends, and all that is sacred, to be deposited in lands hostile and unknown, there are not words enough to convey the agony, despair, and bewilderment, the confusion in mind, body, and spirit, the fear and apprehension that surely seized these innocents.

The *Maafa*—a Kiswahili term for the Middle Passage and impending African Holocaust—was an unspeakable and world-altering horror for untold millions. Out of the belly of the beast, the macabre would be forever seared into the memory of the captives, a memory passed on to their children and their children's children. Questions were without ceasing: How could human beings be so evil? How could one group of people justify treating other people like this? What manner of creatures were these Europeans called Spanish and Portuguese, Dutch and French, Saxon and Dane? For Africa's dispersed, our foremothers and forefathers, a nefarious nightmare, hell on Earth, had begun.

The year 1619 and the settlement of Jamestown, Virginia, are often chosen as the time and place to refer to the beginnings of African America, despite historical accounts that date back one century before, to the territory that would become South Carolina and the first recorded acts of Black resistance on this side of the *grandywaters* (the Atlantic Ocean) in 1526.[3] Thus began for Africans in this land, the uprooted of many cultures, religions, and tongues, a unifying assessment of the meaning of their involuntary presence in a strange land and a fundamental recognition that freedom would not be freely given but arduously won—and never enough.

CIVIL RIGHTS AND BLACK CONSCIOUSNESS

By 1965, almost 350 years after Jamestown, the children of Africa in America numbered well over twenty million. It is almost a cliché to say that the civil rights years were unlike any other period in the history of the nation. But the truth is seldom as neat or simple as it sounds. Hard lessons had to be learned as African Americans gradually disabused themselves of moderate notions about White America with continuing racial discrimination, the status quo ante, and an at-best cautious federal government. Young women and men such as Diane Nash, Ruby Doris Smith, Prathia Hall Wynn, Anne Moody, James Bevel, James Lawson, Bob Moses, and John Lewis pressed the adult generation to assume a less gradualist and more militant and activist posture. Shortly before his death, Martin Luther King Jr. offered these prescient thoughts on the power and meaning that young people brought to the insurgent liberation struggle:

> Young Negroes had traditionally imitated whites in dress, conduct, and thought in a rigid, middle-class pattern. . . . Now they ceased imitating and began initiating. Leadership passed into the hands of [Blacks], and their white allies began learning from them. This was a revolutionary and wholesome development for both.[4]

As the sixties went on, youthful militancy deepened and solidified, challenging more and more of the ideology, customs, and practices of Black complacency and White supremacy. Sit-ins at lunch counters, kneel-ins at churches, wade-ins at beaches, sleep-ins at motels, and freedom rides across interstate lines transformed the national landscape. College students, high school students, and elementary school children courageously withstood the punishment meted out in hundreds of cities, towns, and rural communities and withstood the political indifference emanating from the corridors of power in Washington, DC.

The leaders of the Student Nonviolent Coordinating Committee were a hard core of emboldened and impassioned students who—along with their White allies—plunged into civil rights work. For the most part, they were first-generation Black college students, Northern as well as Southern, who quickly drew around them the poor, unemployed youth of the rural areas, elevating the movement to populist stature and broadening and deepening the meaning of Black emancipation with their youthful audacity and radicalism. The "shock troops of the movement" continued to grow and metamorphose and change, as the freedom movement passed out of the South and to the North and West and raised the provocative and necessary call for "Black Power."

These were the children of those great fallen heroes, Martin and Malcolm and Medgar, and of women warriors such as Ella Baker, Septima Clark, Fannie Lou Hamer, Myrlie Evers, Betty Shabazz, Rosa Parks, Jo Ann Robinson, Coretta Scott King, and Queen Mother Audley Moore. It is important, too, that we not underestimate the influence of such African stalwarts as Jomo Kenyatta, Julius Nyerere, Sékou Touré, Patrice Lumumba, and Kwame Nkrumah. Stokely Carmichael, Angela Davis, Eldridge Cleaver, Kathleen Cleaver, Huey Newton, Elaine Brown, Erika Huggins, David Hilliard, Francis Carter-Hilliard, Frances Beal, and Assata Shakur were among the growing number of young Black leaders who did not agree with the strategies of the elders but cared enough to answer the call, to summon the courage, to become active participants in the struggle to change their own lives and the lives of their communities.

These were also the fierce young warriors of well-known groups such as the Black Panther Party for Self Defense, the Black Liberation Army, the Republic of New Africa, and the African Peoples Party. In response to the triple threat of sexual, class, and racial oppression, "comrade sisters" developed the Black Women's Liberation Committee and the Black Woman's United Front. Laborers organized the Detroit Revolutionary Union Movement and the League of Revolutionary Black Workers; socialists established the February 1st Movement; cultural nationalists founded the United Slaves (or U.S.); and religious nationalists started the Shrine of the Black Madonna. And there were countless local groups at the grassroots. These young people, gang members, high school and college students, literally became the carriers of the fire—not so much the destruction of urban explosions that was exploited by some and misrepresented by others—but women and men who carried in their hearts and minds the burning embers of justice and the relentless fires of liberation. Theirs was a searing anger and fearlessness that refused to accept the status quo, the taken-for-granted business as usual. They believed enough in the possibility of societal change to "fight the power," to try to rebel. (Is it any wonder that the defiant message struck by the Isley Brothers would resurface years later in the seminal rap anthem by Public Enemy?)

The echoes of urban rebellion carried over well into the seventies. On hundreds of college campuses, African American students organized and fought for change in curriculum, administration, admissions policies, racist pedagogy, and educational ethos. Black history classes and Black studies programs emerged, swiftly followed by ethnic studies, women's studies, and a growing consciousness about our African and Two-Thirds World connectedness. They drank from the deep, intellectual, and philosophical wells of Frantz Fanon, Cheik Anta Diop, John Henrik Clarke, Walter Rodney, Chancellor Williams, and countless others. But there was more to come, far more, a tremendous outpouring of artistic energy, which served to connect Black politics, Black Power, and Black consciousness with the masses. At the heart of this magnificent outpouring were such poets as Mari Evans, Ed Bullins, Askia Muhammad Touré, June Jordan, Haki Madhubuti, Amiri Baraka, Kalamu ya Salaam—and Muhammad Ali. Black collegians, movement activists, and community people turned to these prophetic voices who, like them, were seeking to re-create themselves and the nation. Holding out their hands, reaching out with their lives, refusing to let their own woundedness prevent them from making essential connections, these artists found poetry in the people, among the people, with the people, for the people, by the people, as they sought to live out the serious and glorious meaning of their beautiful Black gift.

Black women were especially prominent among the artist-activists, from Sonia Sanchez to Nikki Giovanni and Carolyn Rodgers to reencounters with Margaret Walker, Maya Angelou, and Gwendolyn Brooks. Into the present, their voices can still be heard singing, shouting, wailing, compressing anger, sorrow, and promise into the cadences of their poetic utterances. And there were the musicians of that not-so-distant time, Mahalia Jackson, John Coltrane, Sun Ra, Aretha Franklin, James Brown, Marvin Gaye, Nina Simone, the Impressions, the O'Jays, Stevie Wonder, Gill Scott-Herron, the Last Poets, Bob Marley and the Wailers, and Sweet Honey in the Rock, who opened us to new and provocative ways of oppositional engagement and democratizing self-understanding. To their leadings and promptings and more, a generation listened and learned and danced and fought—and prayed.

RAP AND HIP HOP

That was three decades ago. Today, we are once again undergoing fundamental and incontestable generational and societal change. Now as then, there is division and tension, conflict and change, rivalry and respect, old school and new school, within African America. I, for one, cannot rap, scratch, graffiti, deejay, emcee, or flow. Those who know me would probably say that I don't dance all that well either. However, I see the same divine presence that was at work during the era of civil rights and Black consciousness pervasive in Hip Hop music and Hip Hop culture today. I see it in the growth, innovativeness, and empowerment of my own young adult children, and I see it everywhere. I see it in the oral, musical, and cultural traditions as old as African drumbeats now turned into new art forms. I see it in our largely uncelebrated, ever resourceful and resilient, intergenerational strength. I am the affirmation of our past. I bear witness to our future. I am the transmission of ancestral memory. I am the premonition of Hip Hop.

I am in full agreement with Patricia Hill Collins, who sees the end of civil rights and Black Power and the ascendancy of Hip Hop as being marked by a shift from a color-conscious racism that relied on a system of racial segregation to an apparently color-blind racism that promised equal opportunities yet provided no lasting avenues for African American advancement. All protests notwithstanding, "the new colorblind racism claimed not to see race yet managed to replicate racial hierarchy as effectively as the racial segregation of old."[5] African American youth, in all their ways, stand at ground zero of a complex of intersectionalities including race, gender, sex, ethnicity, class, environment, and more. In the glare of the mass media, in their bodies and with their very lives, they symbolize the contradictions of the new racism.

Just beyond the mass media's pornographic obsession with and magnification of the excesses of contemporary urban Black life—sex, violence, drugs, antiauthoritarian and materialistic life (a real and contradictory consciousness that we ignore to our own peril)—there exists a larger Hip Hop lifestyle, a deeper and oppositional mode of expression that struggles to live within society's tension and seeks to give voice to young people long denied their say. It is the creative power of this generation, the perennial prerogative of the young, the right to be culturally subversive, to potentially transform themselves and the world around them. It is historically represented in the rhymes of KRS-One, Chuck D, Tupac Shakur, and Biggie Smalls. It is manifested in the antisexist message of MC Lyte, Sister Souljah, and Salt-N-Pepa. It is embedded in the metonyms of the Million Man March anthem "Where Ya at Y'All." It flows from the Hip Hop feminism of Queen Latifah, Eve, Missy Elliott, and Lauryn Hill. It is the higher knowledge characterized by Common, the members of De La Soul, the Roots, Mos Def, Talib Kweli, Dead Prez, Nas, and A Tribe Called Quest. It is the spoken-word tapestries woven by Jessica Care Moore and Sarah Jones. It is the power, passion, and poetry of Kanye West, Maxwell, John Legend, Kardinal Offishall, and Anthony Hamilton. It is the sultry, sophisticated, and expressive soul of Mary J. Blige, Erykah Badu, Jill Scott, and Destiny's Child. It is the uncommon compositions and lyric declarations of Alicia Keys, Me'Shell NdegéOcello, and India.Arie.

Regrettably, not everyone agrees with this assessment. There are powerful discussions for us to have about whether cultural potential still exists for organizing young people to transform themselves and their community. In simple terms, do we prefer serious Black Panthers or serious drug dealers and addicts? Do we prefer to establish serious agendas for Black communities or become Black clones of White mainstream America? Are there perhaps other choices? Lest we forget, no generation is perfect, and none of us are exempt from critique. But for complex reasons, now more than ever, the great divides of race, gender, sexuality, and class are falling along the fault line of intergenerational misgivings and distrust.

This is certainly the case where African America is concerned. All too often, the civil rights generation is ready to decry the amnesia and irresponsibility of the Hip Hop generation. With equal eloquence and even greater defiance, the Hip Hop generation trumpets the death of all civil rights sensibilities. (However, I am always amazed to meet young Black women and men who distance themselves from Hip Hop and rap.) Somewhere between these oppositional views and antithetical stances lies the much-needed cross-generational recognition that we as a people are only as strong as our weakest link. Simply stated, we need the lessons of civil rights and Hip Hop. Civil rights is African America's sacred legacy. Hip Hop is this era's sacred hope.

A myriad of complex social realities define the world of the Hip Hop generation, from globalization and resegregation in the public sphere to deradicalization and commercialization in religious places. Despite what some critics have said, today's young people are no less spiritual than their predecessors but live in a time when the loss of faith in social institutions—no less religious ones—is disturbing, understandable, and epidemic. Many Hip Hop heads speak truth to power saying, "I'm spiritual but I'm not religious." Whatever else one may make of Mase—who left the Hip Hop world at the height of his success in 1999, started his own ministry here in Atlanta (SANE—Saving a Nation Endangered Church International), returned to the rap scene with his *Welcome Back* album (by his previous standards neither a critical nor commercial success), and reportedly defected to 50 Cents's G-Unit and his original gangsta roots (Murder Mase), all while still maintaining the status of pastor—his story mirrors the seldom-recognized but vast and aching spiritual void found in much of Hip Hop America.[6]

Like the Rev. Al Green before him, Rev. Run of Run-DMC fame is navigating the worlds of the sacred and profane with his CD *Distortion*. In 2004, the aspiring minister Kurtis Blow sought to bring his turntables into two renowned Harlem churches. In 2005, Kanye West struck multiplatinum with the triple video and megahit release "Jesus Walks" (to say nothing of his head-turning *Rolling Stones* cover).[7] The versatility of Faith Evans is heard on Donald Lawrence's award-winning gospel album *I Speak Life*. Famed rapper and actor LL Cool J features gospel artists Mary Mary on his 2006 disk *Todd Smith*.

Christianity is hardly the only religion game in town. As Imani Perry notes in *Prophets of the Hood*, the submerged underground of rap is populated with the religiopolitical lyrics of groups such as Brand Nubian and the Poor Righteous Teachers, informed by Islam and other religious traditions.[8] To the point, there is a passionate quest for something deeper and more authentic than what often passes for religion in the current generation. If the Black faith community would serve the present age, it requires a far greater commitment to social struggle and a deeper dedication to young people than what is currently the case. Questionable theology, dubious politics, hierarchical practices, misogynistic behavior, mythic untruths, excessive materialism, and an utter captivity to custom are the hallmark of many African American congregations in the twenty-first century. It could even be said that Hip Hop had to be born because, among other reasons, Black believers were no longer being faithful to their own calling.

If Hip Hop would claim its rightful place as the successor of the civil rights movement—and I think it must—there are at least four factors that have to be considered. We have already discussed the need to join Hip Hop and faith where coexistence is possible and where mutual integrity and respect can be maintained. In the second place, Hip Hop will have to establish a more intentional economic and political sensibility than what currently exists. Bakari Kitwana lays out the beginnings of such a constructive blueprint in *The Hip Hop Generation*.[9] Unfortunately, his otherwise-progressive political platform suffers from lack of a much-needed gendered perspective.[10]

With Hip Hop, a twenty-first-century multibillion-dollar industry, and with a proliferation of artists counted among its millionaires, the entrepreneurial spirit of artists such as Master P, Jermaine Dupri, Queen Latifah, and P. Diddy (with various levels of wealth and street legitimacy all) must be encouraged to assume a more progressive economic and leadership presence in African American communities. It is interesting to note, for example, the growing stable of Hip Hop superstars who are now part owners of professional basketball franchises, including Jay-Z (NBA, New Jersey Nets), Nelly (NBA, Charlotte Bobcats), Usher (NBA, Cleveland Cavaliers), and Michelle Williams of Destiny's Child (WNBA, Chicago Sky). That the NBA/WNBA is wildly successful in its marketing campaign to Hip Hop America goes without saying.[11] What remains to be seen is whether and to what degree Hip Hop moguls will similarly commit to doing good for the 'hood, to investing in economic development and growth in local Black communities.[12]

On a more visceral level, the celebration of "Versace values," "many mansions," and "Nike ethics," while signifying and counterhegemonic on its face, effectively reinforces norms of economic disparity that disproportionately affect Black people. The Hip Hop nation must be careful to attend to root causes and never lose sight of its own organic and creative roots, for the great and final portent of capitalist production and commodification—cultural displacement—is co-optation and assimilation of the Hip Hop aesthetic itself. On both a theoretical and a political level, Hip Hop has the capacity to enjoin a movement again, to challenge and critique the social and economic devastation being wrought in Black communities everywhere. The pivotal question is whether Hip Hop culture yet knows the extent of its own potential to model local, national, and global change.

Third, the possibility of a progressive political philosophy has become more apparent of late. "Why," the standout song from rap lyricist Jadakiss featuring Anthony Hamilton, asks questions about a lot of things that he thinks people all over the world want to know.[13] Even more famously known are the televised comments of Kanye West (who was featured on a 2005 cover of *Time* magazine as "the smartest man in hip-hop") after the natural and social destruction left in the wake of Hurricane Katrina.[14] Kanye got it right with his refreshingly candid and provocative statement: "President Bush does not care about Black people."[15] Right enough that a remake of his song "Gold Digger" (renamed "George Bush Don't Like Black People") became an underground hit.

At the same time, West's statement needs to be nuanced and complicated—the permanent Black poor are but one of a number of communities who are devalued by America's political process for lack of political capital. West did not set out to be a role model with his words, but like much of Black America, he was hurt and enraged that in 2005 it was still alright to denigrate and neglect poor people, the majority of whom looked like him. In the spirit of Hip Hop, West gained further street credibility with his spontaneous improvisation. By engaging in subversive verse and unscripted critique, he contested the political boundaries, placing principles over profit and morals over money, for at least one dark shining moment. Soon thereafter, Master P launched Team Rescue to assist evacuees. Sean "P. Diddy" Combs and Jay-Z donated $1 million to the Red Cross, as well as clothing from their respective companies. In the aftermath of Katrina, one may hope that we will now see the emergence of a real and substantive Hip Hop politics (although we still await a like response from the Hip Hop community to West's indictment of the genre's homophobia).[16] More mainstream but constructive efforts have come from Russell Simmons's Hip-Hop Action Network and P. Diddy's "Vote or Die!" initiative, both of which contributed to an upswing in the numbers of eighteen- to twenty-nine-year-olds who voted in the 2004 presidential election.

Finally, Hip Hop must engage in honest and critical self-interrogation for the promotion of sexist, misogynistic, and homophobic tendencies among too many of its creators, composers, and consumers. In this connection, one need only refer to Nelly's now infamous "Tip Drill" video, in which he swipes a credit card through a woman's backside, or Buju Banton's equally repulsive and homophobic anthem "Boom Bye-Bye," which decrees gays "haffi dead" ("have to die"). At the same time, too many non–Hip Hop heads are quick to overlook the very real and constructive dimensions of youth culture and rap and Hip Hop in their rush to disrespect the lifestyle and uncritically perpetuate bourgeois values. Racist and patriarchal society has helped to create a climate where young Black women are seen as promiscuous reproductive machines and where young Black men are viewed with animal and criminal contempt.

On one hand, Hip Hop as contested culture is highly marketable and salaciously satisfying to its consumer base. On the other, its purveyors are vilified daily as the primal and hypersexual antithesis of privileged White culture. This is why in "middle America," patronage of the form by White (and not a few Brown and Black) youth—youth who frequent suburban malls and soccer fields and attend "good schools"—becomes problematic when their indulgence lasts more than a season, while for White, Brown, and Black poor and working-class youth it is a different (or rather indifferent) story altogether.   In   hegemonic-capitalist-White-supremacist-patriarchal-heterosexist culture, unregulated Black female bodies and embedded Black male domination are interconnected representations that function to justify new and evermore-subtle (and not-so-subtle) forms of race relations management.[17] Much more could be said on this subject, but I offer this concluding observation: By companioning together young Black women and young Black men, as equals and comrades, as lovers and friends, Hip Hop can unsettle the present and enter the future self-determining, conscientized, creative, and whole. When joined as allies—Latino/Latinas, indigenous peoples, poor people, same- and opposite-gender-loving people, racial-ethnic immigrant people, progressive people, cross-generational people, faith-filled people—a just and inclusive world may finally become possible.

From civil rights to Hip Hop—these are the two great cornerstones of the modern African American freedom movement: Civil rights laid the groundwork for the transformation of society. Hip Hop now has the opportunity to reinvent the future of the United States and the world and take us there.

NOTES

1. The Distinguished Lecture Series at Spelman College, February 23, 2006.
2. See, for instance, Michael A. Gomez, *Reversing Sail: A History of the African Diaspora* (Cambridge, UK: Cambridge University Press, 2005), 72.
3. For further background, read Vincent Harding's magisterial history *There Is a River: The Black Struggle for Freedom in America* (New York: Harcourt Brace Jovanovich, 1981), and John Hope Franklin's classic *From Slavery to Freedom: A History of Negro Americans*, 8th ed. (New York: Knopf, 2000).
4. Martin Luther King Jr., *The Trumpet of Conscience* (New York: Harper & Row, 1968), 46.
5. Patricia Hill Collins, *From Black Power to Hip Hop: Racism, Nationalism, and Feminism* (Philadelphia: Temple University Press, 2006), 3.
6. Efrem Smith and Phil Jackson have initiated an important discussion of the relationship between Hip Hop and Christian faith in their recent book *The Hip-Hop Church: Connecting with the Movement Shaping Our Culture* (Downers Grove, IL: InterVarsity Press, 2006). Michael Eric Dyson offers early important parallels in his *Between God and Gangsta Rap: Bearing Witness to Black Culture* (New York: Oxford University Press, 1996).
7. Lola Ogunnaike, "The Passion of Kanye West," *Rolling Stone*, February 9, 2006.
8. Imani Perry, *Prophets of the Hood: Politics and Poetics in Hip-Hop* (Durham, NC: Duke University Press, 2004), 148–54.
9. Bakari Kitwana, *The Hip-Hop Generation: Young Blacks and the Crisis in African American Culture* (New York: BasicCivitas Books, 2002). Other notable Hip Hop authors and cultural critics include Todd Boyd, *The New H.N.I.C.: The Death of Civil Rights and the Reign of Hip-Hop* (New York: NYU Press, 2002); Mark Anthony Neale, *New Black Man* (New York: Routledge, 2005); and Derrick P. Alridge and James B. Stewart, eds., "The History of Hip-Hop," a special issue of the *Journal of African American History* 90, no. 3 (2005). Not to be forgotten is the Hip Hop literary anthem by Sister Souljah, *The Coldest Winter Ever* (New York: Pocket Books, 1999). A number of popular Hip Hop autobiographies have been published as well.
10. One thinks, in this regard, of such scholars as the aforementioned Perry, Gwendolyn D. Pough, *Check It While I Wreck It: Black Womanhood, Hip-Hop Culture, and the Public Sphere* (Boston: Northeastern University Press, 2004); Patricia Hill Collins, *Black Sexual Politics: African Americans, Gender, and the New Racism* (New York: Routledge, 2005); Joan Morgan, *When Chickenheads Come Home to Roost: My Life as a Hip-Hop Feminist* (New York: Simon & Schuster, 1999); and the classic work by Tricia Rose, *Black Noise: Rap Music in Contemporary America* (Middletown, CT: Wesleyan University Press, 1994), among others.
11. Part ownership in the NBA, while typically 15 percent or less, can pay major dividends for the NBA/WNBA and Hip Hop industries. See "NBA Markets to Urban Crowd with Superstar Owners," *ESPN*, March 2, 2005, http://sports.espn.go.com/espn/wire?section=nba&id=2003468.
12. Hip Hop impresario Russell Simmons and other artists and entrepreneurs were recently profiled for their growing grassroots philanthropy in *Worth* (April 16, 2006): 57–64.
13. Jadakiss, "Why," from the album *Kiss of Death*, Ruff Riders, 2004.

14. On the aftermath of Katrina, see Alton B. Pollard III, "Wade in the Water: A Meditation on Race, Class, and Katrina," in *The Sky Is Crying: Race, Class, and Natural Disaster*, ed. Cheryl Kirk-Duggan (Nashville, TN: Abingdon Press, 2006).

15. Kanye West, *A Concert for Hurricane Relief*, NBC telethon, September 2, 2005.

16. Hear and read the MTV interview "All Eyes on Kanye West," http://www.mtv.com/bands/w/west_kanye/news_feature_081805/index3.jhtml.

17. While I extend the analogy further, bell hooks is well known for coining the phrase "imperialist white-supremacist capitalist patriarchy" to describe the interlocking political systems that are foundational to the extant social order. See her provocative essay "Sexism and Misogyny: Who Takes the Rap? Misogyny, Gangsta Rap, and the Piano," *Z* magazine (February 1994), and e-commentary "Understanding Patriarchy," at http://arizona.indymedia.org/news/2004/07/20613.php.

Chapter Two

Dissed-Enfranchised: The Black Church under the Steeple

Joshua Hutchinson

The Black Church is in denial.

Many critics of the church and Black Religion have charged that the Black Church has its head in the sand. Others challenge that the Black Church is ignorant of the ever-changing environment that it purports to operate in or that the Black Church is an island in the River Denial refusing to bridge itself to the very communities that it claims to serve. I argue, however, that the Black Church is an isolated nation of wealth in the Ocean of Denial, refusing to join, address, or even concern itself with the many ills that still plague the Black Community.

The very organization that has been the epicenter of the Black Community since the days of slavery chooses to preach financial prosperity over brotherhood and sisterhood. The result of this, both within and beyond the church, is an era where fathers *and* mothers are absent from the home. Their children are left to their own devices of violence and torture. Both parent and child and those persons in between are seeking a false sense of being in sex, drugs, and money, items that aren't being addressed by the Black Church. HIV and AIDS are epidemics in our community along with other diseases that are products of poor health and nutrition, and the Black Church still chooses not to address them. Drug use and the distribution of drugs is a pandemic in our community, and the Black Church on the whole still chooses not to address these items either. While the popularity of prosperity is allegedly increasing, poverty and poor health care still reign supreme within our community.

Many of these tribulations have been sitting on the proverbial table for several decades. Yet, in saying this, none of these tribulations have been fully addressed en masse and in force. It is almost as if the Black Church is waiting for these topics to go stale, if not disintegrate. Rather, it has evolved into a cancer-ridden mass that nobody chooses to acknowledge. Still, it is the very thing we cannot ignore . . . anymore.

The sad reality is that the Black Church and the Black Community can come together to resolve (or at minimum recognize) these cancers but, to this point, have not done so. Regrettably, we are a people divided within a church and a community between the haves and the have-nots, the young and the old, but ultimately brother/sister against brother/sister.

An archivist once stated that the effect of a generation today was caused by something that happened two generations ago. Our parents tried to differ from their parents, and we likewise do the same. In essence, we are the product of the chain of events that our grandparents set forth with our parents.

Sounds elementary?

Sure.

The theory is elementary, but the complications come when the grandparent generation (the Civil Rights Generation, as it is respectfully christened) and the Hip Hop Generation (the latest generation) face off in the community as well as the church. The Civil Rights Generation looks at the fruits of its labor—that is, the Hip Hop Generation—and finds few buoys of pleasantries in the general sea of disappointment. While the Hip Hop Generation pays homage to its elders, it too has much displeasure, mostly in the state of abandonment. This—along with the transitional generation caught in the middle (a parental generation that can link itself to either generation)—causes three generations to be disenfranchised based on the timeless battle of tradition versus innovation.

In previous generations since the days of slavery, the Black Church has slowly undergone a change from the religious pillar it was on the plantation to the social and political platform it served in many communities during the Civil Rights Movement. The social and political activism from that era created a spawn that has transformed the Black Church into a conglomerate, in step with American capitalism. In this latest adjustment, the natural attempt was to be the successor of the social and political avenues that the Civil Rights Generation laid forth in agreement with the religious and spiritual foundation from the past. Unfortunately, the state of the Black Church today is more in conjunction with the merchants that Jesus eventually drove out of the temple in Jerusalem. The Black Church no longer offers a place of spiritual growth, religious stance, or social beaconing. And the political views of the Black Church, in spite of some conflicting stances that are blatantly against the Black Community, have chosen political parties of all things rather than be political in position, as it once was.

Because of the ailments mentioned here, the Black Church has pulled away from the Black Community. Moreover, the ever-prevalent gap between churchgoer and nonchurchgoer has altered into a state where it has become more of a customer-to-business relationship using God's name as a tagline, rather than a parishioner-to-pastor relationship that has dominated the centuries. The generational split of the Black Church is the result of the fact that neither of the two finite generations—the Civil Rights Generation and the Hip Hop Generation—have a stronghold on the Black Church.

This brings several questions to mind: If neither generation has a stronghold on the Black Church, who is in control of the current state of the Black Church? If the Black Community is no longer the focus of the Black Church, who or what is? The two-prong question then becomes this: Is the current direction of the Black Church something we aspire to follow, and who has the right to worship under the steeple in this current direction?

The current dilemma, if it can truly be called that, concerning the Black Church is that neither the Civil Rights Generation nor the Hip Hop Generation has control of it. Yet, both generations are looking for the other to correct the current state. Luckless to say, both and neither of the generations have control. Not absolute control. The power appears to lie in the transitional generation: the parental generation, caught between the epitomes of the Civil Rights Generation and the Hip Hop Generation. Of course, this isn't necessarily a surprise, nor much different from the changing of the guards, so to speak. What is unique about this transition is that these two generations have the largest discrepancy than any other period in African American history, leaving this transitional generation to referee between the Civil Right Generation and the Hip Hop Generation while trying to construct a plan that caters to both ends of the spectrum.

The reason for the huge discrepancy between the two generations is that the Hip Hop Generation is the aftereffect of integration. It is the only generation to date to never experience a period of segregation or separation outside of its tolerable form. Because of this, the Hip Hop generation has no strong sense of community and church, primary items lost in the project of integration that were further destroyed by drugs entering the communities, as well as by various other economic prospects. Therefore, the sense of unity that had been the pillar of Black lineage since the time of slavery was broken after the Civil Right Era.

Neither generation, like many generations beforehand, knows how to talk to the other—thus leaving the people caught between these two generations to act as translator of tradition and originality, which proves to be more of a feat since there is one generation that remembers the struggles of great oppression and a generation that has never experienced it in its true essence.

The problem with this transitional generation is that it failed to find a median between the two standing generations. The Civil Rights Generation, after being granted legal equality, soon began its work to make it a part of the American social fabric. The emerging Hip Hop Generation, however, was faced with another set of problems: street violence and drugs flooding into the community. Though the benefits of integration outweighed segregation, it too came with much backlash, weakening the overall Black Community. The Black Church, then in the hands of the Civil Rights Generation, began to lose clout in the vanishing community as it became more evident that it was losing touch with the ever-changing landscape.

Passing the church on to its children, the transitional generation, in a state of crisis, faced two major burdens: items from the past and items from the then present—thus leaving two extreme contrasting variables that in no way could be dealt with in the same manner or even at the same time.

And here is where the fallout began. The transitional generation saw and understood to large degrees what struggles their parents, the Civil Rights Generation, went through for equality. Because of this, the transitional generation had a blueprint of how to fight battles that went against discrimination—the leading reason why the Black Church can mobilize against discrimination over any other topic facing it or the Black Community. However, to tackle the issues of the forthcoming generation (the Hip Hop generation), the transitional generation gave its children, sadly, the best advice it had to offer, which was the message of "go to church" with no real mode of defense against a fading community. The Hip Hop Generation felt defeated since the church, during the Civil Rights Era, was used to forge boycotts, sit-ins, marches, campaigns, and other organizations against the ills of that time.

The key element that the Hip Hop Generation and the transitional generation lacked to even attempt to stage those kinds of events was a steadfast sense of community. It never became a cohesive ingredient, for various reasons that stemmed back to the disenfranchisement of the Black Community during the Civil Rights Era. When the Hip Hop Generation was able to turn community tragedies into glorious amounts of wealth without any connection to the Black Church, the Black Church changed its tone in turn. It began to abandon its community support, and it began to take a more "individualistic" approach, falling more by the wayside on many issues that, ironically, still connect the disenfranchised Black Community.

A great example of this is the HIV/AIDS epidemic ravaging the Black Community and, in many respects, the Black Church. We are the highest minority infected with new cases each year, yet and still, the Black Church is treating it like the gay White disease it was initially branded more than twenty years ago. Church leadership acts as if the ills of the Black Community have no connection to the Black Church when, in fact, the Black

Church could have been the greatest active prevention educator against the epidemic, as a way to say that it is in tune with the needs and the ills of the community, as it did during the Civil Rights Era, instead of sitting comfortably in a culture of denial. While the Black Church can pat itself on the back in the role that it has played in the Civil Rights Movement, it must understand that the same Black Community is in the battle for its life right now.

As for this individualist doctrine adopted by many within the Black Church, it overshadows a community-based, communal message; it also lacks any strong message in the sense of family. So what is left? There are several factors left, including the Black Community, but most, if not all, of the factors have been deemed too "controversial" or too heavy for the church as a whole to handle. So, it has chosen one individualistic goal that is sought after by just about everybody—financial prosperity.

The message of financial prosperity has been the blessing and the curse of the Black Church. It appeals to newfound wealth gained by the Hip Hop Generation and the transitional generation to remove itself from isolation of money to an association of it rather than a place of divine growth.

The downfall of that message is that most of these people are walking away from the church with a feeling that God has blessed them with financial wealth, rather than finding the blessing in waking up each day and in spiritual growth. This isn't to say that the Black Church in its entirety is operating under this umbrella or all the others things that I mention here. As a matter of fact, various aspects of the Black Church are shying away from this financial monstrosity that it has grown into—particularly the Civil Rights Generation, which still has that strong sense of community and brotherhood/sisterhood, and the Hip Hop Generation, which is diligently seeking spirituality and meaning to life—causing a disenfranchisement of the church, one that hasn't been seen since the Civil Right Era.[1] The stronghold in the latter part of that argument is that God does not pay anyone to believe in Him or His message. And to put a Hip Hop spin to it: God's message has never been about "getting rich or die trying" but rather about doing His will.[2]

It must be understood that the intent of the financial prosperity message was not to disenfranchise the poor or disenfranchise the community even further. It was to utilize the newfound wealth and distribute it back into the hands of the community who needs it. Unfortunately, the movement that was intended to be a weed-and-seed project grew into a competition of materialism, losing its main and subsidiary purposes and losing the people it was meant to serve in the process.

The question isn't necessarily who has the stronghold of the church or if one particular group has the right to control its direction, because the Black Church has disenfranchised into so many various branches to serve the various needs of the community—in the state of disenfranchisement—that in spite of that, we might see, in regard to the Black Community as well as the Black Church, that neither really exists anymore.

What does exist is a collective of individuals gathering together—not coming together—with individualistic mentalities refusing to join, address, or even concern itself with one another, for the simple reasons that we as individuals have to face that we need more than ourselves to survive and that we are flawed individuals in our makeshift "perfect" world, adding another variable that we have become languid in investing our energies and our resources to build something that requires us to work for the greater good ahead of ourselves.

There is no simple, concrete answer in uniting the Black Church or the Black Community, except to say that each disenfranchised body must take the initiative to acknowledge that there is a problem in our community and in our church—that, no, we are not a cohesive unit and it will be that way until we, as individuals in this individualistic state, make that change. We must not look to our so-called leaders to take the initiative in correcting this problem, because many of them have proven to be unworthy of carrying that burden, and in some cases, it is just too heavy for them to carry alone. We must start our own initiative and realize that it starts at home before it can grow anywhere else. In doing this, we must accept that this sector of ourselves, our family, has viewpoints and outlooks based on its experience. We must appreciate that our family members' belief system, regardless of how different it is from our own, has just as much merit—if not more—than our own voice. Once we become steadfast in that message and sensitively address the ills of our own families can we then consider building a sturdy bridge toward another cohesive family until we have built many bridges toward a brotherhood/sisterhood, a community and a church. From there, we can begin to build bridges toward other disenfranchised bodies with a collective communal cohesiveness brought together by our individualities to turn the isolated nation called the Black Church into a nation of wealth that is well connected and accessible to everyone, tackling the ills of the community and the church as a family.

NOTES

1. Many local and national Black Churches massively split on progression and nonprogression of the African American race in society. Denominations such as the Progressive National Baptist Convention, Inc. (founded in 1961) and others emerged from these major differences in opinions.

2. A reference to the street edict proposed by numerous rap artists, including 50 Cent, who in 2003 released the multiplatinum award-winning recording *Get Rich or Die Tryin'* on the Aftermath/Interscope label.

Chapter Three

Chasing a Dream Deferred: From Movement to Culture

Emmett G. Price III

During the height of the Civil Rights Movement, revolutionary playwright and activist Lorraine Hansberry used history as her guide, and reality as her muse, to craft one of the most culturally potent and socially critical works of the twentieth and twenty-first centuries. Based on her middle-class experiences with segregation, discrimination, and her family's legal battles to integrate the Washington Park area of the South Side of Chicago, *A Raisin in the Sun* highly publicized a series of layered challenges within the lives and experiences of Black folk, then and now.[1] Responding to Langston Hughes's perplexing yet poignant rhetorical question, "What happens to a dream deferred?" Hansberry offers her response.[2] Debuting in 1959, *A Raisin in the Sun* achieved over five hundred performances on Broadway, and it remains as the first Broadway play written by a Black women (Hansberry) and directed by a Black man (Lloyd Richards). The play, as a dominant work within the American canon, has taken a life of its own via onstage production, film, and television.[3]

The "dream" for liberty, justice, and equality was one that Hughes often wrote and spoke about in his numerous musings, poems, plays, and other creative works. Born in 1902, James Mercer Langston Hughes would emerge as one of the leading voices of the Harlem Renaissance, the revolutionary moment in history that was an essential component of the Black freedom struggle and a leading catalytic force for the formal Civil Rights Movement. Hughes, a cultural nationalist and race conscious activist captured the essence of the desired result of the Black freedom struggle as the fulfillment of the "dream." A dream that was initiated by the first displaced Africans in the previously settled "New World." It is the same dream that the Reverend Dr. Prathia Hall Wynn would inspire the Reverend Dr. Martin Luther King Jr. to speak about.[4] Twenty years later, the East-West All Stars expressed the same dream in their call for a national end to gang violence, with "Self-

21

Destruction."[5] In many ways, it is the same dream that Biggie Smalls explored in "Juicy," where he emphatically and imaginatively expressed what going from "negative to positive" looked and felt like.[6] The Black Eyed Peas recapitulated the dream as they asked candid questions in their now-classic hit "Where Is the Love?"[7] It is the purpose of this chapter to reimage the connectivity between the Civil Rights Movement and Hip Hop Culture and to reveal the role of the Black Church in bridging the growing generational divide.

In *A Raisin in the Sun*, the Younger family depicts the generational conflict within the Black family during the post–World War II Black freedom struggle—namely, the Civil Rights Movement. Embedded with issues of women's liberation, contemporary ideals of Black beauty, and a superficial admiration of all things "African," the desire for social and economic mobility permeates the storyline as Walter Lee Younger (representing the next generation) dreams of economic opportunity while his sister Beneatha Younger (also representing the next generation) dreams of gender equality and women's rights. The family values are anchored by Lena Younger, the devout Christian mother whose source of strength is found in her unwavering faith and her firmly rooted traditional family values that rely on a high respect for hierarchy, authority, and order. As the three-act narrative unfolds, we find scene after scene where the generational conflicts expose a tension between Lena and her two children (Walter and Beneatha). From her first entrance in the script, commenting on her "children and they tempers," to her captivating closure of the final scene, positing that Walter Lee "finally come into his manhood today, didn't he? Kind of like a rainbow after the rain." Lena is a clear representation of the aesthetic and tradition of the Civil Rights Movement generation.[8]

Lena's firm yet nurturing spirit is indicative of the phenomenal women of the 1950s and 1960s who not only anchored the family but often held sole responsibility for raising the next generation. Understated yet affirmed in the persona of Lena was the role of the Black Church as the center of the Black family of the Civil Rights Generation.[9] Although it would be an overstatement to insinuate that all Black families went to church or that all Black families were Christian, what is clear is that the church (physically, spiritually, and symbolically) played a central role in the lives and beliefs of African Americans during the period. This assertion is affirmed toward the end of act I, scene 1 as Beneatha challenges her mother's religiosity with her own atheistic expressions of nonbelief. Outraged by Benethea's revocation of not only Lena's belief, but that of generations of ancestors, Lena strikes Benethea across the face and repeatedly demands spontaneous acknowledgment of the existence of God.[10]

Lena's response is a powerful slap to Beneatha's face, followed by,

Now—you say after me, in my mother's house there is still God. (There is a long pause and Beneatha stares at the floor wordlessly. Lena repeats the phrase with precision and cool emotion.) In my mother's house there is still God. [11]

Although the church never appears prominently in a specific scene, the numerous colloquialisms and metaphors invoking the presence of the church ("Thank God!" "Praise God!" and "Thank you Jesus") reveal the power and presence of the Black Church within the infrastructure of the Black Family values and tradition during the Civil Rights Era. [12] These same values and traditions serve as the source of much generational struggle and divide.

The Civil Rights Movement was a definitive moment in history when individuals, collectives, and organizations focused on specific political, social, and economic issues that would collectively lead to liberty, justice, and equality. Using formulaic strictures of resistance, the children, young adults, parents, and elders of the movement (of various hues and socioeconomic situations) progressed toward the desired impact of change. The ethos of the movement was based in the lived atrocities of people of color (and others) and the clarion call to join as brothers and sisters to "fight back" and demand "Respect." "Respect" here equated to the desired goal of liberty, justice, and equality, which can also be understood as the realization of the dream. The life cycle of the movement began centuries before the climactic *Brown vs. Topeka Board of Education* Supreme Court case, which often is mistakenly recorded as the catalyst for the movement. In fact, the works of Nat Turner, Denmark Vessey, Sojourner Truth, Harriet Tubman, Marcus Garvey, Martin Delany, and others established the foothold on what would emerge during the 1950s and 1960s as the Civil Rights Movement. It was this historical legacy that established a perplexing pathology within the Black community. The pathology revealed that the communities under the umbrella of Blackness relied and expressed loyalty in one charismatic leader at a time. In moments of multiple leaders simultaneously emerging, a clear polemic was created in the hearts and minds of the community, as the underlying standard of the pathology was one leader at a time. This pathology revealed that the result of communal work should be communal gain; thus, any time that victory was exhorted and that one arose from among the community as benefiting more so than the rest of the people, the individual was often ostracized. This cultural socialization relied on the communal values and beliefs that the thoughts and opinions of the whole outweighed the individual—and certainly minority—views within the community. This pathology created a multitude of friction within the movement and perhaps led to its demise. Within the pathology, the central focus on progress robbed the movement of its ability to self-reflect, self-assess, and self-correct. In fact, most movements operate in the same vein, and thus, their life cycles are similar: They peak and then quickly dissolve due to a lack of foundational integrity and built-in sustainability. Folks were so busy fighting that they rarely came home to debrief, particularly with their children, who were often thrown into the heat of the battle without really understanding the costs of waging war. This would return to haunt the Civil Rights Generation as the Hip Hop Generation would arise, afflicted and impacted by these decisions. Equally challenging to the Hip Hop Generation was the lack of return on the investment of cultural, social, and economic warfare. Folks were so busy fighting that they did not effectively prepare for the fruits (success) of their labor. Instead of fighting and preparing for the potential spoils of victory, the victorious cultural warriors won the war, went home, and left the spoils of victory on the battlefield. This reality was most impactful on the next generation of young people, who witnessed and participated in multiple levels of the engagement only to return home to poverty, homelessness, narcotics, guns, police brutality, and an even more unjust and inequitable system of life under the governmental policies that would only become more detrimental with the emergence of Reaganomics.[13]

Walter's struggle to enter his manhood was partially precipitated by the traditional rules of the previous generation, where young people did not participate in adult affairs and "grown folks business was for grown folks." His inability to see the "behind the scenes" of his father's growth only continued the cycle of diminishing returns of the Black Family. Beneatha's clear revolt against her mother's aesthetic comes from a lack of appreciation built on a lack of understanding why her mother did what she did and the failure of her mother to effectively share her dreams with her children. Symbolically representing the emerging generation (in this case, the Hip Hop Generation), Walter and Beneatha demonstrate the passionate des.re to continue the movement within the next generation without understanding the ethos or pathology of the movement. They want for the family to be successful, and individually, they desire to lead that charge in their own unique ways, but they don't have the grounding to see their desires/dreams emerge as realities. Similarly, the creativity and innovation that led to the evolution of Hip Hop Culture was driven by a sincere and empowering place, but the foundation and sustainability of the culture was never properly established. In many ways, although the expressions that have been codified as Hip Hop Culture have demonstrated their collective power, I propose that Hip Hop is a cultural moment on a diachronical timeline of the Black Freedom Struggle, from slavery to the present, and can be equally defined as a part of a greater cultural movement. My goal is not to diminish the power position of Hip Hop as a culture but to reveal an even more powerful position that Hip Hop has as a continuation of the cultural movement of Black folks (and others) toward liberty, justice, and equality.

In his recent treatise *Tradition and the Black Atlantic: Critical Theory in the African Diaspora*, Henry Louis Gates Jr. takes the idea of a cultural movement to another level as he explores the Diasporic continuum placing the evolutions and creations within Black America as a cultural moment on the diachronical timeline of the African experience.[14] Here I define a cultural movement as intentional and collective progression based on agreed-upon beliefs, values, ideologies, and traditions. Cultural movements occur when a majority defines the need to change or mutate. Based on the needs, concerns, desires, and demands of the majority or dominant community members, the entire population (and its creative expressions) makes a shift, creating a changing tide. The result serves as the source material of subsequently defining the cultural movement. In this vain, Hip Hop is a part of an established trajectory that moves from one generation to another and beyond. Each generation struggles to identify itself, not only in its own terms, but in its own system of dress, syntax, savvy, sensibilities, and certainly its own language. Reflectively, the original composers, arrangers, and performers of the spirituals could have very well codified their cultural creations as a culture. There was a definitive style of dress (not by choice), a unique and innovative style of dance, cuisine, and language. In effect, if separation and individualization were a major goal of the slaves during this era, there would have been a stand-alone spirituals culture as opposed to a broader slave culture. Similarly, the composers, lyricists, and musicians (including vocalists) during the blues era equally could have defined their creative expressions as a stand-alone culture, for all the potential elements were eventually recognized as exceptional creations. From jazz to R&B, to soul and beyond, each genre of African American music—because of its cultural connectivity as well as its inclination to speak to the needs, concerns, and desires of its central audience—could have been established as a sole culture. Previous generations, however, were not concerned with cornering the marketplace or establishing new industry-oriented paradigms; they were busy fighting for survival and preparing the ground for the seed of each new generation. Lena, when presented with the opportunity for financial means, deferred her dreams to provide access and opportunity to a better future for her children and, subsequently, her grandson. Unlike Lena, Walter and Beneatha were both determined to break free of the family curse (legacy) to make a name for themselves as independent, bold explorers into unchartered terrain: Walter as a small business proprietor and Beneatha as a doctor in Africa.

Hip Hop by all means is a culture! To assert that it is not would be ludicrous. Nevertheless, it is also a part of a larger Diasporic cultural system that is connected to both its past and its future. Like Walter and Beneatha, Hip Hop has had the privilege to lean on the supports of the spirituals, blues, jazz, R&B, soul, and all the inner voices of these broad genres. They all were borne out of the need to respond to systemic oppression. They all serve as a voice of hope in hopeless life cycles, and they all push toward, in part, the desires for liberty, justice, and equality. Similar to Walter and Beneatha, Hip Hop has had the privilege to experiment and explore options and paths different from those of its predecessors. Some of these options and paths include self-definition and self-discovery, which allowed for variance away from family traditions and values and toward external influences. Hip Hop ventured to the roulette table of capitalism and partnered with consumerism in ways and manners that its ancestors never had the option or the desire to attain. As with Walter and Beneatha, the desire to depart from the family nucleus to create its own existence created more tension and frustration and expounded on an inherent generational divide. Essentially, because Hip Hop desired to see itself as a culture and not as simultaneously connected to the cultural legacy and heritage of its past, it has taken on the worst of the ethos and pathology of the previous generation. Each generation should desire, and be groomed, to be more effective, more efficient, and more successful than the past. Each successive generation should learn of the ways of previous generations and build on to the legacy. Each successive generation should honor the rich cultural heritage from which it sprang while simultaneously expanding it. Culture is a living organism and can easily be diverted from its initial birth rite, whereas cultural movements are groomed and girded by a centripetal force that allows it to navigate the challenging terrains of change while remaining constantly focused on its prime objective—in this case, the realization of the dream.

For Hip Hop as a cultural movement, the desired goal remains the attainment of liberty, justice, and equality. For past generations, this alone has been the central focus of all endeavors. As a culture, Hip Hop has a central focus on making money and being known; the influence of capitalism and commodification is evident as third-party, external forces as well. These are the same values of Corporate America. Hansberry understood this challenge even in her time as she cleverly crafted the part of Walter Lee Younger. Act II, scene 2, closes with Walter expressing to his son Travis his new revelation of what respect should look and feel like. Not only has Walter clearly redefined the definition of respect, but he has also challenged the traditional values of his family. His fantasy-driven expression of respect exemplifies the class-oriented challenges between and within the generations. Walter, a driver for a wealthy White family, desires to have people working for him. Likewise, his personal investment in the fantasy is based on his imaginative decree that money buys you wealth . . . and apparently a few other things as well, such as college entrance (at seventeen) and entrée to the profession of one's choice. Walter's articulation of his dream also reveals the departure from communal thinking to individualistic thinking. Although he mentions aspects of his fantasy that pertain to himself, his wife, and his son, his dream is for three individual and independent people and not for the family unit as a whole. In effect, Walter was not privy to the prophetic musings of two Hip Hop sages—the Notorious B.I.G., who poignantly and succinctly offered the tragic statement "Mo money Mo problems," and 50 Cent, who clearly warned us that the code of conduct was to "Get Rich or Die Tryin'."[15]

Upon discovering that his dream for the future exploded right in his face, Walter quickly invokes the God of his mother and her generation. Angry at his unproven trust in Willy and their failed business venture, Walter calls on God and falls to the floor as if he had been physically beaten. Out of all the emotions that are expressed, perhaps the most striking is his invocation of God and Hansberry's note directing him to challenge the reader and viewer to ponder whether he is looking for Willy or looking for God. This subtle innuendo acknowledges the power and presence of God in times of destitution, despair, and drastic need. Throughout *A Raisin in the Sun* and throughout the entire existence of Hip Hop Culture, the presence of God is invoked through the institution of the Black Church. What becomes quite evident after some pondering is that the Black Church remains the only space that can serve as neutral territory to bridge the generations in a manner to not only recognize the growing detachment but usher in a much-needed season of generational healing. The Black Church, due to its challenged past and forgiven future, remains the only space with the strength and courage to facilitate generational reconciliation. Created under duress, the Black Church is the only space that can safely reorient all generations to respect one another in a manner to diffuse the dilemma of the generational divide. The Black Church is the only institution within the communities of color that is willing to invite in the dried, festering, reeking, crusted, and sagging dreams of yesterday, today, and tomorrow to rehabilitate each with a renewed sense of hope, power, and purpose. The Black Church is the only space that can play a key role in reversing the detonation clock on the self-imploding dreams of ALL generations. No other institution, with all its faults, challenges, and failures, can issue the challenge to all generations and receive a response. Regardless of one's faith journey, religious conviction, or spiritual inclination, the Black Church is a part of the Black experience in the United States, and its presence and power can avail to all who are willing to explore the possibility of grace. The Black Church is the healing ground that can serve ALL with the hope of finally realizing and receiving the fruits of centuries of dreams.

What happens to a dream deferred? It waits for action!

NOTES

1. Hansberry grew up in a home of a prestigious Black middle-class family who bought property and moved into the Washington Park subdivision of Woodlawn on the South Side of Chicago during the mid-to-late 1930s. As a result of the racial discrimination that ensued, Hansberry's father, Carl Augustus Hansberry, a prominent real estate broker, filed legal action that would eventually rise to the US Supreme Court with a ruling that remains a landmark decision and continues to impact civil procedure to this day (*Hansberry vs. Lee* 311 US 32 [1940]). The move and the experience with the legal system inspired Lorraine Hansberry's creation of *A Raisin in the Sun*.

2. In Langston Hughes's "Harlem: A Dream Deferred," published in 1951 as part of the collection, *Montage of a Dream Deferred* (New York: Henry Holt), Hughes leads with the question "What happens to a dream deferred?"

3. The 1959 cast included Sidney Poitier (Walter), Claudia McNeil (Lena), Ruby Dee (Ruth), Glynn Turman (Travis), and Diana Sands (Beneatha). The 1961 film version, released by Columbia Pictures with a screenplay written by Hansberry, included the original Broadway cast with the additions of Louis Gossett Jr., Ivan Dixon, and John Fiedler. In 1973, after Hansberry's passing, her ex-husband Robert Nemiroff converted the play into a musical, which won the Tony Award for Best Musical (1974). In 1989, based on an off-Broadway revival of the play by the Roundabout Theater, the play was adapted as a movie made for television starring Danny Glover (Walter), Starletta DuPois (Ruth), Ester Rolle (Lena), and Kim Yancey (Beneatha). In 2004, the play returned to Broadway with a cast of Sean "Diddy" Combs (Walter), Phylicia Rashad (Ruth), and Sanaa Lathan (Beneatha). The same cast later starred in the 2008 made-for-television movie, which premiered on ABC. As a play, this is one of the most popular works read and analyzed in high schools across the country.

4. The Reverend Dr. Prathia Hall Wynn was often recognized behind the scenes as inspiring Dr. King's use of the "I have a dream" phrase. Dr. Hall, as she was most often recognized, was an ordained Baptist minister (1977) and pastor of Mount Sharon Baptist Church in Philadelphia. A Freedom Rider with the Student Nonviolent Coordinating Committee, Dr. Hall was a popular civil rights speaker and activist. In addition to her many accolades and accomplishments, the professor and university administrator held the prestigious Martin Luther King Jr. Chair in Social Ethics at Boston University School of Theology. She passed away in 2002.

5. East-West All Stars released "Self Destruction" in 1989 on the Jive label in an effort to raise money to halt gang violence and to spread the message that rap artists from both coasts were coming together to bring an end to gang violence.

6. "Juicy" was released by the Notorious B.I.G. on his 1994 debut album, *Ready to Die*, on the Bad Boy/Arista label.

7. "Where Is the Love?" was released on the Black Eyed Peas' 2003 album, *Elephunk*, on the A&M/will.i.am/Interscope labels.

8. Lorraine Hansberry, *A Raisin in the Sun* (New York: Vintage Books, 1994 [1958]), 40, 151.

9. In this context, the Black Church is inclusive and includes the expressions of faith that have a clear cultural nationalistic appeal, including the Nation of Islam and Five Percent Nation of Gods and Earth and others that have the best interest of Blacks and Black families as a core area of interest.

10. Hansberry, *A Raisin in the Sun*, 51 (Hansberry's emphasis).

11. Hansberry, *A Raisin in the Sun*, 51.

12. In act I, scene 1, alone there are six references to God, faith, Christianity, and the like. These occur on pages 41, 46, 47, 49, 50–52, and 53. It is clear that the church was an important aspect of the Black family as portrayed by Hansberry.

13. *Reagonomics* is a term that captures the economic policies of President Ronald Reagan during the 1980s. His policies were, in effect, more advantageous to the rich and wealthy while being disastrous for impoverished and working-class families.

14. Henry Louis Gates Jr., *Tradition and the Black Atlantic: Critical Theory in the African Diaspora* (New York: Basic Civitas, 2010), xiv.

15. "Mo Money Mo Problems" was released on B.I.G.'s 1997 Bad Boy/Arista release *Life after Dark*. "Get Rich or Die Tryin'" was the title track on 50 Cent's 2003 release on the Aftermath/Shady/Interscope label.

Part II

Hip Hop Culture and the Black Church in Dialogue

Chapter Four

Deep Calls to Deep: Beginning Explorations of the Dialogue between the Black Church and Hip Hop

Charles L. Howard

Within the dialogical space between diverse Christian faith expressions and an international Hip Hop cultural movement, we find an open cypha with the lyrical chemistry of the best rap groups and duos of the last three decades but, at the same time, with the Battle MC ferocity of the most-heated beefs and rivalries. The relationship between Christianity and Hip Hop has been one mostly played out on television, with images of bulldozers running over 2 Live Crew Records, preachers condemning rap from the pulpit, and MCs dismissing the church on the mic. Yet, there is a far deeper engagement and interlocking that occurred since the earliest days of Hip Hop. As the dance between Hip Hop and Islam (Nation, 5%, Sunni, and others) has matured and seen various manifestations, Hip Hop and Christianity, particularly the Black Church, have navigated their way through deep, sometimes bumpy, but always powerful waters. Commentary has been made about the negative reactions that religious leaders (usually the church) have made toward Hip Hop (especially rap music).[1] Likewise, criticism has come from the ranks of Hip Hop toward religious establishments.[2] Here, the complex intersection between Christianity and Hip Hop is explored with special attention focused toward Gospel Rap and Gospel Rappers, as well as mainstream rappers that make Christian faith claims and expressions.

These contact points, intersections, and integrations are vital. Hip Hop and Communities/Expressions of Faith are two of the most crucial parts of our society today, with the tremendous influence and presence they both hold. A greater understanding of the two (especially a greater understanding of each other) will provide some strategy and insight on how Hip Hop and Faith can work together to continue to bring about much-needed positive change.

SYLVIA AND THE SPIRIT

The name Sylvia Robinson is unfamiliar to many. Yet, she is properly described as the "Mother of Hip Hop."[3] Robinson is the one credited with first recording the music that would, in Hip Hop journalist James Spady's words, "spawn a multibillion-dollar industry."[4]

In the powerful book *Street Conscious Rap* (with Dr. H. Samy Alim and Charles Lee), Spady interviewed Robinson and provided space for her amazing and perhaps surprising story to be told. Although her narrative does not describe the inception of Hip Hop, it does describe the birth/delivery of Hip Hop into the greater world. The presence of her faith in this narrative, about how she decided to record the rap music she had heard, is profound.

> Well really it was a revelation from God. I was at a disco one night in Harlem . . . [at a club called Harlem World]. My sister was having a birthday party for me and it wasn't even my birthday. She was managing the place and she wanted to drum up business. She knew I had been very depressed at the time because I was going through a very sad time in my life and she was having this party for me. I didn't want to go out. I said, "I can't disappoint her." So I made myself go that evening and while I was there, you know. I use to ask God. I said, "You know every time I was in trouble I could always pick up my guitar and write a hit record." . . . I was sitting up in the balcony and I saw all these kids out on the floor. . . . And here was a fellow talking on the Mic with music playing and I saw if he told them to do this or do that, they did it. . . . All of a sudden I felt a chill all over my body and a voice said to me, "You put that on tape and You'll be out of all the trouble you've ever been in." And all at once, I felt the chills all over my body, like the Holy Spirit overcoming me. And that's how that happened. It was really a Revelation of God how that happened.[5]

In the beginning, there was God, right there at the advent of Hip Hop. The description of her experience hearing the Sugar Hill Gang at Harlem World night club is shockingly Marian, with her speaking of "the Holy Sprit overcoming her."[6] To present the origins of Hip Hop from a strictly Christian perspective would be misleading and misrepresentative, yet it is important to point out that at this definitive moment, Christianity was engaging with Hip Hop in a confirming and moving way.

CROSSROADS

It may be beneficial to look at this complex space where Hip Hop and Christianity meet, by examining the concepts of Christian Rap and the Christian Rapper and then Christianity within Rap/Hip Hop.

Attempting to place MCs in categories and genres has proven to be a difficult, if not wasteful, effort. An example of this is referenced in how hard it has been to lock down and define the concept of the "gangsta rapper." Are gangsta rappers artists who talk about violence and have guns in their music videos? Are gangsta rappers artists who get caught in unfortunate circumstances and become engaged with the law? Are gangsta rappers artists who used to be caught up in street life, still rap about it, but have since reformed their ways? Could gangsta rappers even be MCs who rhyme about things they've never known.

Similarly, the "conscious rapper" is another label that has brought misunderstanding, with MCs talking about socially and politically relevant issues such as police brutality while still having exploitative and demeaning lyrics on their tracks. Where is there space for a conscious rapper that gets a little gangsta or for the gangsta rapper that speaks wisdom on the microphone? (And who's to say that the so-called gangsta rapper isn't "dropping science" and raising consciousness no matter what he or she says?) What do we do with MCs such as Will Smith or Trina? Are they gangsta, conscious, neither, or both?

Many people have discovered that putting MCs and groups under the title of Christian Rap is somewhat easier. I argue here that the walls of the Christian Rap house are more permeable than they seem.

There are often two paths to Christian Rap and Holy Hip Hop. Worship of God is an important part of the Christian's life. Music is an important means of doing this for many. Some churches and individuals find traditional hymns to be an effective and meaningful way to worship. Others prefer chanting in one of the forms used by those in certain religious communities. Still many prefer what has come to be known as praise songs, with a variety of musical instrumental accompaniment. Others prefer spirituals and traditional gospel songs sung by choirs. Particular cultural differences around the world have influenced the way that God is sung about and sung to by all, throughout the Christian Diaspora. From Puerto Rico to Ghana, from China to the Bronx, the musical expressions of Christianity are wide and varied.

It is not unusual for one to move from a local church or denomination or just a personal devotional style because of a personal musical preference. In the present era, some prefer to worship through Christian Rap music. For some it is a matter of taste, and for others it is a matter of expressing a part of who they are in the way that they worship God. Without making generalizations, many Christians who are or were into rock music might understandably prefer praise music with guitars and drums over robed choirs and organs. This path can be described as moving from faith to devotional/cultural style because it entails the believer (the Christian) starting as a Christian and then seeking or being drawn to a particular worship style.

Another path to Christian Rap and Hip Hop can entail the individual starting from her or his cultural/social location and then moving into a life of faith. In this case, a member of the Hip Hop Nation might move into a life of Christian faith, bringing with him or her the realities and styles of the Hip Hop cultural movement. Instead of searching for a devotional style with which to worship God, individuals bring the desired style with them, applying that style to the new faith/religion. This is the path that members of the Philadelphia-based rap group/ministry Cross Movement take. Within this profound exchange with a group that may be remembered as one of the pioneer Christian Rap groups, they were influenced and inspired by the likes of Big Daddy Kane, KRS-1, the Beastie Boys, Eric B, and numerous others representing an ecumenical composition of the Hip Hop Universe (Christian, Jewish, Muslim, Buddhist, and others) and the way that these expressions of Faith maintain a sublyrical dialogue with one another.

Still, Christian Rap or Gospel Rap, as some refer to it, remains difficult to define. It might be easier to first consider what a Christian Rapper is. Many can conceptualize some kind of picture in our minds when asked what a rapper is. We have images of an MC, a woman or a man manipulating language, often rhymed language, sometimes over a beat. Some tell stories of "the way it is" or "the way it should be" or "the way they would like it to be." Others recite lyrics with the pure intent of entertaining the listener. Defining the rapper is not terribly difficult, though there might be slight differences from person to person.

A Christian is slightly more difficult to define. Generally, it is one who is a follower, believer, and worshipper of Jesus of Nazareth, whom he or she believes is the Christ/Messiah. A Christian commits one's life to follow Jesus by striving to obey His commands written in what is believed to be Holy Scripture. The believer trusts in His Love to be salvific, which He especially expressed on the cross. Last, Christians worship Christ not as just a Holy man or prophet but as God Himself. Self-proclamation and public declaration of one's self as a Christian is often imperative. This self-expression is an important part of not only Christianity but also Hip Hop.

A Christian Rapper is one who is a Christian and happens to be an MC. Is it a sister or brother who goes to church faithfully and fits into our definition of what a rapper is? Or is it one who raps about Christian themes in his or her music? What if he or she is a Christian who also raps but never mentions Jesus or any Christian themes in the lyrics?

Along with those who self-identify as Christian Rappers, we can also merge MCs who include lyrics that positively reflect on Jesus. However, it should be noted that one need not mention Jesus directly or by name in the lyrics to be a Christian Rapper, just as a Christian preacher need not mention Jesus in every sermon to be considered a Christian Minister. Likewise, there is an evangelistic aspect that often seems to be common among those who are commonly known as Christian Rappers. An example of this is the popular group from Philadelphia mentioned earlier, known as the Cross Movement. All would recognize these brothers as MCs. Their abilities on the microphone can certainly be compared to any other mainstream artists, and they stand tall in a Philadelphia roll call of great MCs and musicians. They are also Christian men. They all profess Jesus as their Lord and truly worship Him as their God. Their lyrics, while exploring different aspects of life, consistently touch on Biblical issues and sound theological principles. But there is more: there is an evangelistic aspect to their lyrics. They incorporate a teaching aspect of their ministry/movement, which may have been modeled on the teaching (edutainment) of KRS-1 and some of the early 5% Nation MCs.[7] Evangelism can be defined literally as bringing the Good News (of Christ and His love). Teaching and evangelizing have an important difference. Some might rap about Jesus as a person, but the Cross Movement encourages others to adopt this way of life and this faith.

Another example of this is the Catholic Priest MC Father Stan Fortuna. Not only is this MC a priest, but he is a monk as well (a Friar of the Franciscan Order). Often serving as a featured guest or host on EWTN, the Catholic television and radio network, he rhymes with tremendous skills while encouraging listeners to follow Jesus and Love God. Other MCs, such as BB Jay, T-Bone, and the Grits, are of this tradition of lyrical evangelists.

NOISE AND SPIRIT

The groundbreaking collaboration led by Dr. Anthony Pinn and captured in *Noise and Spirit* provides a unique intellectual cypha for scholars to explore some of the relationships between rap music and a variety of faith traditions. The first essay is by a scholar named Garth Kasimu Baker-Fletcher, and it is entitled "African American Christian Rap: Facing Truth and Resisting It." Baker-Fletcher's essay is a well-written exploration into the traditionally described Gospel Rap corner of Hip Hop. Yet a critical eye might see his piece as being limited in its scope and consideration of Christianity and Rap. Baker-Fletcher's consideration of Christian Rap mentions only those who explicitly declare themselves to be Gospel Rappers. Pinn challenges this in his introduction when he says,

> In addition to explicit moments that reflect a type of hip-hop evangelicalism, there are also more "shadowed" engagements with religious themes and religious traditions in rap music, often lyrically fused in metaphors, signs, and symbols.[8]

Baker-Fletcher misses a large part of the rap community that might legitimately be considered Christian Rappers. Or rather, does he intentionally draw a line between the secular and the sacred?

> L.G. Wise, BB Jay, Lil Raskull, King Cyz, E-Roc, ad Easop all were homies from the streetz. The feeling, tone and attitude of their rap music is similar to that of secular rappers like Eminem, Dr. Dre, Snoop Dog, Notorious B.I.G., Tupac Shakur, Bone Thugs-n-Harmony, and Ja Rule. Their overall sound still "reaches homies" because they still sound like homies—just sanctified![9]

This passage brings out a painful question that begs to answered: Are not the latter-mentioned artists "sanctified" too? What is it that makes the former sanctified and the latter not? Is it baptism or church membership? Apparently not, since Snoop was baptized and even sang in the church choir at one time! Is it rapping about Jesus? Does that mean Kanye West should be mentioned on the first list? Or rather is it the way that they live their lives? What does that mean for ministers and Christians who find themselves caught in some of the very terrible public scandals that we see from time to time? Certainly God's grace is extended to both lists. And is it not by grace that we are sanctified?

So then what shall we do about the MCs that rhyme about Jesus at times during their lyrics but not during every track? Furthermore, what about those who rhyme about Jesus but are not actively encouraging others to follow Jesus as their Lord and God? Are they Christian Rappers?

When Hip Hop was a teenager, still exploring the country and still getting to know itself, a young performer named MC Hammer was the premier artist in the rap genre. Hammer was famous for tracks such as "Turn This Mother Out," "Let's Get It Started," and the classic "Can't Touch This," which sampled Rick James's famous song "Super Freak." His music was popular and his videos influenced the way that we moved and dressed during that period of Hip Hop history (and a portion of American history). He was accepted as a mainstream rapper who was not within a particular subgenre (gangsta or conscious rap, etc.). But then he released a track called "Pray," in which the hook was "We've got to pray just to make it today."[10] At this point, was Hammer a Christian Rapper? He was an MC who professed Jesus as his Savior and God, but he rhymed about Christian issues on only one or two tracks, and in the song "Pray," he did not actually mention Jesus's name (he says "Lord"). There are few if any that would have classified him as a Christian Rapper at that point, but when he began to make appearances on a Christian television station[11] and then came out with another album more explicitly Christocentric, he was considered a Christian Rapper.

What about Rev. Run? He's an ordained minister and an MC. Run DMC came out with an album after Run became a minister, and not all of his lyrics on this album reflected his adoration of Christ. He was not found on any of the tracks to be encouraging listeners to adopt faithful lives confessing Jesus as their Lord and their savior, though one could still make a strong argument about Rev. Run being a Christian Rapper.

There are other MCs who were once "mainstream" (nonreligious) but later in their careers and lives focused on their Christian faith, such as MCs from 2 Live Crew, Play of Kid 'n Play, and how could one not mention the journey that Pastor Mason Bertha has taken. The rapper named MA$E has gone from being the prince of Bad Boy Records to Inspirational Christian speaker/pastor and back to MTV rapper in the matter of a less than a decade. Even KRS-1's rap career took a very religious turn after years of being a part of the mainstream.

But what of those MCs who explore their Christian faith while they remain mainstream and continue to rap about things that most would not associate with Christianity? What of those rappers who are not necessarily encouraging others to pursue a particular faith life but are just wrestling with some of the hard realities of life from a religious paradigm? Rather than be evangelists, they could be considered theologians.

THE JESUS PIECE

The night before he died, Christopher Wallace—known in the rap world as the Notorious B.I.G.—performed at the eleventh annual Soul Train Awards. The author of the book *Unbelievable* describes what happened when the Notorious B.I.G. returned to his room and watched the taped show.

> A few moments later, Wallace saw himself on the screen. He was expecting the boos (which he received from some at the live show), but the television broadcast polite applause. Anyway the people in the room were more focused on the gold plated diamond-crusted likeness of Jesus hanging around Biggie's neck. It glimmered in the stage lights. "The Jesus piece is banging'," Wallace said happily.
>
> G (Gregory Young—his driver) laughed, "It's crazy son!" he yelled. "It's off the hook!"
>
> I asked Wallace if the piece was meaningful to him or just a cool accessory.
>
> "I think that if there were more people that were into the Lord, there would be a lot less sh** going on in the world," he said.

"I think people need to realize that there are tests and obstacles that everyone has to go through. A lot of niggas want to give up and do wrong, but they don't even think that God is in their corner. What I respect about God is that He always steers you in the right direction."

He rolled up his sleeve to show me the fresh tattoo on his inside right forearm, in the form of a weathered parchment were the verses of Psalm 23.

"The Lord is my light and my salvation, whom shall I fear?

The Lord is the truth of my life, of whom shall I be afraid?

When the wicked, even my enemies and foes, came upon me to bite my flesh, they stumbled and fell."

"This is how I feel sometimes." [12]

Whether this makes the Notorious B.I.G. a Christian Rapper is not as important as pointing out the fact that there was real theology going on within this man's mind and heart, theology at its rawest definition—"God talk." The Notorious B.I.G. was considering his place in life and our society in relationship to God and Jesus in particular.

Kanye West's debut album *College Dropout* brought many radio hits, such as "Through the Wire" or "They All Fall Down." [13] At the same time, on a track that he produced for Twista, he could be heard saying, "I could make you a celebrity overnight." His tracks produced for Alicia Keys and other artists were still getting airplay at that time, as were many others. But he also had a song called "Jesus Walks," which was getting a lot of airplay and attention on many mainstream Hip Hop and R&B stations. [14] The lyrics on this classic track describe how the MC wants Jesus to walk with him through the different challenges that life might bring. He goes on to make the scandalously true statement that Jesus even walks with "hustlers, killers, murderers, drug dealers, even strippers." [15]

What do we do with a song like that? During a concert in Philadelphia during the spring of 2004, West performed "Jesus Walks" as one of his final songs. I will never forget looking at the stage watching Kanye, Damon Dash, and many other Roc-a-Fella Records representatives with their hands in the air, dancing to this track. At this point, whether Kanye is a Christian Rapper is not what the focus needs to be but rather the fact that one can bare witness, in a very clear way, to the presence of Christianity within Hip Hop. This track should be given the attention it deserves as a song that not only mentions Jesus but makes a very strong and very deep statement about God's love for even the "hustlers, killers, murderers, drug dealers, even the strippers." This is huge for someone to make the assertion that might be obvious to some but heretical to others—that Jesus walks even with the criminals of our society.

It would appear that within Hip Hop there is a fine line between the blasphemous (utterly disrespectful to God) and the brilliant, as well as perhaps the sinner and the saint. Rather than viewing things as being on either side of the fine line, it may be more productive and more faithful to consider things and people as being "in process" rather than sacred or profane.

Sadly, there are movements that are gaining force to destroy Hip Hop culture or at least sever the relationship between the Black Church and Hip Hop. Elder G. Craige Lewis of EX Ministries is but one example of those who see it as their mission to "expose the enemy" that is infiltrating the church through Hip Hop.[16] He has had a most profound exchange with The Ambassador (of Cross Movement), also a believer about the relationship that the church should have with Hip Hop. Lewis's reaction to Hip Hop, Spirit-led or not, is just what many in the Hip Hop world have come to expect from clergy: one that is judgmental and critical rather than welcoming, affirming, or challenging in love. Still, he is adding to the dialogue that is just now gaining distance and velocity between the Black Church and Hip Hop.

While it is far easier to see the presence of Islam within the history and current expressions of Hip Hop, there has been and continues to be a strong representation of not only Christian Rappers but rappers who are rhyming about Christian themes and theologically wrestling with Christian issues. There is clearly a presence of Christianity within Hip Hop.

Among many things, Hip Hop can be described as self-defining. It is also transcendent of ethnicities and cultures. It has the potential to exercise a prophetic gifting—speaking directly to society just what needs to be said. There is indeed room for that in the church. Just as Hip Hop brings this critical engagement to the world stage in politics, entertainment, and other aspects of human existence, it is beginning to show influence in the faith.

A Prophetic voice? Coming through Hip Hop? I can only imagine that similar words were said about Martin Luther King Jr., the students who organized a campaign of sit-ins during the 1950s and 1960s, and the thousands of others who spoke truth to power in various ways (including music) during the last century. Perhaps the most ironic turn will come when Hip Hop, perhaps the most exploited global movement in regard to commodification, begins to speak out in a louder voice about the chains of capitalism and neoliberal globalization. Then we will know that God really is speaking through Hip Hop, because most of the world will try to destroy it.

So what now? Only God knows. Perhaps that which was traditionally secular and traditionally sacred will be less and less distinguishable—and whether that is a positive thing will surely be debated. Perhaps there will be more songs like "Jesus Walks" or more rappers like MA$E and Rev. Run. Maybe there will be more worship services with rap- and Hip Hop–inspired dance. Maybe groups like the Cross Movement and lyricist ministers like BB Jay will get more spin on the radio or on television. Maybe not. Maybe religion will no longer be a welcome topic or welcomed participant in Hip Hop spheres? Maybe Hip Hop will forever be banned from approaching

Christian alters. Whatever the future may bring, realized engagement or broken relationship, I pray that the conversation continues because both these complex institutions have much to offer each other and much to offer the world together. More important, there is the great opportunity to bring glory to God by walking, with understanding, hand in hand through the various intersections that the streets of life may bring.

NOTES

1. The images of pastors driving bulldozers over the recordings of rap group 2 Live Crew or its cases with Christian conservative group American Family Association stand as examples of this.

2. For example, the song "B.I.B.L.E. (Basic Instruction Before Leaving Earth)," written and performed by the Gza, offers criticism toward not only churchgoers but many held beliefs and practices of Christianity. "B.I.B.L.E." was released on the *Liquid Sword Instrumentals* album on the Think Differently label in 2008.

3. James Spady, "Lean Back: Re-membering Religion, Culture, History, and Fam in the Hip Hop Global Community," written in 2005 and to be featured in the soon-to-be-published book by Spady, *The Cypha* (Umum Press).

4. Spady, "Lean Back."

5. James G. Spady, Charles G. Lee, and H. Samy Alim, *Street Conscious Rap* (Philadelphia: Umum/Loh 1999), 86–87.

6. The use of the term *Marian* makes reference to the characteristics of Mary, a friend and disciple of Jesus.

7. In 1990 Boogie Down Productions, led by KRS-One, released the album *Edutainment* on the Jive/RCA label. *Edutainment* is a combination of "education" and "entertainment."

8. Anthony Pinn, *Noise and Spirit* (New York: New York University Press, 2003), 19.

9. Pinn, *Noise and Spirit*, 42.

10. MC Hammer released "Pray" on the 1990 Capitol Records release *Please Hammer, Don't Hurt 'Em*.

11. The Trinity Broadcasting Network during the early twenty-first century.

12. Cheo Hadari Coker, *Unbelievable: The Life, Death, and Afterlife of Notorious B.I.G.* (Three Rivers Press, 2004).

13. Kanye West released *College Dropout* in 2004 on the Roc-A-Fella label.

14. "Jesus Walks" was also on the *College Dropout* album.

15. A line from the chorus of "Jesus Walks."

16. According to the description of EX Ministries (led by Elder G. Craige Lewis), one area of specialization is "exposing the enemy."

Chapter Five

Rap Music as Prophetic Utterance

Cynthia B. Belt

Since the beginning of my time in ministry, I have had a burning desire to deal with issues that relate to Black youth. Losing a nephew to gang violence shortly before his fifteenth birthday in 1993 and losing my own son at the age of twenty-three to AIDS in 1996 has made me acutely aware of the need for the Black Church to be intentional about its ministry to young people. It is no longer appropriate to dismiss the large numbers of unchurched Black youth as lazy, valueless, self-destructive, or violent. These are *our* children, *our* daughters and sons, *our* future. We must be willing to risk new understandings and new interpretative methods, and we must be willing to wrestle with the biblical text and sometimes lose. The Black Church can no longer afford to blindly and uncritically accept traditional interpretations of scripture, nor can it continue to blindly follow the traditions of generations past. God is calling us to a new thing, even in this generation that many have labeled as lost. In Isaiah 43:18–19a, God says,

> Forget about what happened long ago! Don't think about the past. I am creating something new. There it is! Do you see it? (Contemporary English Version)

I believe that we must be willing to see what God is doing in and through our youth.

I have often struggled with ways to articulate the gospel message that would make it relevant to young people. In 1998, I had the privilege of starting a new church in an urban neighborhood. This church was mostly made up of young people between the ages of twelve and seventeen. Each week, God did a new thing in me and in them as we struggled together to hear what God was revealing to us. I learned to study the music of young people, particularly rap or Hip Hop, as well as their poetry, short stories, movies, and the language of young people to hear God's prophetic word through them. As I have wrestled with the text, labored over sermons and

Bible study, and allowed young people a significant part in my ministry, my sense of the prophetic and the sacred has changed. The goal of this chapter is to examine a form of cultural expression—namely, rap music—and to look at its validity for biblical interpretation. After laying some foundational history and perspective, I take the lyrics of rap artist Tupac Shakur and discuss points of convergence with the Hebrew Bible prophetic tradition. For some of these lyrics, there are no specific biblical quotations; however, the prophetic tone and prophetic themes are consistent with the words of the Hebrew prophets. For the gospel to begin to impact and transform our communities, the church must take on new forms and speak a new language. It is my belief that language is intrinsically linked to biblical interpretation. That is, we view the words of the Bible and hear the message of the Bible through lenses of our language. Walter Brueggeman says that we must "recognize how singularly words, speech, language, and phrase shape the consciousness and define reality."[1]

In the Book of Acts, the Bible says that after the Holy Spirit was given, the disciples began to speak with "new tongues" and that each person hearing the message of Jesus Christ heard the gospel in his or her own language.[2] It is clear from this passage that the persons hearing the message accepted its validity because they heard of God's wonderful deeds in ways that spoke to the reality of their racial/ethnic identities. No doubt, each person present at Pentecost was familiar with the Greek language. Greek was the language of the marketplace. Probably, many were familiar with Hebrew or Aramaic because these were the languages of the scriptures. However, it is clear that each person was able to respond to God's message of saving grace because each heard it in her or his own language.

As we approach the twenty-first century, the church must again be willing to risk "speaking in tongues" for the sake of the gospel. J. Deotis Roberts says that we must look for new, nontraditional ways of doing ministry if we desire to reach Black youth, particularly those in hostile urban environments:

> Ministering to underclass black youth is a real challenge. First of all, the minister needs to be aware of the existence of this group of young people. He or she must enter their world. . . . There must follow a deep sense of caring for underclass youth. One has to find a means of encounter into the life-world of these young people. There are no traditional approaches to these youth.[3]

Black youth have adopted their own language as a form of cultural revolution that seeks to deny the oppression of Eurocentric society. The use of this language is pervasive and persistent. Even suburban Black youth and White youth who speak standard English know the language of the street and can converse in it freely.[4] The blunt, coded language of enslavement that signified to White slave masters—"Everybody talkin' 'bout heaven ain't goin' there"—has evolved into today's bold, confrontational in-your-face Hip Hop language.[5] There is a rawness to the language of the streets that mirrors the rawness of life on the streets. Crime, drugs, violence, unemployment, and unyielding frustration are elemental to the lives of many Black youth, and this is reflected in the content of their language. This language constitutes a form of resistance and self-identification for those who are completely marginalized.[6] The church can never hope to reach these young people with a watered-down, sugarcoated gospel that denies the reality of oppression and racism in our society.

According to Mike Dyson, urban streets are operating in what he calls a *juvenocracy*:

> the domination of black and Latino domestic and urban life by mostly male figures under the age of 25 who wield considerable economic, social, and moral influence. A juvenocracy may consist of drug gangs, street crews, loosely organized groups, and individual youths who engage in illicit activity. They operate outside the bounds of the moral and political economies of traditional homes and neighborhoods.[7]

Dyson goes on to express three factors that he feels have led to the rise in this juvenocracy. First, he describes the proliferation of violence in our lives. Among television, news, and music, American culture is inundated with visions of violence, in some cases twenty-four hours a day. For me, this proliferation of violence, even in programming directed at the very young, creates a culture where humans are considered expendable and violence, a badge of honor. Of course, Black bodies are, and have always been, the most expendable. Second, Dyson sites the emergence of the economy of crack. He feels that this economy has shifted power from traditional sources (i.e., working adults) to young Black and Latino males. The third and final factor for Dyson is the rise in the culture of the gun in America. Our love affair with weapons has endangered our youth.[8]

I would add to Dyson's factors a fourth. The decline of the influence of the church in the Black community has had a negative impact on our young people. Instead of reaching out to our youth as we once did, much of the church has recoiled in fear and condemnation. The Black Church, for the most part, has stuck its head in the sand and allowed a corrupt society to educate, nurture, and model for our young people its core values. We have condemned our young people, particularly musicians and specifically rappers, yet we offer nothing of substance to compel them toward another course of action. We have failed to deal with the issues of survival, simply staying alive from one day to the next, that confront many of our youngest children. We have also been blind to the systematic economic oppression of the poor, many of whom are people of color. How can the church begin to provide ministry that is both sensitive to the real issues facing many of its people and true to the transformational power of the gospel of Jesus Christ? I think we begin by removing the blinders and facing the harsh truth about life in many of our cities. Music, particularly rap music, provides us with a prophetic warning and a picturesque view of life in the ghetto.

Music has long been used by African Americans as resistance and social protest. James Cone explains that music has been a consistent form of self-identification and social expression for African Americans since slavery:

> Music has been and continues to be the most significant creative art expression of African Americans. Blacks sing and play music (in their churches and at juke-joint parties) as a way of coping with life's contradictions and of celebrating its triumphs. We sing when we are happy and when we are sad; when we get a job and when we lose one; when we protest for our rights and when the formal achievement of them makes no difference in the quality of our life. Singing is the medium through which we talk to each other and make known our perspectives on life to the world. It is our way of recording and reflecting on our experiences—the good and the bad, the personal and the political, the sacred and the secular.[9]

He goes on to say,

> Today, a new form of musical discourse has emerged in the black community. It's called "rap" music. It is musical-talk, extremely popular among young people who are searching for meaning in a world that has no place for them.[10]

As a form of social protest, rap music is a statement of class-conscious self-expression. It uses the language of the streets in ways that resist the institutionalized oppression of the underclass, and it provides a voice for those who would otherwise be silenced. According to Cornel West,

> Black rap music is primarily the musical expression of the paradoxical cry of desperation and celebration of the black underclass and poor working class, a cry which openly acknowledges and confronts the wave of personal cold-heartedness, criminal cruelty, and existential hopelessness in the black ghettos of Afro-America.[11]

Rap music—particularly gangsta rap, with its profanity and violence—represents a form of protest that is unique to this generation in that it does not seek legitimacy within the mainstream culture. Tupac Shakur described it this way:

> Hip hop music is really a reaction to the failures and the fallacies of the so-called civil rights movement. A lot of these people say, "we can vote now, we can sit on the bus, in the restaurant," but we don't own the bus, we don't own the restaurant.[12]

The response to this dilemma is alienation—and this alienation is felt by White youth as well as Black youth. At its best, rap music draws attention to the cultural realities of ghetto life, which mainstream Americans would rather ignore. Rap also gives a voice to the alienation and disillusionment felt by many Black youth. According to West Coast–based rapper Ice-T, "the ghetto is, at worst, the product of deliberately oppressive policies, at best, the result of racist neglect."[13] It is incumbent on mainstream society, particularly the Black Church, to acknowledge the validity of the lived experience of many in our inner cities and low-income communities. We cannot set at liberty those whom we feel are bound by their own vices, nor can we proclaim deliverance to those whom we ourselves keep in chains. The gospel of Jesus Christ can transform only those realities we acknowledge and diligently seek to transform.

The rap group Bone Thugs-n-Harmony encapsulates the reality of ghetto life in its song "1st of Tha Month," which candidly reflects those joyous days when the welfare checks arrive.[14] One member of the group comments on the difficulty of ghetto life:

> The first of the month was great because you knew you were gonna eat dinner.
> I was on welfare my whole life until I turned 18. It's a way of life in the ghetto.
> Ain't nothin but poverty here.[15]

In this interview, the group admitted to selling drugs to survive. Members said that they were happy now to be in a position that allowed them to leave the drug culture behind. They stated their commitment to give back to their community and help others leave the drug culture as well. However, they acknowledged what many mainstream Americans refuse to believe—that the current economy of the inner city is largely supported by the drug culture. While we decry the atrocities of drug use and drug dealing, we continue to support policies that keep large numbers of inner-city residents unemployed and underemployed.

Of particular interest to me are the often-prophetic lyrics of Tupac Shakur. He has become an alternative religious icon for many young people. On his posthumous CD *Makevelli: The Don Killuminati*, Tupac is pictured hanging on a cross, and youth now expect his return.[16] Along with other rap artists, Tupac uses quasi-religious themes in his lyrics to express his frustration with American society and his condemnation of the religious establishment. He is a self-proclaimed prophetic voice for many marginalized Black youth. As I experienced the raw power of his songs and his lyrics, I was reminded of the prophets Isaiah, Jeremiah, Amos, Malcolm X, and Martin Luther King Jr. It should not be surprising, however, that Tupac's lyrics have a prophetic edge.

Tupac Shakur was born on June 16, 1971, to Alice Williams and Billy Garland. Both were founding members of the national Black Panther Party based in New York in the 1960s. Alice took the name Afeni Shakur after she married a man named Mutulu Shakur when Tupac was a toddler, and she gave her son the name Tupac Amaru after a warrior and the last Inca chief to be tortured and murdered by Spanish conquistadores. It means "Shining Serpent," which was an Incan symbol for wisdom and courage. "Shakur" is Arabic for "Thankful to God." Both Tupac's father and stepfather were activists in the Black Panther Party and were wanted off and on by the law. Tupac learned early in his life to distrust police and other White officials. His godfather was Elmer "Geronimo" Pratt, a deputy minister in the Black Panther Party. Tupac was groomed early on to be an activist, to be engaged in political resistance, and to be a prophet for his people. He would later say of himself that he continued in the footsteps of Geronimo Pratt, Afeni and the Black Panthers, Mutulu Shakur, and Lumumba Shakur. He referred to them in his lyrics as political prisoners.

After two years in Baltimore, where he attended the Baltimore High School for the Arts, Tupac and his family moved to Marin City, California. It was in this community that Tupac was exposed to drugs, prostitution, and all the other ills of ghetto life. It was also at this time that his mother became a cocaine addict. When he felt that he could no longer handle his mother's addiction, he moved out of her apartment and into an abandoned building with a group of boys. Homeless, he eventually dropped out of school at the age of 17. After working a series of odd jobs, he sold crack on the street to get by. It was out of this environment that Tupac began to rap and finally got a break in the rap industry and eventually in movies. The seeds of his prophetic destiny began to take root.[17]

Years after his death, young people all over the world remain convinced that rapper Tupac Shakur is still alive. The title of his posthumous CD *Makevelli: The Don Killuminati* calls to mind the story of one who faked his own death. However, the picture of Shakur on the CD (he is featured hanging on a cross) and the allusions to his foreknowledge of his death in the cuts released after his death link this young man with the Messiah, Jesus Christ, the one who did rise from the dead. Even in the title of this CD, Tupac alludes to biblical themes. The full title is *The Don Killuminati—The 7 Day Theory*, a clear allusion to the biblical story of creation. Tupac himself considered his music spiritual. He likened his lyrics to the old Negro spirituals,

> except for the fact that I'm not saying, "We shall overcome." I'm saying, we *are* overcome.[18]

Many of Tupac's songs have religious overtones, but three in particular caught my attention: "Blasphemy," from *The Don Killuminati*; "So Many Tears," from *Me against the World*; and "Words of Wisdom," from *2pocolypse*.[19] Tupac stands squarely within the tradition of the Black preacher in his use of scripture and the biblical stories to critique an unjust, insensitive society. He is prophetic in the sense that he accomplishes the task that Walter Brueggeman describes for prophetic ministry: "to nurture, nourish, and evoke a consciousness and perception alternative to the consciousness and perception of the dominant culture around us."[20]

Tupac's lyrics, which give a no-holds-barred account of ghetto life, adequately do what Brueggeman describes as cutting through the numbness of our religious self-deception—namely, the notion that all is well in "Christian" America. In the song "Cradle to the Grave," Tupac offers a well-constructed critique on economic injustice in America. From images of alcoholism, narcotics peddling, and abuse to the effects of trying to survive in this "hell on earth," his poignant examination of many examples suffering in the reality of poverty is effective.[21]

Tupac's songs offer to Black folk—and, indeed, to all who would name the name of Jesus—an opportunity to evaluate who we are in God, in light of the masses whom we have written off as Generation X. In this, he accomplishes the threefold task of the prophetic as described by Brueggeman: first, to offer symbols that are adequate to the horror and massiveness of the experience, which evokes numbness and requires denial; second, to bring to public expression those very fears and terrors that have been denied so long and suppressed so deeply that we do not know they are there; and, third, to speak metaphorically but concretely about the real deathliness that hovers over us and gnaws within us.[22] He exposes White America's fears of Black masculinity, succinctly expresses the realities of poverty as experienced by Blacks in the ghetto, and articulates the hopes and frustrations of Black youth.

In "Words of Wisdom" the rapper expresses the horrible reality of a permanent lower class that has been systematically denied access to jobs, education, and due process.[23] Our fear—particularly those of us who have arrived at the so-called middle class—is that we will be relegated to these ranks ourselves; that is why it is so difficult to face. The American dream is an illusion, a hoax, craftily woven by a person's intent on prospering at the expense of others. But for many, it is more comfortable to chase a false dream than to dream a new world.

"Blasphemy" begins with a gospel preacher talking about Jesus's return and the need to "get right" with God by accepting Jesus Christ as personal savior.[24] The rapper expresses his disdain for preachers who convey this message without acknowledging the harsh reality of ghetto life. For Tupac, the preacher is a liar when he or she preaches about persons going to hell and does nothing to alter the reality that the life of a crackhead is eternal fire. The rapper also questions the preacher who labels Blacks in the ghetto as evil without seeing the evil of the society that perpetuates their meager existence. Reflecting on Tupac's stimulating lyrics, how do we as the Black Church continue to justify preaching and evangelizing in a manner that labels some as "none of God's people?"

Surprisingly, the rapper acknowledges Jesus's own goodness and says that Jesus should understand the circumstances that give rise to "thug life." Tupac's direct narrative to Jesus, specifically, is not only a tremendous attribute of his own spiritual inquiry but, more important, a direct challenge to the church. He also says that he hopes heaven is not just another door to more misery. In the final analysis, God is portrayed as one who looks on the heart and understands the purity within. Also implicit in this song is a rejection of those who preach one message for ghetto youth and another for themselves.

Tupac also uses the Exodus story in this song. He equates his quest, and that of his boyz, with Moses and the Exodus. He alludes to Pharaoh's demise in the Red Sea, offering an interesting perspective to those who might listen; Tupac knew much about the Bible. He even ministers, so to speak, as it is clear that he wants those who hear his words to know that they have an identity in God and that God has owned them as God's own children. For Tupac, God has heard the cries of God's children, and God's response is to raise up a "A Thug Nation" to bring judgment on the oppressors. He clearly sees even his illegal activity as an act of prophetic resistance to a society that refuses to acknowledge his value as a human being.

Tupac also equates himself with Jesus Christ in "Blasphemy." I believe that here he is saying, similar to James Cone, that Jesus was a person of color, born to a Black woman. What Tupac does here is make Jesus a part of the struggle of Blacks against the oppressive forces of ghetto life. Jesus is a brotha, a homey, one of the boyz in the hood. He and his boyz are fighting devils and being crucified because of it. Yet the Black Church refuses to hear these words.

In his song "So Many Tears," from the album *Me against the World*, Tupac opens with a paraphrase of the Twenty-Third Psalm.[25] With the opening paraphrase and throughout this song, Tupac pleads his case to God and offers up the story of his life both tragically and poetically. Like the psalmist, Tupac exposes his anger at those who oppress him and wonders if God will see him through this hell on earth. However, Tupac is unable to say like the Psalmist, "I shall fear no evil, for thou art with me."[26] He must offer his plaintive plea, asking God to walk with him because he is unsure of how God will judge him in the end. The lyrics of this song are reminiscent of Psalm 119:81–84, which reads,

I long for you to rescue me! Your word is my only hope. I am worn out from waiting for you to keep your word. When will you have mercy? My life is wasting away like a dried-up wineskin, but I have not forgotten your teachings. I am your servant! How long must I suffer? When will you punish those troublemakers? (Contemporary English Version)

This is the plaintive plea of one calling out to God for deliverance from intense oppression.

When I first read the lyrics to "So Many Tears," the psalmist came to mind. However, when I actually experienced the song, my mind went to Jeremiah 8:21–9:1:

Since my people are crushed, I am crushed; I mourn, and horror grips me. Is there no balm in Gilead? Is there no physician there? Why then is there no healing for the wound of my people? Oh, that my head were a spring of water and my eyes a fountain of tears! I would weep day and night for the slain of my people. (Contemporary English Version)

Like Jeremiah, Tupac expresses grief over the plight of his people. He understands like Brueggeman that the "proper idiom for the prophet in cutting through the royal numbness and denial is the language of grief."[27] Tupac and those prophetic rappers who followed him must mourn aloud and grieve because the Black community is unable or unwilling to do so. When our sons and daughters must ask the question "Will I make it to old age?" we should be grieving and demanding some change in our society.

As a critique of society, Tupac uses both his lyrics and his song titles to get his point across. The song "Blasphemy" decries a religion and a society that talks about righteousness and does not deal justly with the poor. Tupac asked, are we to cry when members who persecute us, namely the police, die? Like the prophet Amos, who preached a critique of Israel's society, Tupac calls us into accountability for our refusal to hear the cries of the poor and the oppressed. Like Isaiah, he is also critiquing God's people, the church, for its refusal to stand for the rights of the poor and the oppressed.[28] Just as our foreparents sang, "Everybody talkin' 'bout heaven ain't goin' there," Tupac proclaims that we are probably already in hell, misguided, disillusioned, and operating in the wrong mission.

Similar to Isaiah, Jeremiah, Ezekiel, and Amos, Tupac suggests in his lyrics that America will be judged for the way that it has oppressed people of color. In his song "Words of Wisdom," Tupac charges the entire country with the various crimes that have been scapegoated on young Black males specifically and urban communities of color in general: rape, murder, assault, robbery, and false imprisonment. Further, he concludes by finding America guilty of all charges. Similar words can be found in the writings of all the prophets. This is a call to accountability demanding that justice be served.

Like Amos, Tupac challenges the systematic abuse of the poor and identifies the heavy taxation that occurs for people with limited, fixed, or no income. Amos 5:10–12, 24 is clearly invoked:

> You people hate judges and honest witnesses; you abuse the poor and demand heavy taxes from them. You have built expensive homes, but you won't enjoy them; you have planted vineyards, but you will get no wine. I am the LORD, and I know your terrible sins. You cheat honest people and take bribes; you rob the poor of justice. But let justice and fairness flow like a river that never runs dry. (Contemporary English Version)

Tupac goes on to claim that the very persons that America has oppressed have now become the country's worst nightmare.

Again in his song "Words of Wisdom," Tupac tries to stir hope by calling those who are oppressed to fight back. He challenges the oppressed to not succumb to fear but find a new meaning in survival. He even implores them to develop a self-definition of life and reality, one where words such as "nigga" can be redefined to mean "Never Ignorant Getting Goals Accomplished." Tupac expresses the need of the oppressed to take a stand. In this, he stands in the tradition of Malcolm X, calling people of color to wake up and realize what is going on around them. It is a call to consciousness and a call to community.

Tupac is also doing what Brueggeman describes as "mining the memory of his people and educating them to use the tools of hope."[29] Tupac understood that the act of naming is essential to the building of hope in the Black community. He must rename and reclaim the very words that the oppressor has used to describe his people. A nigga is no longer the object of the White man's contempt. The horrors of the ghetto are real, but when brothas and sistas stop fighting one another and begin to remove the blinders, they will be able to fight and die like persons of honor.

Later in this song, he redefines the reality of Blacks in the ghetto by giving a vision of what can be if we begin to reach back to our own sense of history and community. He also rejects the leaders that have been acceptable to the oppressors and opts instead for identification with the more radical leader, Malcolm X. His position is one we should heed. The King presented in our textbooks is not the radical King who denounced the Vietnam War and the condition of Blacks in the ghetto. We must wonder why we must settle for a watered-down version of one leader when our history is filled with women and men who have opposed the forces of oppression.

Finally, Tupac expresses in his lyrics hope in a God who will look beyond the circumstances of ghetto life and see the purity within those persons trapped in the maze of ghetto life. In "Blasphemy," "So Many Tears," and "Cradle to the Grave," Tupac articulates his hope in a God that is different from the God preached in most of society. Tupac is clinging to the God of the oppressed—the one who chose to identify with sinners, dope dealers, and prostitutes.

How can the church respond to the prophetic voice of rappers such as Tupac Shakur and to the masses of underprivileged youth who consider him their spokesperson? Again, I turn to Brueggeman for the words. The church must add its voice and begin to speak prophetic words, not against rappers, but in concert with them, giving their expressions validity and power to speak as the voice of God. "The church must offer symbols that are adequate to contradict the situation of hopelessness" within which our young people find themselves.[30] We cannot continue to co-opt the power of the gospel message and domesticate Jesus—the same Jesus who came into the temple courtyard, took up a whip, turned over tables, and shouted, "My father's house is a house of prayer, and you have made it into a den of thieves."[31]

Like the Gadarene demoniac, Black youth are possessed with a legion of demons.[32] Oppression, poverty, and racism have combined to create mighty chains that continue to bind them. In disproportionate numbers, Black youth are consigned to the tombs—the tombs of prison, addiction, unemployment, illiteracy, and much more. The Black Church must once again speak a word of deliverance to the dispossessed, a word of hope to the hopeless, and a word of warning to the world that seeks to keep our youth bound. Just as the graveyard symbolized death for the demoniac, Black youth have been consigned to the ghetto, which has become a culture of death. Many young people will quickly say that they will probably not live to be old. However, the biblical witness of the demoniac reminds us that even within the context of death, the graveyard, Jesus can speak, deliver, and restore.

I believe that the church must discard the rhetoric that has sustained it in the past and risk speaking in tongues to reach young people. Dare we say that Jesus is a brotha, a homey, one of the boyz? Can we tell God in worship and in prayer that God's got it going on, that God is all that and a bag of chips, and that we give God God's props? Is it too offensive to us to rewrite the parables so that they fit the culture and experience of our youth? I don't think so. In fact, I believe that it is the only way we can truly offer Jesus as a relevant hope, not only for Black youth, but for many of the poor and oppressed of our nation.

NOTES

1. Walter Brueggeman, *The Prophetic Imagination* (Philadelphia: Fortress Press, 1978), 66.

2. Acts 2:4.

3. J. Deotis Roberts, *The Prophethood of Black Believers: An African American Political Theology for Ministry* (Louisville, KY: Westminster/John Knox Press, 1994), 59.

4. Cornel West, *Prophetic Fragments: Illuminations of the Crisis in American Religion and Culture* (Grand Rapids, MI: William B. Eerdman's Publishing Company, 1988), 177.

5. Refers to the Negro spiritual "Ev'rybody talkin' 'bout heav'n ain't goin'." Although there are numerous interpretations of the vernacular spelling and even more arrangements of the spiritual, the connotation of the expression is clear in the title.

6. Tricia Rose, "Orality and Technology: Rap Music and Afro-American Cultural Resistance," in *Popular Music and Society*, ed. R. Serge Densoff (Bowling Green, OH: Bowling Green State University, 1989), 37.

7. Michael E. Dyson, *Race Rules: Navigating the Color Line* (New York: Vintage Books, 1997), 140–41.

8. Dyson, *Race Rules*, 143.

9. James Cone, *The Spirituals and the Blues* (Maryknoll, NY: Orbis, 1995), 129.

10. Cone, *The Spirituals and the Blues*, 129–30.

11. West, *Prophetic Fragments*, 186.

12. Cathy Scott, *The Killing of Tupac Shakur* (Las Vegas, NV: Huntington Press, 1997), 132.

13. Michael Eric Dyson, *Between God and Gansta Rap: Bearing Witness to Black Culture* (New York: Oxford University Press, 1996), 184–87.

14. Bone Thugs-n-Harmony released "1st of tha Month" in 1995 on the Ruthless Records recording *E 1999 Eternal*.

15. A. J. Woodson, "Behold the Brothaz Bone," in *Word Up!* (Paramus, NJ: Word Up!, 1997), 40–41.

16. The posthumous recording *The Don Killuminati: The 7 Day Theory* was released on November 5, 1996, on the Death Row/Interscope label.

17. Scott, *The Killing of Tupac Shakur*, 63–75.

18. Scott, *The Killing of Tupac Shakur*, 178.

19. *Me against the World* was released on the Jive/Interscope label in 1995, and *2pocolpyse Now* was released in 1991 on the Jive/Interscope label.

20. Brueggeman, *The Prophetic Imagination*, 13.

21. "Cradle to the Grave" was released on *Thug Life Volume 1*, the 1994 release by the group Thug Life (led by Tupac Shakur) on the Interscope label.

22. Brueggeman, *The Prophetic Imagination*, 49–50.

23. "Words of Wisdom" was released as part of the *2Pacalypse Now* project.

24. "Blasphemy" was released as part of *The Don Killuminati: The 7 Day Theory* project.

25. *Me against the World* was released in 1995 on the Amaru/Jive/Interscope label.

26. Psalm 23:4.

27. Brueggeman, *The Prophetic Imagination*, 51.

28. Isaiah 1:21–23.

29. Brueggeman, *The Prophetic Imagination*, 66.

30. Brueggeman, *The Prophetic Imagination*, 66.

31. Mark 11:15–17, Matthew 21:12, and John 2:15–16.

32. Matthew 8:28–34, Mark 5:1–20, and Luke 8:26–39.

Chapter Six

Binding the Straw Man: Hip Hop, African American Protestant Religion, and the Dilemma of Dialogue

Lerone A. Martin

African American religious history reveals a unique relationship between the Black Church and popular culture, particularly popular music. Thomas Dorsey's innovations in Gospel music and Rosetta Tharpe's controversial popularizing of Gospel music are two examples that attest to the peculiarity of this historically tenuous relationship.[1]

One thing that is certain, concerning our present historical moment, is that rap music, like other forms of Black popular music of the past, has seized the imagination of a generation across the globe and has exacted a significant influence on American culture and simultaneously on African American life.[2] This emergence of Hip Hop has reshaped and continues to reshape African American identities, communities, and cultural practices. African American Protestant churches are put into a familiar situation—namely, facing the challenge of grappling with their relationship to Black popular music and culture. Our contemporary challenge should first be understood in light of the storied history between Black popular music and Black sacred music. From this place, the question must be asked: How can African American faith communities address and respond to Hip Hop music and culture in a manner that is faithful to the mission of Jesus Christ and that correspondingly addresses the realities of African American life? The aim of this chapter, then, is to help African American faith communities reframe their approach, discussion, understanding, and relationship to Hip Hop music in hopes of overcoming the dilemma of dialogue between Black faith communities and Hip Hop culture.

There is a critical mass of individual churches and ministries that have embraced Hip Hop culture and the effect that it has had on African American communities. These ministries, in there own ways, have negotiated faith with

the popular music of our day. Such is evidenced by a change in worship and
faith practices, religious imagination, and religious discourse.[3] Numerous
ministries and churches remind us that if the church is to remain faithful to
the mission of Jesus Christ, there must exist a continual dialogue between
faith communities and the realities of their respective communities.
However, before any meaningful dialogue can take place, Hip Hop must be
redeemed from the demonization it has endured. Let me be clear, I do not
have any delusions of grandeur nor romanticism of Hip Hop. I too am deeply
disturbed and vexed by Hip Hop's championing of homophobia, misogyny,
violence, and sexism. However, it is important to note that Hip Hop has
always been a "fragmented universe of political rap (Public Enemy), street
provocateurs (NWA), Afrocentrics (Brand Nubian), and even comics (Biz
Markie)."[4] The difficulty arises in that, similar to the representative images
of African American churches, the rap music images that bombard our
airwaves are often the ones saturated with first-person singular messages of
immediate gratification, product endorsement, and sundry expressions of
"bling bling." To typify African American Protestant religion and Hip Hop
solely based on such images is to miss the larger picture.

Black faith communities, along with C. Delores Tucker, Senator Bob
Dole, Tipper Gore, Bill Cosby, John McWhorter, and countless others, have
been influential in using these demonizing vices to construct a Hip Hop
"straw man."[5] This straw man serves as a scapegoat and a convenient culprit
in the midst of perilous times. The persistence of the Hip Hop straw man
should not be surprising to us, seeing that we dwell in the midst of an age
where political and religious scapegoats abound. By constructing this Hip
Hop straw man and all its mythic scarecrow dimensions, African American
Protestant religion has hindered the exploration and conception of Hip Hop
as a ripe field, full of viable and creative expression for faith in the twenty-
first century. This opposition has primarily expressed itself in three ways
within African American faith communities: the offensive, the defensive, and
resistance. By examining these three oppositional stances and exposing the
"straw" that they contribute to the dilemma of dialogue, we will be able to
reframe the conversation. Binding the straw man will help to clear the path
for fruitful dialogue concerning Hip Hop and its relationship to the Black
Church.

HIP HOP'S STRAW ORIGIN: THE OFFENSIVE

The first oppositional stance is best understood as an "offensive" expression.
It is best characterized by the zealous employment of wholesale theological
and cultural "warfare" (the term used by its adherents) against Hip Hop and

the media. By exposing Hip Hop's "evil" origins and its sinister vehicle, the media, this stance has as its goal the disarming of the "evil" and destructive hold of the media and Hip Hop upon African American culture. This effort is seen as the paramount battle for the hearts and minds of African American youth. Oddly enough, through the relentless selling of various forms of media (books, CDs, DVDs), this faith expression espouses an offensive against Hip Hop in any of the various expressions.[6]

What this camp fails to consider is the very context in which Hip Hop was birthed. By focusing on Hip Hop's vices and resulting "evil," it fails to recognize or address the persistence of the very "evil" conditions that gave birth to Hip Hop. The socioeconomic background of the birth of rap music in the late 1970s and the characterization of its adolescents of the 1980s are best summed by Michael Eric Dyson:

> The bitter belly of the 70s . . . the fallout was felt in restructured automobile industries and collapsed steel mills. It was extended in exported employment to foreign markets. . . . There was the depletion of social services to reverse the material ruin of black life. Later, public spaces for black recreation were gutted by Reaganomics or violently transformed by lethal drug economies. Hip Hop was born in these bleak conditions[7]

Black faith communities who mount an offensive against Hip Hop tend, or rather should I say, force themselves to ignore that Hip Hop's birth took place alongside the establishment of Black and Brown ghettoes. Such neighborhoods of concentrated poverty were constructed by Whites in hopes of controlling burgeoning minority populations, and they were solidified through a series of legalized institutional practices, private behaviors, and public policies.[8] As if this weren't enough, Hip Hop's budding adolescence consisted of being confronted with the economic environment of the Reagan era and all its setbacks in minority housing, health and welfare concerns, and urban public education. The urban neighborhoods of the Reagan era provided a supportive structural and environmental alcove for the emergence of an "oppositional culture."[9] Hip Hop is a manifestation of this oppositional culture, not the womb of this culture.

Typifying this stance, self-professed Christian Bill Cosby commented on the influence of Hip Hop on African American youth:

> The debauchery in BET videos became the strongest influence on black people in their teens and early twenties, replacing the values and models of success that went missing with absent voices of parents and civil rights leaders.[10]

While the significant influence of Hip Hop can rarely be denied, situating Hip Hop as the strongest influence that contributes to our current "paradise lost" posits a ludicrous "golden day" narrative of African American culture.

This narrative ignores, for instance, the effects of dilapidated public schools, biased public school funding, and the realities of working poor families in impoverished communities. To ignore such origins or the environment that gave birth to Hip Hop mislabels the faith community's concerns of evil practices and secondly creates a systemic misunderstanding of Hip Hop and its place in the chronological evolution of Black popular music.

Hip Hop's origin speaks to the creative genius of African Americans faced with dire circumstances. By saying nothing of rap music's environmental incubator is tantamount to indicting a victim for crying out. When it is understood this way, one can really hear the prophetic antagonistic utterances of Grand Master Flash and the Furious Five or the pop culture indictments of Jay Z.[11] Rap music can then be understood as the passionate murmurings of oppositional voices expressing themselves in various kinds of ways in the midst of a hostile environment. The violence and sexism that plague Hip Hop testify to the anger and lack of regard for human life that were and continue to be engendered within these contexts. Through varying expressions of Hip Hop, as controversial as they may be, artists testify to a sentiment of people grappling with the overwhelming sense of despair while trying to maintain a sense of human dignity.

Again, the ways in which this struggle for human dignity finds words is oftentimes plagued with the "isms" mentioned previously. However, our faith communities must lend an ear and dialogue with this resounding sound of struggle and pain if it intends to minister to the realities of African American life. To demonize such voices is to throw out a crying naked baby with the bath water. African American faith communities can no longer harbor full opposition to Hip Hop, for it is not the virus that plagues our communities. Rather Hip Hop is the outbreaking of a fever caused by the social and economic viruses that were injected, created, and maintained within African American communities. The fever has manifested itself to notify us to what is going on within our communities. While the symptomatic fever of Hip Hop is running extremely high, faith communities cannot lose sight of the cultural "viruses" that cause the "fever"—to which we now turn our attention.

HIP HOP'S STRAW "CULTURE": THE DEFENSIVE

The second response of many African American church communities toward Hip Hop can be described as "defensive." This strategy draws the ecclesiastical and theological line in the sand and refuses any type of change or dialogue with Hip Hop that does not involve one side lecturing the other. Such faith communities resent rap music on the grounds that it represents

Hip Hop culture—a culture that indulges and prides itself upon the cultural rituals and norms of sexism, patriarchy, homophobia, violence, and misogyny. If we look at this stance closely, we can see the straw contribution of this cultural argument.

Hip Hop culture and rap music are not the only cultural forms that are plagued with "isms." The "sin" of Hip Hop culture is that its existence explicitly brings out the "isms" that our culture and institutions seldom talk about or like to recognize. To this end, Hip Hop calls into question the romanticism of the past. For example, Juan Williams, in his recent book *Enough*, states that in an interview with Bill Cosby, the famed actor and comedian commented,

> When I grew up in Philadelphia, a man who got a woman pregnant without marrying her often left town or went in the military or to a reform school. Now it is acceptable behavior, celebrated in hip hop's corrosive culture. [12]

These comments shed light on the "sin" of Hip Hop and the problem of a romanticized cultural past. While leaving town or entering the military is hardly a "civil" response to having a child out of wedlock, how does it differentiate from Cosby's indictment of Hip Hop's current culture? In both situations, the father is not present in the child's life in a substantive way, so we are left to choose from a "civil and honorable" abandonment or just plain abandonment. This is just one example of how "rap crudely exposes harmful beliefs and practices that are often maintained with deceptive civility in much of mainstream society, including many black communities," particularly African American Churches. [13]

Let us be clear, sexism, patriarchy, and homophobia are explicitly spelled out within the lyrics of the majority of rap lyrics by larger-than-life, diamond-encrusted celebrities. However, these same values are implicitly expressed within the practices and discourses of many faith communities. We need to look no further than our local faith communities' patriarchal leaderships and larger-than-life celebrity pastors who possess their own "bling-bling" proclivities. The only distinction seems to be that within our faith communities, these vices are carried out under the guise of sanctified hierarchies and righteous indignations that are then baptized in authoritative biblical interpretation. Simply put, faith communities that oppose Hip Hop on the grounds of its "corrosive culture" are really holding the Hip Hop generation accountable for not embracing sanitized, institutionally acceptable forms of these vices. [14]

HIP HOP'S INTENT: RESISTANCE

The third perspective, resistance, is closely related to the aforementioned perspectives in its result. This perspective is best described as "apathetic" or indifferent to Hip Hop culture. Whereas the two aforementioned groups chose to mobilize against Hip Hop in some way, this perspective deems dialogue with Hip Hop and discussions such as those put forth in this book as inappropriate and lacking serious value to African American Protestant religion. Instead of drawing any lines in the sand, such groups seemingly choose to just stick their ecclesiastical heads in it. This perspective is found within faith communities and can be seen in the resistance of teachers, religious scholars, and seminaries to even acknowledge the dilemma. Little can be said about those who embrace this ignorance, save those who choose to bury their heads and risk suffocating in irrelevancy. Our communities are riddled with ecclesiastical edifices of prior prominence that refuse to change and dialogue with the realities of their respective surrounding communities. Such churches are now limping along toward their own extinction on the crutches of "what used to be." The struggle of African American communities to understand if and how faith and Hip Hop intersect is entirely too dire for our faith communities to embrace apathy, rigidity, and ignorance. By refusing to reimagine the way that faith and ministry are expressed and embodied in the midst of a culture strongly enamored with Hip Hop is to refuse to responsibly address the specific social and cultural realities of the masses of African American people. The result of which is irrelevancy and extinction.

CONCLUSION

It has been said that one without a memory is like one who looks in the mirror and then walks away forgetting what she or he has seen. This amnesia plagues us, as we forget that patriarchy, homophobia, and sexism are insignias of American culture as a whole, not just Hip Hop. Rap music is not the oxygen of homophobia, sexism, and misogyny; rather, it is simply our society's and faith community's "mirror mirror on the wall." Attacking, scapegoating, and ignoring Hip Hop is tantamount to "shattering" the mirror. Unfortunately, maybe this is indeed the agenda of some African American churches.

Thomas Dorsey, the "father of Gospel music," once said that the blues were as important to a person feeling bad as "Nearer My God to Thee." I'm not talking about popularity; I'm talking about inside the individual . . . where there is some secret down there that they didn't bring out. . . . When you cry out, that is something down there that should have come out a long time ago.[15]

Hip Hop, like the blues, grows out of the depths of African American experience. Hip Hop, with all of its debauchery, is indeed a voice calling out in the wilderness of African American life. Unashamedly and in aggressive fashion, it is articulating the racist, sexist, homophobic, materialistic, and capitalistic "secrets" of America that were hidden in civility. Hip Hop's voice is a constant reminder that there is something deep within our nation and faith communities that should have been dealt with a long time ago. To bind the straw man, faith communities must dialogue with Hip Hop and concern ourselves not with liberation from Hip Hop but with freeing our society and faith communities at large from sexism, misogyny, hypermasculinity, and violence.

NOTES

1. On Thomas Dorsey, see Michael W. Harris, *The Rise of Gospel Blues: The Music of Thomas Andrew Dorsey in the Urban Church* (New York: Oxford University Press, 1992). On Rosetta Tharpe, see Jerma A. Jackson, *Singing in My Soul: Black Gospel Music in a Secular Age* (Chapel Hill: University of North Carolina Press, 2004). Both these texts attest to the controversial and popular relationship between African American religion and popular music.

2. Cornel West, *Democracy Matters* (New York: Penguin Press, 2004), 183.

3. For some examples, see *Jet*, August 28, 2006.

4. Ethan Brown, *Queens Reigns Supreme* (New York: Anchor Books, 2005), 112.

5. Within the discipline of logic, the "straw man fallacy" is one of the most noted and best recognized forms of incorrect reasoning. In layperson's terms, it is when one purposefully bases his or her argument on a distorted or misrepresented perception of the other person's claim.

6. See, for example, G. Craige Lewis's DVD *The Truth behind Hip Hop*, http://www.exministries.com/. The webpage boasts the celebration of the destruction of over one million CDs worldwide. Accessed September 23, 2006.

7. Michael Eric Dyson, *Between God and Gangsta Rap* (New York: Oxford University Press, 1996), 177. In this text, Dyson puts forth this argument in regard to Gangsta Rap.

8. Douglas S. Massey and Nancy A. Denton, *American Apartheid* (Cambridge, MA: Harvard University Press, 1993), 10.

9. Massey and Denton, *American Apartheid*, 13.

10. Juan Williams, *Enough* (New York: Crown, 2006), 136.

11. For example, songs such as "The Message" by Grand Master Flash and the Furious Five released in 1982 on Sugar Hill Records. Others, such as "Renegade" or "Izzo (H.O.V.A)" by Jay-Z, were released on his 2001 Roc-A-Fella Records album *The Blueprint*.

12. Williams, *Enough*, 145.

13. Dyson, *Between God and Gangsta Rap*, 177.

14. Mark Anthony Neal, *New Black Man* (New York: Routledge, 2005), 9.

15. Nick Salvatore, *Singing in a Strange Land: C.L. Franklin, the Black Church, and the Transformation of America* (New York: Little, Brown, 2005), 32.

Chapter Seven

Sermon: "Kick Your Delilah to the Curb"

Sherman A. Gordon

This morning's scriptural reference is Judges 16:4–9, 13–17 (emphasis on 16–17a).

Some time later, he fell in love with a woman in the Valley of Sorek whose name was Delilah. The rulers of the Philistines went to her and said, "See if you can lure him into showing you the secret of his great strength and how we can overpower him so we may tie him up and subdue him. Each one of us will give you eleven hundred shekels of silver." So Delilah said to Samson, "Tell me the secret of your great strength and how you can be tied up and subdued." Samson answered her, "If anyone ties me with seven fresh bowstrings that have not been dried, I'll become as weak as any other man." Then the rulers of the Philistines brought her seven fresh bowstrings that had not been dried, and she tied him with them. With men hidden in the room, she called to him, "Samson, the Philistines are upon you!" But he snapped the bowstrings as easily as a piece of string snaps when it comes close to a flame. So the secret of his strength was not discovered.

Delilah then said to Samson, "All this time you have been making a fool of me and lying to me. Tell me how you can be tied." He replied, "If you weave the seven braids of my head into the fabric on the loom and tighten it with the pin, I'll become as weak as any other man." So while he was sleeping, Delilah took the seven braids of his head, wove them into the fabric and tightened it with the pin. Again she called to him, "Samson, the Philistines are upon you!" He awoke from his sleep and pulled up the pin and the loom, with the fabric. Then she said to him, "How can you say, 'I love you,' when you won't confide in me? This is the third time you have made a fool of me and haven't told me the secret of your great strength." With such nagging she prodded him day after day until he was sick to death of it. So he told her everything. "No razor has ever been used on my head," he said, "because I have been a Nazirite dedicated to God from my mother's womb. If my head were shaved, my strength would leave me, and I would become as weak as any other man." (New International Version)

In our text, we find a couple, no, a man and a woman named Samson and Delilah, whose story is more famous than Shakespeare's Romeo and Juliet, Anthony and Cleopatra, Othello and Desdemona, yes, even more famous than Janet Jackson and Jermaine Dupree. In our text, we find a man who was robust, a model of health, full of vigor, young, energetic, quick on his feet, sharp in his head, a man who could rip a lion apart with his bare hands and a martial artist in his use of the jawbone. He was a committed man. He was a Nazirite. As a Nazirite, he had committed, dedicated, and devoted his life to a lifestyle that obligated him to refrain from touching a dead body, abstain from drinking alcohol, and vowed to never allow a razor to come upon his head. This was not only Samson's yearly resolution but a resolution made from birth. Yet Samson, like many of us, found himself coming up short.

Preachers, teachers, and lecturers have preached and taught on Samson for centuries. They like to paint the picture that Samson's ultimate fall was because of his dealing with Delilah. What is it about human nature that when we fall, we quickly want to blame it on someone else? You remember Adam, "Lord, it's that woman." Adam blamed Eve. Eve blamed the serpent, and the serpent sought to place his blame on God. Many naively suggest that had Samson never fooled around with Delilah, he would have never faced the fate he encountered. However, I am prepared to argue that while it may not have been Delilah, it would have been a "Halle Berry." For understand that Samson's real problem was not so much with a lady from the Valley of Sorek, which means "choice vine," a valley where men would stop on their journey from Jerusalem to the Mediterranean Sea to indulge themselves in the world's oldest profession of prostitution, but Samson's real problem was from the valley of within. Samson had personal problems that he just could not seem to get a grip on. On the outside, everything looked fine, but on the inside, when it came to the valley of within, Samson was "tore up from the floor up." He was a public success but a private failure.

Now, be sure that in our text, Delilah was a woman; in fact she was all woman—"hips, lips, and fingertips." Like the grapes being plucked from the vine, Delilah was a plump and precious jewel. Like the sweet savory taste of maple syrup, so was Delilah. However, in today's exegesis of the text, we must understand that Delilah does not always have to be a woman! Truth be told, Samson's problem was not a woman named Delilah; in fact, his problem was not women at all. His real pressing problem was his inability to control his sexual desire!!! He just could not get enough love, and it was not even love he got or was after. Remember the fourteenth chapter of Judges: Samson went down to the land of Timnah of the house of the Philistines; he saw a woman, did not even know her, but said, "I want her." Men and women, you have to be careful of wanting everything that looks good to you. For everything that looks good to you is not good for you. You better investigate before you participate. Consider the sixteenth chapter, where we open up with Samson having left the house of another prostitute in the city of Gaza. My brothers and sisters, Samson's "Delilah" was sex, but your Delilah may be, can be, and could be anything that you allow to control you. Anything that you just can not get enough of is a Delilah. Anything that has you so addicted that you keep coming back, running back, and looking back for more, even though that thing is hazardous to your health, is a Delilah. Delilah was hazardous to Samson's health, but like a lost dog, like a dog chasing its tail, like a dog in heat, Samson kept going back for more. Four times, Delilah tricked him, played him, yet he kept going back, over and over. Ladies, if you've been in an abusive relationship, don't keep going back for more. Don't be like Samson. Samson was sprung. I didn't say it; the Bible said it. Look at the text. Time after time, Samson kept running back. What is it that no matter how you try, you find yourself constantly running back to it!

What is it that at night when you think no one is looking, you struggle with it? For Samson, it was Delilah and sex, but for you, could it be the crack pipe? Weed? Pornography? Adultery? Fornication? Maybe it's not a lady named Delilah but a man named Daryl. Whatever your Delilah is, you need to kick it to the curb.

Allow me to offer up three reasons why you have to kick your Delilah to the curb. First of all, you have to rid yourself of Delilah, because if you don't . . .

Delilah will control you. Consider verse 6. A careful look at Delilah reveals that she really did not try to hide her intentions. She came straight out. Samson, what is your power supply? What can I do to weaken you? How can I bind and afflict you? How can I control you? As strong as Samson was, as wise as he was, perhaps because Delilah was bootylicious, showed a little leg, and revealed a little cleavage, he lost control of his mind and body. A man who knew that his strength came from the Lord, knew that his strength rested in the Lord, knew that all he had came from the Lord, yet in the moment of physical anticipation, he developed spiritual amnesia. I find it interesting what Samson told Delilah in that seventh verse: "If you bind me, if you control me, I will become weak." Samson did not say, "I will lose all my power at once"; he said, "If you bind me, if you control me, I will become weak." One thing about sin: it does not zap all your power at once. Sin is like a terrible cold or flu. You do not start out all sick and messed up; it is a sniffle here and a sniffle there. Samson told Delilah one thing, but she took that one thing and subconsciously began to control him. One thing was the beginning of his end. If you are going to scale new heights, you cannot risk giving Satan an inch. When Satan approaches you asking, "Where is your strength?" Tell him or her that all of your help cometh from the lord.

Second, you have to kick Delilah to the curb because if you don't . . .

Delilah will confuse you. Look at verses 16–17a. Delilah pressed Samson so much that he became frustrated, angered, and confused. Simply put, Satan's job is to confuse you and cause you to toss back and forth like a ship out on the sea. The apostle Paul said, "When I desire to do good, I find myself doing evil." The devil can mess up your mind so much that he will have you thinking that the only thing that matters in life is experiencing self-gratifying acts of pleasure. A confused mind will make you stay longer at a place than you should, make you pay more than you intended, and cause you to go farther than you had planned. Samson fooled around with Delilah way more than he should have, and destruction was headed his way.

Last, you have to get a grip on Delilah because, if not, . . .

Delilah will cripple you. Look at verse 19. Samson with his seven locks symbolized a man complete as long as he remained in God. In Delilah's hand and lap, as his locks were snipped away, Samson became weaker by the moment and incomplete. Anytime you fool around with the devil, anytime you sleep around with the devil literally or spiritually, you risk losing your strength, you risk losing a blessing, you risk becoming spiritually impaired. Samson lost his strength fooling around with Delilah. Samson became crippled by the forces of evil. Thank God that's not how Samson's story ends.

Judges 16:30 informs us that after the love games had been played, after Samson had played a fool, after he had died to the flesh, after he grew tired of being controlled, confused, and crippled by Delilah, God granted him the power to conquer his Delilah. In fact, Samson would conquer more in a day than he had his entire lifetime. I want to tell someone that as soon as you decide to conquer your Delilah instead of being controlled, confused, and crippled by it, you will begin to experience more than you ever have before. When you conquer your Delilah, when you die to the flesh, you will triumph victoriously in Christ. So go ahead, kick Delilah out of your life and tell her, tell him, tell whatever problem that was holding you in captivity, "Enough is enough." Tell your Delilah that you are under new management and that mess, stress, and chaos no longer have a place in your life. Get rid of it and don't turn back. My brothers and sisters, kick your Delilah to the curb!

Chapter Eight

Thou Shall Have No Other Gods before Me: Myths, Idols, and Generational Healing

Shaundra Cunningham

One of the most foundational staples of Judeo-Christianity is the Decalogue, or Ten Commandments. Before children learn to read or write, Sunday school lessons, children's church, and youth activities instill the import and value of the Ten Commandments as an ethical and moral code by which to live. That was certainly the case for me. Birthed in the Black Church as the daughter of a Baptist preacher and an elementary school teacher but raised in an ecumenical environment via my father's years as an Air Force chaplain, I can attest to the emphasis placed on these tenets for Catholics and Protestants. References in Deuteronomy 5:6–7 and Exodus 20:2–3 proclaim the first commandment: "I am the Lord your God, who brought you out of the land of Egypt, out of the house of slavery; you shall have no other gods before me." The primary point is an unequivocal commitment to the one and only God, Yahweh, as depicted through the Israelites storied history in the Hebrew Bible. This principle continues to be taught with vigor today.

My curiosity has consistently been piqued by the language that demands total allegiance to God while acknowledging the presence of other gods. It is as if even God conceded that people would have warring loyalties. This locus of desiring complete devotion provides the framework for theologian Paul Tillich's definition of faith. In his classic work *Dynamics of Faith*, Tillich declares that "faith is the state of being ultimately concerned," and he posits that everyone has faith because every person is ultimately concerned about something.[1] The source of a person or group's ultimate concern becomes its god. The first commandment coupled with Deuteronomy 6:5, "You shall love the Lord your God with all your heart, and with all your soul, and with all your might," describes the dynamic of faith for Tillich. He is not concerned with the content per se but with the phenomenon of how faith involves the total surrender of a person. According to Tillich, that which "concerns one ultimately becomes holy." If a person elevates that which is transitory and finite (cars, money, success, etc.) to the level of ultimacy, then it is considered idolatrous faith.[2] I find Tillich's definition of faith refreshing as it broadens the scope beyond any sectarian belief or doctrine and focuses on the dynamic of how faith works regardless of its source or god.

Inasmuch as we live in a country built on mythologies composed of symbols and gods—some good and others nefarious—that govern perceptions and impact public policy, I consider this serious business. Myths have cultural currency; thus, they have the power to influence and shape public discourse. In the case of Hip Hop, more often than not, certain myths, such as angry Black boys or promiscuous Black girls, gain traction as the dominant narratives and set "in motion whirlwinds of images used in the cultural production of evil."[3] These images uphold vicious stereotypes that often have life-or-death consequences. While I certainly will not negate the structural forces of oppression at work against Hip Hop culture along with the Black Church, this chapter examines the gods or sources of ultimate concern that continue to grip each and the ways in which "worship" or allegiance gets pledged by those involved.

I posit that three gods are prevalent in Hip Hop: the god of money, power, and respect; the god of sex; and the god of relevance and eternal youth. I also spotlight and examine three gods within the Black Church: the god of patriarchal language, the god of heterosexism and homophobia, and the god of male leadership. My thesis is that Hip Hop and the Black Church share forms of idolatrous faith and that if they can be more transparent and honest with themselves and each other, it might create a space for dialogue and generational healing. Furthermore, I demonstrate how both remain stifled to an extent by the perpetuity of certain hackneyed archetypes and myths imposed by others that affect our self-understandings and love for one another.

THE GODS OF HIP HOP

The God of Money, Power, and Respect

Back in 1998, during the height of Bad Boy Record's run as arguably the most influential rap label at the time, its former trio, the Lox, released a smash single and debut album bearing the same name entitled "Money, Power, & Respect." With great bravado, Lil' Kim opens the song declaring her "belief" in the straightforward process of acquiring money, then power, and finally respect . . . in that order. Hip Hop's storied history reveals that in its nascent stages, rappers didn't start out glorifying materialism and market-driven barometers of success with such emphasis. More records revolved around having fun, dancing, macking, and providing a countercultural space for young Black and Brown voices to be heard. Not to display selective amnesia (because there were songs that dealt with the accumulation of riches), but it was not nearly as industry-wide.

Fast-forward to the present and the evidence of the Lox's megahit is ubiquitous. Virtually every other song in rotation on the radio and one of the last standing video countdowns, BET's *106 & Park*, feature artists bragging about their finances, embellishing their power, and highlighting the respect they deem is due.[4] Songs such as Birdman's "I Get Money," Chris Brown's braggadocious "Look at Me Now," and Lloyd Banks's "Beamer, Benz, or Bentley" are reflective of this constant need to reinforce the mythology of money, power, and respect.[5] Now the upshot is that many of these artists are entrepreneurs and uplift and employ others as they progress. This was the case when MC Hammer declared bankruptcy in 1996.[6] Forbes estimated his net worth at $33 million in 1990, but due to his extravagance, along with his infamous one-hundred-person backstage entourage composed largely of friends and family, he lost it all.

Although MC Hammer's management skills were abysmal, the reality is that he and other artists single-handedly provided jobs for many through their endeavors. While we certainly need to encourage entrepreneurship, we cannot dismiss the damage such narratives have on perceptions and on diminishing the magnanimous aspirations for our youth. Tricia Rose's brilliant analysis in her latest book *The Hip Hop Wars* reiterates my point that "big money comes from the successful fashioning of alluring and rhetorically powerful stories that normalize and often even celebrate images of black people as thuggish, promiscuous, sexist, and violent."[7] Thus, we cannot dismiss or become numb to the negative chain effect that this mythology has on society as a whole and our kids.

Further, to recall an insightful quip in his HBO stand-up *Never Scared*, Chris Rock reminds us of the big picture reality of these rappers' and athletes' places in the pantheon of multinational corporate control:[8] "There are no wealthy black or brown people in America. We got some rich ones; we don't got no fuckin' wealth! People go, well what's the difference? Here's the difference: Shaq is rich, the White man that signs his check is wealthy."[9] Even with all the boasting and bragging done by many rappers, they have not acquired wealth; neither have we as Black people. Hence, we all must stay vigilant in checking this idolatrous god that serves as a smokescreen for the sad reality that, on the whole, Blacks still struggle to realize the vision of Proverbs 13:22 that "a good man [or woman] leaves an inheritance for his children's children." For various reasons, we still don't have money, power, or much respect.

The God of Sex

Sex sells. We hear this adage over and over again from advertising agencies and marketing executives, and it appears to ring true. Everywhere one turns, sexual images prevail, even in the oddest of places. I am an avid sports fan, and it never ceases to amaze me how strategically placed hypersexualized cheerleaders, commercials, and network promotional intros and outros objectify women as fleshpots of desire and fantasy. On television and in movies, we see glaring instances of forced sex appeal that do not impact the plot but simply serve as eye candy. Now I appreciate a good romance as much as the next person, but far too many movies insult their actresses with certain scenes that serve no point other than to objectify their body as a sexual/sensual prop. For instance, the recent squabbles about the dismissal of Megan Fox from Michael Bay's movie *Transformers: Dark of the Moon* reveals this reality and the tension that many actresses may feel. Before the leading man, Shia LeBeouf, started backtracking on his comments, he declared to the *Los Angeles Times* "Hero Complex" blog, "Mike films women in a way that appeals to a 16-year-old sexuality. It's summer. It's Michael's style. And I think [Fox] never got comfortable with it."[10] Clearly then, this issue is much larger than one industry and permeates every facet of society, but that doesn't mean Hip Hop is off the hook.

To say misogyny and degrading archetypes of beauty still reign supreme throughout all of Hip Hop's mediums is an understatement. As Hip Hop continues to create enormous profits for corporate conglomerates, industry executives will continue to green-light projects that follow the myth that sex sells. Similar to the movie industry, a project that would gain traction and popularity regardless of tasteless portrayals of women manages to force them anyway. On occasion, female wardrobes and cosmetics become the drivers for women across the world (within and beyond the industry). A clear example is the case of the copycat leotard that many female artists don thanks to Beyonce's infamous 2008 video "Single Ladies." I keep wondering, when is this trend going to end? Instead of showcasing a unique and innovative sense of style, whatever that may be, more women in music have adopted these grown-women onesies in an attempt to follow the path blazed by the reigning queen of R&B and Hip Hop—defined, of course, by her money, power, and respect.[11] We certainly can't dismiss the pressure that comes from industry executives, but the onus also falls on the artists themselves. It's evident that gender equity remains a muddled terrain by which women are subjected to the "beauty myth," as coined by Naomi Wolf, and sometimes willingly corroborate the worst of "black sexual politics," as defined by Patricia Hill Collins.[12]

To avoid a one-sided, cynical attempt to throw women under the bus, we cannot escape the function that men serve in regenerating this god of sex and the myth that it is necessary to sell. Far too many lyrics from men and women in rap music suggest hypersexuality, of which I argue 90% or better are condescending toward women. To be fair, there are plenty of songs that risk showing male vulnerability and feelings regarding relationships, such as Jay-Z's "Song Cry" and Kanye West's "Heartless."[13] But overall, certain images of male fantasy and raw vulgarity, such as T-Pain's summer hit "Booty Work," continue to dominate the landscape.[14] Tracey Sharpley-Whiting argues that spaces for young Black women in "commercial hip hop are categorically one-dimensional. Beauty is nothing short of the helpmate to sex; and we have become reducible to our sexuality as the predominate arbiter of our reality."[15] More often than not, women are inserted into music videos for the sole purpose of being pawns of hypersexuality. And the same goes for men in music videos; several close-up shots of chiseled brothers are standard backdrops on the ladies' side. These images of women and men help uphold the myth that sex is needed to sell and also impacts relational dynamics and approaches among the sexes.

The God of Relevance and Eternal Youth

The last god of Hip Hop is that of relevance and eternal youth—that is, a heightened preoccupation with having buzz and projecting that which is appealing to young audiences. For many male rappers, this takes the form of feigned rebelliousness and constant nostalgic tales suggesting that one is still a hustler or living a hard life; yet, their corporate deals and luxurious lifestyles are anything but rebellious. They have learned to play the game, and many play it very well! To be specific, simply notice the age of two preeminent Hip Hop moguls: Jay-Z and P. Diddy. Both of them are over forty years old; Jay-Z's birthday is December 4, 1969, and P. Diddy's birthday is November 4, 1969, exactly one month apart. To be frank, these are some "mature" dudes who clearly make shrewd business moves; yet, one might not realize it based on their videos and press coverage.

There seems to be a resistance to moving beyond the typical aforementioned gods of money, power, and respect along with sex. As a caveat, P. Diddy's latest album with Dirty Money, *Last Train to Paris*, did deal with love and emotions, though to mixed reviews.[16] And one can always count on artists such as Common, Talib Kweli, and Lupe Fiasco to mix up the monotony and offer fresh perspectives on well-worn themes. But this desire to keep the façade of being eternally youthful seems to truly grip the industry as an ultimate concern in an unhealthy way. I was amusingly glad to hear Kevin Hart validate this claim during his opening monologue as host of the 2011 BET Awards.[17] He called out P. Diddy and said that he should act his age with regard to his constant name changes. Another instance is Mariah Carey's new advertisement for her perfume trio Lollipop Splash the Remix, which raised quite a few eyebrows as she posed with florescent colors accented to project a weird pubescent mood. To see a forty-plus-year-old woman "present herself as an aging tween with a butterfly fetish" makes one wonder, "Isn't Mariah too old for this act?"[18] The fact is—she is! And she's not alone.

My favorite online destination for all things Hip Hop is www.allhiphop.com. It also seems to be one of the pioneers for launching a dedicated space for online rumors, which has now morphed into major business with the onslaught of gossip blogs all over. That said, on AllHipHop.com, its rumor man goes by the name illseed. After running down the latest gossip and rumors that the streets whisper in his ears, he ends most of his posts with a mantra that speaks to the god of relevance: "They keep us talking, but if we stop talking about them then they should worry!"[19] His signature quote sums it all up. Certain artists, such as 50 Cent, create controversy through random and trivial "beefs" or conflict just to get their name back in the spotlight. Others have even stooped to leaking nude photos, like Chris Brown, to generate buzz.[20] Then the saying that nothing breeds good music like personal drama seems to be true as scandal, hardship, and breakups help boost anticipation. Consequently, it's all a machine with a larger web of powers at work but also with willing buy-in from artists themselves. Especially in this age of Twitter and Facebook, artists and all of us now have platforms by which to be our own global marketing honchos.

The act of naming can be a powerful tool that leads to heightened awareness and eventually to transformation. The aforementioned gods are rooted in fleeting, finite dimensions, which make them idolatrous by Paul Tillich's standard. It's encouraging to see a song like "The Wobble" become an instant line dance classic because it gets back to the fun and community that Hip Hop can spark.[21] Nonetheless, I hope Hip Hop can be more self-critical and produce more conscious and heartfelt images and lyrics that would shift these gods and rupture the false notion that only such products sell. I think one of the reasons why Lauryn Hill was so groundbreaking and why people still await her return is that she proved Emilie Townes's quip that indeed "the story *can* be told another way."[22]

THE GODS OF THE BLACK CHURCH

The God of Patriarchal Language

The Black Church spends a great deal of time explicitly and implicitly championing the first commandment, but it too has elevated more than a few notions to the level of gods, which have become idols. The first is the battle over language. Perhaps it shouldn't be called a "battle," because most Black Churches don't consider it an issue. As the saying goes, it is what it is. God as Father remains the only metaphor for appropriating the divine in God talk, both in and beyond the church even when hymns, anthems, negro spirituals, gospel lyrics, and the Bible suggest other options. In Sallie McFague's dated but still relevant book *Models of God*, the author highlights the metaphors and models of God as mother, lover, and friend, in contrast to the dominant image of Father God.[23] To borrow her questions, "what sort of divine love is suggested by each model [of God]? What kind of divine activity is implied by this love? What does each kind of love say about existence in our world?"[24] It is a good practice to take inventory of how we do what we do in liturgy, in sermons, in prayer, and beyond.

This has long been a battle waged by womanist and feminist theologians and ethicists, along with plenty of male scholars and preachers who are committed to more inclusive God talk. But for many, it's simply a moot point, and for others, it's blasphemous to even suggest any model other than God as Father. This issue was at the core of the United Church of Christ's publication of a new hymn book, *The New Century Hymnal*, in 1995. According to accounts of friends who are United Church of Christ ministers, one of the first questions that a prospective member will ask before joining a new fellowship is which hymnal it uses. Some people simply don't want inclusive language added to traditional hymns, and I can understand and empathize with that view for varied reasons. As Otis Moss III aptly points out, "music is memory to people"; therefore, the "songs we like in church are associated with memory and events. . . . The clash between generations is as much about new and old memories as it is about methodology."[25] That's why I can respect and value the memories and meanings that certain language has carried through the ages for different generations while also suggesting that we could all benefit from a broader worldview for appropriating the divine.

The irony is that we sing songs with lyrics that point to more metaphors than those of strictly Father and yet they don't translate to our linguistic renderings in everyday conversation. We may sing Israel Houghton's "I am a friend of God," but we won't necessarily allow ourselves to make that connection in our self-understanding. How might the church's mission and internal relationships be different if we adapted different models of God? How would gender norms and expectations shift if we utilized more than one image of God in our speech and in our worship experiences? How might we think differently about societal ills and our ability to address them with altered models of God and consequently altered views of ourselves? I've often heard my father and other preachers declare, "God has no hands but your hands, no feet but your feet," in an effort to press the point that we all have work to do. However, many of us still uphold a very paternalistic view of how God operates. I like what theologian Marjorie Suchocki declares:

> Often we Christians have thought that the best relationship to God would be abrogation of our own power by pretending that we do not have it, or by treating it as something shameful, as if the very Godness of God depended upon no one other than God having any power that counted. But what would be so godly about that?[26]

I concur with her sentiment and wonder if shifting the language might adjust our own impulses and acknowledge the power we do have. By relying too much on one image of God the Father, we have effectively turned this metaphor into an idol and failed to address that it is not an exhaustive category, nor can any other model be; but we could greatly benefit from utilizing more frameworks.

The God of Homophobia

Upon a recent visit to a local Black Church and after the welcome and meet-and-greet time to "pass the peace," or lovingly embrace members and visitors, the minister came back and acknowledged birthdays and anniversaries. This is a fairly widespread practice by many churches—regardless of their racial makeup—that provides a platform for communal appreciation and celebration. It is one of my favorite parts of service. Most churches designate a Sunday each month to do this. Well, after singing "Happy Birthday" to the stars of the month, the congregation proceeded to recognize members with wedding anniversaries. This is usually a fun-filled, jovial time of recognition because couples can stand and state the date and either the minister or the couple themselves will make good-humored jokes about the nature of their marriage. Comments like "You've been putting up with Mr. Joe's antics for 20 years" or, if the minister has the gift of history with a couple, "I remember when you got married and couldn't stand dogs but Ms. Jane has managed to turn you into an animal lover," and so forth and so on. This is always a special part of the communal worship experience to witness embodied symbols of love and commitment.

The welcome section also reveals an imbalance, as certain relationships are ignored and rendered invisible—specifically, same-sex loving people. With the exception of a growing number of open and affirming congregations, churches that take seriously their mandate to be progressive on social justice and outreach still fail to reconcile the injustice done towards gays, lesbians, bisexual, and transgendered persons within their midst. It is as if a proverbial "don't ask, don't tell" law lingers over the atmosphere in many Black Churches. Further, the simple fact remains that some of the most faithful, dedicated, and tithing members in the church are often closeted or openly gay, lesbian, bisexual, and transgendered, but they don't count. Many preachers erroneously equate homosexuality to the worst of sins and declare fire-and-brimstone messages of condemnation and eternal punishment. Again, as with patriarchal language, there are plenty of preachers and scholars who don't condone such readings, such as ordained Baptist minister and public intellectual Michael Eric Dyson, just to name a widely known figure. But Horace Griffin's work *Their Own Receive Them Not* chronicles in great detail the split between the Black Church's willingness to address racial discrimination while remaining firm on judging and dehumanizing gay, lesbian, bisexual, and transgendered people instead of celebrating them as God's creation and handiwork.[27]

Even beyond homosexuality, the Black Church often acts as if discussing sexuality at all is taboo. The church constantly teaches arcane views that may have merit but fail to reach people in a way that's honest with the reality of our anthropology. Those that do address the topic often reinforce heterosexism and fail to nuance the matter in a way that leaves space for anything other than Victorian ideals of respectability. This form of idolatrous allegiance to the god of heterosexism and homophobia is probably the most pressing for this era.

The God of Male Leadership

The final god that operates as a source of ultimate concern in the Black Church is that of male leadership. Despite many gains and strides by women in the rank and file of mainline denominations, the fact remains that women are still relegated to associate minister status more often than not. There are many more who are pastors of congregations now than a generation ago, and for that, we cannot pay enough tribute to the trailblazing paths of Jarena Lee, Sojourner Truth, Prathia Hall, Carolyn Ann Knight, Renita Weems, Vashti McKenzie, and countless women who made inroads. But even with their gains, the reality is that far too many churches still seek and desire a male in primary positions of power and authority. According to the National Congregations Study conducted in 2006 and 2007, despite the increase of women attending seminary, it found that women lead only 8% of American congregations and "women are more likely to lead small than large congregations, so only about 5% of American churchgoers attend a congregation led by a woman."[28] Many still uphold a literalist understanding of the controversial texts by Paul in 1 Timothy and 1 Corinthians suggesting that women remain silent and not have authority over men. When put into context, neither of these verses are universal decrees on the role of women, but they nonetheless maintain and solidify the myth that women ought to be submissive and subservient.

As an ordained National Baptist minister, I recognize that depending on the church and context, many still don't affirm women in the pulpit beyond token occasions, such as women's day, missionary day, or youth day. This is evident in the largest annual gathering of African American clergy in the country: the Hampton Ministers' Conference. The Hampton conference is a weeklong spiritual retreat of different lectures, panels, and preachers along with a lineup geared toward choir directors and musicians. I've enjoyed attending this conference on a couple occasions and, like many others, look forward to it with great anticipation. However, in its remarkable ninety-seven-year history, there has only been one female conference president, the Reverend Dr. Susan Johnson Cook. While female ministers have been featured in different slots as preachers and lecturers, the 2011 conference was the first time a woman has been selected as *the* conference preacher in the history of the conference. This is important to note because each slotted speaker has a full house in the arena, but the conference preacher is set apart to speak nightly and thus symbolically becomes the pastor for the pastors for a few days by speaking to their varied needs. For this reason, it is a unique designation to be deemed the conference preacher for the week. The Reverend Dr. Gina Marcia Stewart was the first woman charged to do it. This reality highlights the findings in the study that more women in seminary does not translate to more women in the parish context nor at the institutional level. It is true that many seminary-trained women don't pursue pastoral ministry in a church setting but take other vocational paths; however, there are many who try but get denied because of prejudice and preference for men. This god of male control and leadership needs to be tackled.

FINAL THOUGHTS

I recall hearing Cornel West lament that one of the gravest mistakes of his generation toward my generation is that it preached *success, success, success*, instead of *be great, be great, be great*. There is a huge difference: one speaks of climbing the ladder by any means necessary, and the other speaks of having a certain spirit with one's giftedness. The former stresses rugged individualism; the latter reminds us of context, community, and origins. I appreciate and agree with West's sentiment, but I know that the younger generation is not homogeneous (and neither is the older one) and that all have not adopted success-oriented ways of being.

Both Hip Hop and the Black Church have infinite wisdom to impart to each other and have more in common than they may realize. While I outline three distinct gods for each group, the reality is that I could have easily swapped the gods of Hip Hop with those of the Black Church and vice versa. The church certainly struggles with the god of money, power, and respect, as reflected in prosperity gospel preaching and teaching. But it stretches beyond those who espouse that problematic doctrine, and it impacts those who jockey for position as leading social gospel preachers. The god of sex could also be applied to the Black Church; there's a certain aesthetic and sexualized veneer that is often at work during worship. Not to mention all the literature, books, and conferences that deal with sex, targeting couples along with single Black Christians. The god of relevance and eternal youth loosely applies in that many mainline Black Churches are struggling to stay relevant and endeavoring to keep youth engaged. At times, many pastors face backlash for trying too much innovation and thus have to do a delicate dance of bridging traditional elements with that which will also attract a strong young adult contingent. I take the view that additional reinforcements are not really needed for my generation to get involved with church; rather, a sincere and nonjudgmental congregation is most important.

On the other side, the gods of the Black Church can be applied to Hip Hop. The Hip Hop language reeks of patriarchal dimensions and reinforces certain machismo themes. As with the church, Hip Hop still deals with its own homophobic cloud. Derogatory and dehumanizing terms for gay men and women still get hurled as the rhetorical weapons of choice for insults and bravado posturing. The god of male leadership hardly needs explaining when one examines the corporate executives at major record labels and other executive positions within the growing Hip Hop–dominated recording industry. Further, even the number of women rapping and gaining notoriety seems to have reached a relative stalemate in recent years. Nonetheless, each of these gods could've been switched around, and my argument would still stand.

As it is, on both lists the gods are idolatrous; that is, they don't lead to transcendence or that which is life-giving but reinforce debilitating myths and lies. If both Hip Hop and the Black Church would be open and honest, it could lead to dialogue and a chance for the younger generation to feel affirmed and accepted and allow the more mature generation to feel respected. I can imagine the faces that many young people might have if a deacon or elder in their church admitted his or her struggles or regrets without rushing to spiritualize them with excessive God talk. How might high school dropout rates, violence, and pregnancy rates shift if more church folk were to actually get real? For Hip Hop, how might the music and cultural idiom shift the American landscape if imbued with a sense of holy rage? How might its reach and impact shift if more artists were vulnerable and honest with expressing their pains and worries? To that end, I appreciate Terrie Williams's book *Black Pain: It Just Looks Like We're Not Hurting*.[29] And the subtitle gets to the crux of the matter. Young and old, churchgoers and those who couldn't care less about church—indeed all of us are hurting! Plato says, "Be kind, for everyone you meet is fighting a hard battle" and that is the case for both generations.

Last, both Hip Hop and the Black Church retain a mysterious hold on many Whites who still cling to illusions and falsehoods about our humanity. Both remain typecast for vicious appropriation. Zora Neale Hurston provides a vantage point for why it may still happen. In the April 1950 edition of *Negro Digest*, Hurston wrote an article called "What White Publishers Won't Print," where she opined about the reasons why White publishers wouldn't publish stories on the interior lives of non-Anglo-Saxons. She posited that the reason was that Blacks and all other non-Anglo-Saxons were viewed as exhibits in "the American Museum of Unnatural History."[30] Hurston stated that this is not a physical place but an intangible belief that all non-Anglo-Saxons are uncomplicated stereotypes. "Everybody knows all about them," and so publishers wouldn't print articles that delved into the romantic lives or ideals of Blacks, because they weren't deemed to have the capacity for such subtlety.[31]

> The American Negro exhibit is a group of two. Both of these mechanical toys are built so that their feet eternally shuffle, and their eyes pop and roll. Shuffling feet and those popping, rolling eyes denote the Negro, and no characterization is genuine without this monotony. One is seated on a stump picking away on his banjo and singing and laughing. The other is a most amoral character before a share-cropper's shack mumbling about injustice. Doing this makes him out to be a Negro "intellectual." It is as simple as all that.[32]

I reference Hurston because the two archetypes that she mentions in essence capture the two categories of our study: Hip Hop as the first and the Black Church as the second. Both still reside in the Museum of Unnatural History for many Whites today. We occupy shared space, as both living organisms continue being objectified by those who know little about either. Simply watch commercials, movies, or award telecasts, and it is not uncommon for a Black choir to be thrown into a jingle or to back up an artist that knows little or nothing about Black sacred music. Whenever the "cool factor" is needed, one need simply appropriate Hip Hop and add a rap or break-dance segment. This sort of cultural cycle is sickening and keeps these imaginary but real archetypes of Black folk in motion, as defined through Hurston's museum.

If each side could acknowledge the idolatrous gods that each has vowed allegiances to, it could be a particularly eye-opening and refreshing moment. By doing so, each could challenge the other. Hip Hop can help the church peel back its layers of respectability and stay committed to hearing the cries of youth, the street, and the disenfranchised. On the flip side, the church can challenge Hip Hop to remember its roots and embrace "a more excellent way." Both may never admit it, but they worship at the altar of gods that need to be examined and destroyed. To be fair, both organisms are engaged in practices and ideologies that lead to liberation and deliverance, but these idolatrous gods loom too large to be ignored. Suchocki suggests that "if passive participation in social sin is like a union that isolates, fragments, and destroys, confession becomes the antidote with its own power toward a union that draws together into community."[33] Only transparency and confession can lead this next generation of Hip Hop fans and churchgoers to bridge the gap and work together on pressing social justice and community concerns.

NOTES

1. Paul Tillich, *Dynamics of Faith* (New York: HarperOne, 2001), 13. For the duration of this chapter, I use "G" (God) to distinguish the monotheistic Judeo-Christian supreme deity from "g" (god). Here, "god" retains Tillich's neutral descriptor of the dynamic and function at work.

2. Tillich, *Dynamics of Faith*, 13–14.

3. Emilie Townes, *Womanist Ethics and the Cultural Production of Evil* (New York: Palgrave Macmillan, 2006), 21.

4. BET's *106 & Park* is a top-ten music video show that celebrated its 10th year on October 6, 2010.

5. "I Get Money" was released on Birdman's 2011 Universal Motown recording *Bigger Than Life*. "Look at Me Now" was released on Chris Brown's 2001 Jive Records recording *F.A.M.E.* "Beamer, Benz, or Bentley" was released on Lloyd Banks's 2011 D Bag International recording *Freestyles*.

6. According to the June 24, 1996, issue of *Jet*, MC Hammer's April 1996 filing for bankruptcy was a result of the fact that "he had $137 million in debt with only $9.6 million in assets."

7. Tricia Rose, *The Hip Hop Wars: What We Talk about When We Talk about Hip Hop—and Why It Matters* (New York: Basic Civitas Books, 2008).

8. Chris Rock's 2004 HBO special was recorded live at Constitution Hall in Washington, DC.

9. Chris Rock, *Never Scared* (HBO Home Video, 2004).

10. Rebecca Keegan, "Megan Fox's Absence Changed 'Transformers' Vibe, Says Shia LeBeouf," *Los Angeles Times* "Hero Complex" blog, June 2, 2011.

11. In 2009 Beyonce was ranked number one on the *Forbes* list of "Hollywood's top earning moguls in the making," earning $87 million. Found on http://www.forbes.com .

12. Patricia Hill Collins, *Black Sexual Politics: African Americans, Gender, and the New Racism* (New York: Routledge, 2005).

13. "Song Cry" was released on Jay-Z's 2002 Roc-A-Fella (Def Jam) recording *The Blueprint*. "Heartless" was released on Kanye West's 2008 Roc-A-Fella (Def Jam) recording *808s & Heartbreak*.

14. "Booty Work" was released on T-Pain's 2011 Nappy Boy Entertainment (Jive Records) recording *RevolveR*.

15. T. Denean Sharpley-Whiting, *Pimps Up, Ho's Down: Hip Hop's Hold on Young Black Women* (New York: New York University Press, 2007), 52.

16. *Last Train to Paris* was released in 2010 on Bad Boy Records (Interscope).

17. The BET Awards aired on June 26, 2011.

18. Erin Carlson, "Mariah's New Perfume Ad: Creepy or Cute?" found online at "OMG!" Yahoo blog, posted June 17, 2011.

19. Illseed from the Rumor section on http://www.allhiphop.com; on some of his recent posts, he stopped using it, but for years that was his automatic signature line at the end of his rumor updates.

20. Internet bloggers around the world had reposted the photo by March 4, 2011, creating an international frenzy.

21. "Wobble" was recorded by Atlanta-based rapper V.I.C. and released on his 2008 Reprise recording, *Beast*.

22. Emilie Townes, *Womanist Ethics and the Cultural Production of Evil* (New York: Palgrave Macmillan, 2006), 7.

23. Sallie McFague, *Models of God: Theology for an Ecological, Nuclear Age* (Philadelphia: Fortress Press, 1987).

24. McFague, *Models of God*.

25. Otis Moss III, "Real Big: The Hip Hop Pastor as Postmodern Prophet," in *The Gospel Remix Reaching the Hip Hop Generation*, ed. Ralph C. Watkins (Valley Forge, PA: Judson Press, 2007), 130.

26. Marjorie Hewitt Suchocki, *In God's Presence: Theological Reflections on Prayer* (St. Louis, MO: Chalice Press, 1996), 22–23.

27. Horace Griffin, *Their Own Receive Them Not: African American Lesbians and Gays in Black Churches* (Cleveland, OH: Pilgrim Press, 2006).

28. Mark Chaves, "Mark Chaves: Why Are There (Still!) So Few Women Clergy?" on http://www.faithandleadership.com, posted on July 13, 2009.

29. Terri M. Williams, *Black Pain: It Just Looks Like We're Not Hurting* (New York: Scribner, 2009).

30. Zora Neale Hurston, "What White Publishers Won't Print," *Negro Digest*, 1950.

31. Hurston, "What White Publishers Won't Print."

32. Hurston, "What White Publishers Won't Print."

33. Marjorie Hewitt Suchocki, *In God's Presence: Theological Reflections on Prayer* (St. Louis, MO: Chalice Press, 1996), 82.

Chapter Nine

Hip Hop Children of a Lesser God

Paul Scott

I always find it kind of funny when, accepting an award for his hit "Kill 'Em All; Till They Fall," MC Pullatrigga gets on the mic and says, "First of all, I would like to thank God." Or during a magazine interview, Sexxx Thugstress innocently tells a reporter how her close relationship with her Savior gave her the strength to write "If the Escalade Is Rockin' Don't Be Knockin." As Grandma would say, "Chile let me move 'cause I know that lightnin' is fixin' to strike."

From as far back as history records, African people have had a reverence for the Supreme Being. From the African people who laid the foundation for modern religion to the old lady across the street who never misses a Sunday service—rain, sleet, or snow, we have always had a strong spiritual connection with the Creator. Many of us have vivid memories of receiving our first whippin' for mocking Reverend Jones or Sister Ruth Ann when she got in "the spirit" one Sunday morning. We found out early that playin' with "tha lawd" was a definite No-No!

Historically, music and Spirituality have walked hand in hand as music is more than just something to help us get our party on. It is a divine expression of our respect for the gift of LIFE. It was our spirit-filled song that helped us keep the FAITH, even when we were beaten by the slave master and forced to work in the hot cotton fields from sunup to sundown, and it will be our song that leads us to the LIBERATION of our people from mental slavery. The Spirituality of African people has always been a thorn in the side of the oppressor. Our FAITH has been like that trick birthday candle that no matter how hard you try, you just can't blow it out. We have been like a Spirit-filled energizer bunny playin' an African drum; we just keep going and going.

For many young brotha's and sista's who are disillusioned with organized religion, today Hip Hop has become the faith of choice. Maybe for some, the rules and regulations of the other religions were just too hard to follow, so they turned to the cardinal rule of Hip Hop—"If it feels good, do it"—or, more likely, they simply rejected the idea that they had to have the word of

God interpreted by White Kings and other European writers. So, instead they traded in the King James Version of the Bible for the gospel according to the White-owned media and entertainment industry, who at least had the foresight to put pictures of Black people on the covers of its magazines. So, the LAWS revealed to Moses were traded in for the Ten Crack Commandments of the Notorious B.I.G.

While many rappers reflect "the Life is Hell" philosophy in their lyrics, I doubt very seriously that any other religion outside of Holy Hip Hop considers eternal torment as living in a $5 million mansion with an Olympic-sized swimming pool. However, some rappers are helping to perpetuate the hellish conditions that African people are experiencing globally by aiding our mental enslavement that keeps us under the foot of the White supremacist system. Sadly, many of the brotha's and sista's in Hip Hop are fully aware that they are leading African children down the path of destruction but have made a conscious decision to sell the destiny of our people for thirty pieces of silver or a platinum chain. The problem is that our African Spirituality makes it hard for us to believe that anyone could be so evil as to use our music and Spirituality as a genocidal weapon. Many have underestimated the depths that White supremacists would sink to keep the masses of African people oppressed.

Some will argue that it is "only music," but as the dude from the movie *The Usual Suspects* said, "The greatest trick the devil ever pulled was convincing the world he didn't exist." The oppressor knows that the only way to totally destroy a people is to separate them from their connection to the Creator. Once their Spiritual immune system is broken down, the people are left open to all the vices that plague the planet, drugs, disease, violence, and so on.

When faced with this TRUTH, many young brotha's will defiantly shout, "Only God can judge me!!!!" However, there is such a thing as corporate responsibility, and the actions of one member of the African family affect the whole, including future generations. So to answer the age-old question, "I am my Brother's keeper."

Our African ancestors knew that it was not only the right but the responsibility of the elders to give guidance to the younger generations because it was they who would determine the future of the tribe. But today even, our most learned elders seem to be intimidated by children just because they can quote rap lyrics like the old folks quote scripture. When the adults in the African family stop trying to win a popularity contest with fourteen-year-olds and stand up and speak TRUTH, then will the end of our oppression come.

Most religions have some sort of Judgment Day when TRUTH is revealed, when a person's deeds are weighed in the balance against the Universal principles of Righteousness, a day when LIGHT (KNOWLEDGE) eventually overcomes DARKNESS (LIES). Although some rappers think that they can defy the law of Reciprocity by raising hell all year long and giving out a free turkey at Thanksgiving, rappers Bone Thugs-n-Harmony once asked, "What ya gonna do . . . when judgment comes for you?" So Hip Hop, today, we are at the Crossroads. We must make a decision as to which road we will take—the road to LIBERATION or the road to SLAVERY: the path that will ensure a future for the next generation or the path that will lead to its destruction.

To borrow from an old Public Enemy interlude, "Right vs. Wrong; Good vs. Evil; God vs. the Devil; what side you on?"

Chapter Ten

Sermon: "Bling Bling"

Stephen C. Finley

[9]I saw one of the seven angels who had the bowls filled with the seven last terrible troubles. The angel came to me and said, "Come on! I will show you the one who will be the bride and wife of the Lamb." [10]Then with the help of the Spirit, he took me to the top of a very high mountain. There he showed me the holy city of Jerusalem coming down from God in heaven. [11]The glory of God made the city bright. It was dazzling and crystal clear like a precious jasper stone. [12]The city had a high and thick wall with twelve gates, and each one of them was guarded by an angel. On each of the gates was written the name of one of the twelve tribes of Israel. [13]Three of these gates were on the east, three were on the north, three more were on the south, and the other three were on the west. [14]The city was built on twelve foundation stones. On each of the stones was written the name of one of the Lamb's twelve apostles. [15]The angel who spoke to me had a gold measuring stick to measure the city and its gates and its walls. [16]The city was shaped like a cube, because it was just as high as it was wide. When the angel measured the city, it was about fifteen hundred miles high and fifteen hundred miles wide. [17]Then the angel measured the wall, and by our measurements it was about two hundred sixteen feet high. [18]The wall was built of jasper, and the city was made of pure gold, clear as crystal. [19]Each of the twelve foundations was a precious stone. The first was jasper, the second was sapphire, the third was agate, the fourth was emerald, [20]the fifth was onyx, the sixth was carnelian, the seventh was chrysolite, the eighth was beryl, the ninth was topaz, the tenth was chrysoprase, the eleventh was jacinth, and the twelfth was amethyst. [21]Each of the twelve gates was solid pearl. The streets of the city were pure gold, clear as crystal. (Revelation 21:9–21, Contemporary English Version)

On this third Sunday in the month of February in which we celebrate Black History and on this first Sunday in the Christian season of Lent that lifts up and illuminates the suffering and challenges that Jesus experienced that culminated in his crucifixion, I am excited to be with you. Black History is more than an opportunity for us to recount and remember facts and information, for Black History offers us an opportunity to worship the Divine. This morning we gather to celebrate what God has done in the history of African American people, despite the suffering and challenges. We celebrate the Eternal for the creative activity in our lives. We also gather today to celebrate and worship with young people, as this Sunday has also been declared Youth Sunday. We have shared with them, and they have shared with us through song and speech. Young people need worship, just like the rest of us, because they live in a challenging world and in challenging times. Though they are not often strongly connected with their history and culture these days, it is important for them to be informed that their ancestors have suffered throughout time, just like the Jewish Christians to whom the Book of Revelation was written.

The writer of the book was writing to his people so that he might encourage them to continue in the faith and to impress upon them that God had something better for them than the lives they were living. They were suffering simply because they were former Jews who became Christians in a world that wanted them to embrace its values, and we have suffered just because we are African Americans in a world that does not value who we are but rather seeks to force us to be something else while at the same time commodifying and exploiting our cultural products for their own benefit.

Unfortunately, many of our young people don't understand how much their parents, grandparents, and ancestors had to suffer just because they were Black. Therefore, they don't know how significant God was and still is, for it was God who brought us this far by faith. It was not Abraham Lincoln and the Emancipation Proclamation that made us free from slavery; it was God. It was not people who gave us the rights of human beings and the right to participate in this country as citizens of the earth; it was God. It was neither MTV nor BET that made us artistically gifted; it was God.

But many of our young people have been seduced by the culture. They are wonderful people, who are full of potential, but they have no connection to our spiritual struggle as a people, no understanding of what God had to do to get us here and what we had to do for ourselves. Instead, many of them have adopted the values of the culture. They want the American dream. Even if they do not have full access to the system that will allow them to obtain the wealth and materialism that they desire, their minds are often consumed with what they want and how they will go about getting it. They want riches, and they are guided by a Freudian pleasure principle. In other words, they want the greatest reward, the highest degree of pleasure, with the least amount of work, risk, and pain. The materialism and opulence that they seek they call "bling bling," and too many of them, and us for that matter, will do what we have to do to obtain it, even if it means counting someone else's.

"Bling bling" is a term that seemed to have its origin in the deep South, although the concept itself is universal. The culture of young people all over this country is dominated by the idea of materialistic living. Just ask the young person sitting next to you if he or she knows what "bling bling" is. I am sure that almost all of our young people will be able to explain it to you. Let me see if I can help you with it.

"Bling bling" is what the young people call a lifestyle full of riches and flashy possessions. It means having so much that people recognize you for what you have and what you own, rather than the significant things that you do with your life that bless and benefit human beings. "Bling bling" means owning fancy cars and big houses even if you have to do illegal things to get it. "Bling bling" is wearing expensive designer clothing that emphasizes stuff that adorns your body, rather than the significance and beauty of your body. "Bling bling" requires privileging that which is in one's pocket rather than what's in one's heart. "Bling bling" is wearing lots of jewelry, diamonds, and gold, rather than something more valuable like developing a powerful mind. "Bling bling" is having pockets full of money, more money than one could ever really need so that one has the sense that he or she is important because of what he or she has, rather than who one is. "Bling bling" is the goal in life for many young people, to eat fancy foods, to travel to exotic locations, to pop the cork on expensive bottles of wine whose name one may not even be able to pronounce. "Bling bling" means acquiring all the stuff that we can in life.

Everyday and everywhere our young people go, they are bombarded with images of materialism. I heard one young man on television suggest that he wants all the materialistic stuff that he saw, including the fancy cars and the extravagant jewelry. Everywhere young people look and listen, strategic marketing encourages them to live life for the moment and to desire material possessions. At the same time, I don't want to blame young people for this perspective, for they have had plenty of influence from us and the culture, but that's another sermon for another time. A friend who works with me helped me with an Internet search that illustrated this idea in the music of Hip Hop culture. He introduced me to the song "Bling Bling," by the rap artist B.G.[1] I encourage you to pull up the recording on the Internet at some point and take a listen to the message that our young people are being bombarded with.

My good friend, recording artist Montell Jordan, who was my roommate in college, sang a song called "Once Upon a Time," where he talks about the old days and recounts that he and his woman "had no fancy cars, no diamond rings, no credit cards, no bling bling."[2]

Blu Cantrell seemed frustrated and depressed in her song "So Blue," when she said that she was "trying to find a man, trying to find a ring, trying to find a man, who loves me more than his bling bling."[3]

Rappers Snoop Dogg and J. D. added, "Like uh, boomerang, Dogg Pound game. Hundred thousand dollar chains. What chu say J.D.? Bling bling, money ain't no thang."[4]

I'm sure by now y'all get the idea and the challenges we face and that our young people face as they try to live positive and healthy lives. And we have to admit that "bling bling" as a way of living and a goal for life is not all their fault. Perhaps we have not shared our stories with them sufficiently enough so that they would understand that being Black means that they have a responsibility to God and to the community, to take what they have, their gifts, talents, and strengths, and be the best human beings that they can be and make contributions to their community and world so that it is a better place because of them.

Likewise, they have more now in terms of things they own than what some of our parents and grandparents had in their whole lives. I remember seeing a picture of my grandmother, and she told me that the dress she was wearing was her Sunday dress. She had one good dress, and that was the one that she wore for worship. Our ancestors gave God the best that they had. On the other hand, even some of our churches reflect the values of the culture. Some of our churches will even try to tell us that we are more important to God because of the cars we drive and the houses in which we live. They want us to believe that material stuff ("bling bling") is an indication of one's relationship with God, that the closer one is to God, the more fancy and expensive stuff one should have as evidence. Now let us turn our attention back to the sacred text to see if it offers us any insight on this dynamic.

The writer of the text in the twenty-first chapter of the Book of Revelation was using symbolic language to communicate to his people what he said an angel showed him in a vision. The writer was strict on his community because he knew that his people were suffering persecution and he did not want them to take on the ways of the culture that had oppressed them. He wanted them to continue living in the way that they understood, from their own cultural and religious sources. I suppose that he also recognized that when people live in a culture that is dominated by someone else, where they have been subjugated and treated badly, they have a tendency to take on the ways of those who have had power over them. They begin to act in ways that are contrary to their faith. They live for what they can acquire. They forget who they are. They may even begin to despise themselves. So the writer paints a picture for them of a new reality, a new city, the New Jerusalem.

He said that this city was made with streets of gold and walls with foundations that were made of pure gold that was so clear that it looked like crystal. He said that the city was dazzling, that it shined bright like jasper. The twelve walls or gates of the city, he said, were made of precious stones like sapphires and emeralds, onyx and chrysolite, beryl and topaz, carnelian and amethyst, and other precious stones. He wrote this story because he wanted his people to know that their suffering would not last always. He did not desire to valorize their suffering but rather to inspire them to imagine the possibilities that lay beyond their present condition and to live as if this fantasy was a promise yet to be fulfilled. The writer wanted his community to believe that the beauty that characterized his vision was possible in spite of their suffering. But I want us to know that this story is really a story whose meaning is for our people and their relationship to the Divine. The New Jerusalem represented God's people, and the precious stones and jewels represented what they could be. The text tells us that the city shined because of God's presence. The writer said that God's presence was so great that it lit up the city like jasper and fine jewels, that God's presence was like a very rare jewel that was clear as crystal.

I guess by now some of you might be asking, what does all this mean for African American young people, and what does it mean for me?

I believe that we can learn two important insights from this Scripture. Just like the writer of this text reported that an angel of the Lord showed him a vision for his people, while in the spirit, I too proclaim a vision and the meaning of these things for my community.

As I considered this text deeply, the first thing that became apparent to me is that "bling bling" is a condition of the heart. The text tells us that the city represents the people and that God's glory filled the city with a bright radiance. That means that God wants to influence the hearts of people. God wants to fellowship and "live" with the people so much so that one's being is transformed; one's heart reflects the beauty and goodness of the Creator. You see, the culture tells us that you are somebody based on all the stuff that you have out here. The culture teaches us that you are important based on what jobs you work, in what houses you live, where you were educated, and even what churches you attended, so we spend all of our energy and resources trying to fix up the outside. We want to be associated with the people of the best reputation. We want to wear the most expensive clothing. We want to live in the most opulent homes in the most elite neighborhoods. We want to drive the fanciest cars, and there is nothing wrong with any of that in and of itself. But this text indicates that God would not be impressed by stuff that we use to fill our emptiness on the inside, but on the contrary, God desires pure hearts.

God doesn't say that we have to be perfect. God does not require that we run church laps to prove how religious we are. God does not require that we sound holy and say "Jesus" in every sentence in every conversation that we have with every person. God desires relationships with people to change the condition of their hearts. Yes, God loves people who have good hearts, but God also loves people who's hearts have been broken, so that their hearts might be made beautiful. Unlike the culture, God does not judge us by our failures or by our faults. God judges us by our hearts, not by the artificial and temporal things with which we surround ourselves. We can "bling bling" from now until the next full moon, and it does not make a bit of difference to God that we are important in the world. God does not care that people respect us because of the things that we own. All God wants to know is that we love goodness and righteousness, and if we love God, Jesus told us that we will love our neighbors like we love ourselves. Then God will truly be glorified.

God's glory lit up the city. That means that God is most glorified not in what we have but in hearts that love God and hearts that love people. That's why we like to say that someone who is kind and loving has a "heart that is good as gold." True "bling bling," young people, is a condition of your heart. It means that despite your imperfection, your heart is good so that you do not have to do all this superficial stuff to feel good about yourself and your life.

Some of us grown folk got it all backwards too. We think that God is impressed with the religious stuff that we do in worship, and too often we communicate that to young people. God is not concerned with our religious activity. I can preach every Sunday, and I almost do, but it doesn't mean a thing if my heart is mean and nasty, if I condemn and judge people who are imperfect rather than trying to help them be all that they can be. We can shout and dance and do fifty church laps, but it doesn't mean a thing to God if we are always talking bad about people, if we don't love the people who are considered the most unlovable, those who have had problems in their lives with substances and those who are poor. Some of y'all who read the Bible will recall that Jesus wasn't hanging out with the people who had all the riches and wealth. He spent most of his time with people like me, who messed up in life and needed someone's affirmation, someone to remind me that God loves me and that God would look beyond all my faults and see my needs.

God wants to dwell in the city. God wants to live in the hearts of the people. God wants to shine in the hearts of those who say they practice and pursue justice and righteousness. God wants to radiate from our very souls like precious jewels, from the deepest recesses of our being. God is glorified, not by wealth or social standing. God is glorified in the hearts of men and women, boys and girls, who love God and love people.

When God lives in your heart, God shines in your life like a flawless diamond. God adorns your heart like pure gold and fills your soul with a sparkle, like fine crystal.

When God lives in your heart, we don't have to spend all of our time and energy trying to get something out there to fill the empty spaces in our lives.

When God lives in our hearts, we don't have to worry whether or not we have on the most expensive stuff on our body, because God's glory radiates from deep within our souls and outshines anything that anyone could buy.

When God lives in our hearts, God transforms our hearts and changes our values so that what we do with our lives becomes more important than the stuff we have in our lives.

When God lives in our hearts, we can live freely. We don't have to worry about keeping up with the neighbors, because we trust God to meet all of our needs and even grant us some of our desires.

When God lives in our hearts, we can love one another, even someone who doesn't have all the stuff that we used to think made him important. In fact, we may even find ourselves giving some of the stuff we own to someone else because we believe that Jesus is more than enough.

"Bling bling" is a condition of the heart. God wants our precious jewels, our gold to live in here, in our hearts. The other stuff means nothing if our lives and our souls are empty.

The second insight that we learn from this text is that "bling bling" is who you are, not what you have. Young people and older people, being important to God is more significant than being important to people because of what you own. As we look at this text, we learn that the twelve walls that were made of the precious jewels represented God's people. That means that people are precious and beautiful by virtue of being created by the Divine. "Bling bling" is not what you have; it's who you are. It's an ontological condition. It's a state of being. It's a divine facticity. You are precious to God. You are like rare jewels. You are like twenty-four-carat gold. In God's eyes, you are like jasper and sapphires, agate and emeralds, onyx and carnelian, chrysolite and beryl, topaz and chrysoprase, jacinth and amethyst. You are more important to God, not because of what you have, but because of who you are.

You are God's own, and you are marvelously created. God formed you from the material of the earth, and God breathed into your body the breath of life. God created you in God's own image so that no matter what you have or don't have, you carry with you a spark from the divine fire. You are sacred to God because you are God's sons and his daughters. That means that all the things you really need to be successful in this life are on the inside of your soul. You may have to go to school and be educated. You may face some challenges along the way. But God is for you, and if God is for you, God is more than the world against you. God values us and wants us to be all that we can be in this life.

God's values are different from the values of the culture. The culture teaches us that stuff is important and that people only gain importance in relationship to the stuff that they have or the positions that they hold. God declares that we are important, maybe even more important to God when we have less rather than more. You see, some people have so much down here that they don't even need God. That's why Jesus spent the most of his time with people who were poor, people who were troubled, people who, like some of us, needed affirmation from a heavenly source. God values us because we are God's own creation and the chosen people. People are precious to God. That's why we like to tell people that God so loved the world that God sent God's only son, not to condemn the world, but, through Jesus, reconcile the world to its creator. Young people are very important to God. "Red, yellow, black, and white, they're all precious in his sight. Jesus loves the little children of the world."[5]

Human beings were so important to God that God gave up what was most precious so that human beings might share in relationship with the Divine. Through God, we learned that sometimes we have to give up things that seem important to us to find meaning and to get closer to God and to one another. Some of us have so much stuff surrounding us that we don't have room for God. We fill our lives with all kinds of things because we don't want to deal with the pain that is in our hearts. We are so busy trying to fill our lives with the finer things in life because we fail to realize that we are the finer things in life. Let me remind you again that "bling bling" is who you are, not what you have.

You are the finest jewel that was ever fashioned. You are the brightest star in the sky that radiates like crystal. You are the most beautiful purple amethyst. You may have once looked hard on the outside, like a rock, because life had been difficult for you. But God helped you open up, exposing the brilliant colors of life on the inside. You are the most beautiful green emerald, despite what others may say. God made you Black and Brown and beautiful. When God looks at you, God's eyes twinkle because God has never seen anything as aesthetically pleasing to God's divine senses.

"Bling bling" is who you are not what you have. You belong to God. You are the apple of God's eye. You are worth more to God than all of the riches of the earth.

I want to continue telling young people that they are responsible for their community. It's not enough to live life just so you can get yours. You have a responsibility to God and this community to be the best you can be and to contribute to the conditions in which we live. Your people have suffered, but they suffered because they believed in God enough and they loved you enough that they fought for the right to be human. You are not free by chance. Your freedom as African American young people was paid for by the struggle of those who served God. Like the writer of the Revelation text, they wanted you to have the opportunity to be who you are, not so you could "bling bling" with stuff. They believed that a better day was coming, but they knew that they had to participate in making that new day happen. They wanted to create a new reality, a "new city." That new city that they wanted to create was a new people, who would open their hearts to God and let God dwell with them no matter what challenges they faced.

You have to make the choice whether the "bling bling" of the world will be your goal or whether you will strive for God's riches. God does not care about the gold on your wrist and around your neck. God cares about the gold in your heart. God desires a loving relationship with you. God wants you to love yourself, and God wants you to love people. God also wants you to know that you are important, more important than any precious jewels or anything that this world can offer you. Therefore, you are more valuable than anything material. You don't need to spend all of your energy trying to "bling bling." "Bling bling" is a condition of the heart. To God, you are "bling bling."

How will you choose to live? What bling will you pursue in life? The choice is yours to make.

This sermon was delivered on the occasion of Youth Sunday at Swansboro Baptist Church in Richmond, Virginia, on February 17, 2002. I would like to dedicate this homily to the memory of the Reverend Dr. Miles Jerome Jones, the dean of Black preaching, who influenced African American preaching for more than forty years like no one else, to the Reverend Dr. Charles F. Baugham Sr., to my grandfather, Deacon Lovie D. Ball, to the memory of my grandmother, Flora Mae Lee Ball, to my wife, Rachel Vincent-Finley, PhD, and to Najya.

NOTES

1. "Bling Bling" was released on B.G.'s 1999 Cash Money (Universal) recording *Chopper City in the Ghetto*.

2. "Once upon a Time" was released on Montell Jordan's 1999 Def Jam recording *Get It On . . . Tonite*.

3. "So Blu" was released on Blu Cantrell's 2001 Arista recording *So Blu*.

4. "Bow Wow (That's My Name)," featuring Snoop Dogg and J.D., was released on Bow Wow's 2000 So So Def recording *Beware of Dog*.

5. A quote from the familiar Christian children's song (often considered a nursery rhyme) "Jesus Loves the Little Children." The lyric was composed by Rev. Clare Herbert Woolston (1856–1927) as inspired by Matthew 19:14.

Chapter Eleven

Formality Meets Hip Hop: The Influence of Hip Hop Culture on the Afro-European Church

Shana Mashego

Over the course of the last thirty years, the Hip Hop Culture has greatly influenced and impacted American popular culture and proven to be a major force in the everyday lives of the current generation. The culture of Hip Hop has been far-reaching, with its largest effect taking hold in the communities of color of which it originated. One of the most intriguing areas of Hip Hop's influence, though, has been on the church denominations of the Black community. While many Black megachurches of the last decade have built their church services around the likes and dislikes of the Hip Hop generation, many churches of the Afro-European church tradition—namely, Black-populated churches in the United States belonging to European-born Catholic, Methodist, Lutheran, Episcopal, and Presbyterian traditions—have not been so eager to alter their church services. As a result, some congregations of the Afro-European church tradition have learned that if they do not attract and retain the young people connected to their current congregants—those whose music palates, style of dress, and tastes mirror that of urban rap artists—their churches face inevitable closure. Therefore, some churches of the Afro-European tradition have altered their music liturgies, order of services, dress codes, and service times to attract, retain, and excite prospective members from the Hip Hop generation.

During my experience growing up as a congregant of a Black Catholic Church in southeast Texas, I watched as the inception of Hip Hop culture began to change our church almost completely. As a child of the 1980s, I witnessed the alterations that my church made to accommodate new perspectives regarding our very formal Sunday mass. These changes divided families, friends, and even those in my own household against one another. What began as subtle alterations to our Sunday mass music liturgy developed into the evolution of new masses, all for the sake of retaining congregants. During this time, I also realized that I was a bit different in regard to the traditions of my Black Catholic Church. While having a discussion in my school cafeteria with another Black student, I realized that not having gospel music in our church service was considered unusual. One of my Black friends, a member of a local Black Baptist Church, pointed out to me, "*All* Black people should like gospel music at church! What is wrong with you and your church?" My father and a few of his friends even formed a committee to end what they called "foolish nonsense" in regard to creating changes to our formal Sunday mass. Their meetings included remarks such as "This is ridiculous! Gospel is for churches with loud screaming preachers! What will the White Catholics think of us if we bring *that* music to *our* church? We will only prove to them what they have thought of us all along. . . . They will say we are not really Catholic!" Although the changes did go forward and our church maintained steady growth, we lost many pillars of our congregation to the other Black Catholic Churches on the south side of town. The Catholic churches on the south side did not partake in these so-called necessary changes but remained true to their formal music liturgy and orders of service—until their growth began to halt. They then found themselves in the same position as many Afro-European congregations. It became evident that the new generation demanded change, for without growth, its church would face eventual closure.

THE AFRO-EUROPEAN CHURCH

Since its inception, the church has played a vital role in the Black community. Blacks separating into their own church congregations became a common practice during the late eighteenth century in America, and it was not long before Black congregations became prevalent within Methodist, Presbyterian, Catholic, Lutheran, and Episcopal denominations. Black Churches acted as a space void of racism since the beginning of slavery and still hold a significant place in many communities and certainly within the culture. By law, Blacks were denied access to public space, such as parks, libraries, restaurants, meeting halls, and other public accommodations, so the Black Church came to signify public space.[1]

During the late-eighteenth and early-nineteenth centuries, the Black Methodist movement began. The first separate denomination to be formed by African Americans in the United States was Methodist.[2] After this very important movement in Black Church history, other Black congregations of various denominations began to form. The members of these new churches had the opportunity to be a part of a freely governed association of believers, but to be validated as true Methodist congregations, the new Black Methodist church held fast to the traditions of the European-born Methodist church, including a traditional music liturgy.

Presbyterianism became a part of African American culture during the mid-nineteenth century. John Gloucester was founder of the First African Presbyterian Church in 1807 in Philadelphia. Gloucester was trained for the ministry within a Presbyterian church in Tennessee while he was still a slave.[3] It was from this humble beginning that the Black Presbyterian Church movement began. These churches were in no way independent churches; they had a responsibility to uphold the same practices as the other churches included within their denominational organization. The use of the traditional music liturgy and the traditional order of services in the Black Presbyterian Church gave the Black congregants validation as true Presbyterians. Alteration of the music within the church service was limited to special sacraments, such as Holy Communion or Baptism. Even during these sacraments, the early Black Presbyterian Church followed the standard music liturgy and order of service prescribed for these service additions.

The history of independent Black congregations of the Lutheran church is complex due to the discouragement of Blacks to form their own independent Lutheran churches. Black congregants of the Lutheran church were encouraged to worship along with other White congregants, but this proved problematic for many Blacks because they were forced to sit in pews separate from White congregants. In 1832 Jehu Jones founded St. Paul's Lutheran Church in Philadelphia, the first Black Lutheran Church in the United States.[4] Nearly one hundred years later, St. Philip's Lutheran Church in Detroit, Michigan, the first Black Lutheran Church in the state of Michigan, was formed in 1930 by a group of Black families who held rotating church meetings in their homes. The parish, first recognized as a mission church, shared a pastor with a church in Windsor, Ontario. St. Philip's Lutheran Church moved into a building in the early 1940s and remains in that location today.[5] The tradition of the Black Lutheran Church continues today with widespread congregations in many parts of the United States.

The history of Blacks in the Episcopal Church is rich, interesting, and controversial. In 1792, Absalom Jones, the first Black Episcopal priest in the United States, founded St. Thomas's African Episcopal Church, the first Black Episcopal Church in the United States.[6] While many may argue that the Episcopal denomination fought against the development of independent Black congregations, which in turn caused the founding of the independent Black Methodist Episcopal denomination, it must be noted that the Black Episcopal Church has remained an important component of African American culture.

The Black Catholic Church holds a unique and rich history and finds itself deeply rooted in the history of southern Louisiana and southeast Texas. Due to the strong influence of the French, many slaves populating southern Louisiana territory converted to Catholicism. The monumental St. Augustine Catholic Church in the Treme neighborhood of New Orleans, Louisiana, was dedicated in 1842 as the first Black Catholic Church in the United States. [7]

Although the Black Catholic Church understood the importance of holding on to the traditions of its founders for the sake of authenticity, it may come as some surprise that many Black Catholic Churches have been very progressive in the alteration of their music liturgy and order of services to welcome and accommodate the Hip Hop generation.

Within many Afro-European churches, the tradition of the musical liturgy, which included the music of European classical composers, was expected to remain unchanged, and even today, many of the churches within these denominations have maintained their loyalty to a traditional music liturgy and order of services. Interestingly, it seems that the churches belonging to the Afro-European denominational traditions that have altered their music and services have maintained growth while the churches that have remained true to their traditional roots have faced closure. Perhaps the key to longevity for these churches lies in the ability to compromise or, in many cases, overhaul their services altogether.

As stated before, it seems that many Black Catholic Churches caught on to the idea of alteration to accommodate the Hip Hop generation much sooner than many of the other denominations that compose the Afro-European church tradition. At my church, what began as one gospel song used for the offering or reflection portion of the church service, quickly grew into a separate church service complete with a full band and gospel choir by the late 1980s. It seemed that the new generation responded well to gospel music and grooving instrumental beats during church, and the music ministers of our church had countless meetings with the liturgical officers to make these changes occur.

For example, Sunday mass at my Catholic church would have included two traditional services, one at 7:30 am and another at 11:00 am. Both masses followed the traditional mass order and included music traditionally performed and approved by the parish council, the governing board of the church. The music of the mass was arranged into two categories, the Proper, the parts of the mass where the texts sung differed for each mass, and the Ordinary, the parts of the mass wherein the text remained the same for every mass but the melodies of the text and the accompaniments were allowed to change. The Proper includes the Introit, Gradual, Alleluia, and Communion Verse. [8] The texts of the Proper usually come from the Scriptures and are particular for each mass. For example, the Proper changes based on the mass celebrated; therefore, the Proper for masses during the season of Lent are very different from that of masses during the Advent Season. The Ordinary includes the Gloria, Credo, Sanctus, and Angus Dei.[9] The texts of these sections of the mass do not change, but the melodies and accompaniments can be changed.

Before the early 1980s (circa 1981), the music of my church's masses followed the same musical guidelines as a mass at the Vatican.

BASIC ORDER OF A CATHOLIC MASS

The Introit, Alleluia, Gloria, Credo, Sanctus, Agnus Dei, and Communion verses may have been Gregorian chants, excerpts of masses by Beethoven, Mozart, Obrecht, Bach, or Haydn or compositions written by a priest or monk unknown to us as congregant singers. Around 1982, this all began to change. The first mass, at 7:30 am, continued to follow the traditional format, while the 11:00 am mass underwent slight changes. For example, after the Communion rite, during the Reflection portion of the service, the musician performing the accompaniment for the mass, usually an organist, had the opportunity to display his or her musicianship;[10] therefore, a complex sacred Bach composition may have been performed. After the changes to the service were made, the music performed during the Reflection portion of the service may have been a slow, quiet instrumental Andraé Crouch composition.

By the mid-1980s, the 11:00 am mass changed drastically to include a gospel choir, which stood on the floor on risers in the front of the church near the pulpit, instead of in the choir loft in the balcony of the church. This new gospel choir was featured to sing twice for each service and during the Offertory and Reflection portions of the mass. This service also came complete with a new musician, one familiar with the concept of the overall order of the Catholic mass but with the capability of composing his own arrangements of the Ordinary and the Proper. While the texts of the Ordinary remained the same, the melodies and accompaniments were composed with gospel-styled chords and rhythms. The Proper received similar treatment, with each section altered to follow the new style of gospel-infused melodies and chord structures.

These types of changes began to affect every area of our church service: the priest at the 11:00 am service abandoned his robe and wore a black shirt with a white cleric's collar and black trousers; the dress code for congregants relaxed to include jeans; and the Benediction portion of the service was accompanied by upbeat gospel music.

To my surprise, the congregants of resistance began to change their opinion when they discovered how profitable the changes were. Even my father, a member of the church financial board, began to change his opinion of the service alterations when he viewed financial statements proving the church's security. His barking regarding the changes ceased, and he became satisfied with forfeiting his regular 11:00 am mass, which had undergone major alterations, and he began to attend the traditional mass at 7:30 am, the mass he still attends today. My mother, however, relinquished her traditional loyalties completely and began to attend the 11:00 am mass, which became known as the "Gospel Mass." She even joined the gospel choir, which she explained proved reminiscent of her childhood Baptist roots. My father still affectionately calls her a traitor. The separate mass attendance began long after I had left home and gone to university because, as my father explained, none of his seven children would ever be allowed to attend a "hippity-hop" mass!

Within a small span of time, the Black Catholic Church tradition in my part of the country had undergone major alterations, and it is currently common that most Black-populated Catholic churches of southern Louisiana and southeast Texas offer their congregants the choice of an early morning traditional service, complete with pipe organ and a quiet homily, or a midday mass, complete with charismatic-styled preaching, praise and worship, soul-stirring gospel music, and a relaxed dress code. The young people of my childhood church arrive early and leave the church grounds late due to the inception preservice coffee and after-mass lunches, which challenge the congregational leaders to create plans to accommodate the vehicles overflowing out of their church parking lots. To compete with the megachurches in the community, my childhood church now has three mass services: one for the traditionalist, at 7:30 am; another at 9:00 am, now called the "Gospel Mass," which features music geared toward those with a taste for traditional gospel; and another mass at 11:30 am, now called the "Contemporary Mass." The Contemporary Mass is the newest and most innovative mass offered by the church. This mass was created to attract the younger congregant, between the ages of sixteen and thirty, and it includes a praise team, with the music of the Proper and Ordinary set to the rhythms and melodies of contemporary gospel. While the church of my parents cannot boast the large numbers of congregants of the megachurches within their southeast Texas community, they report consistent attendance near the high two hundreds for all Sunday masses offered. When I was a child of the church, the numbers hovered near the middle three hundreds. This drop in attendance is seen as slight by the parish council, and the steady attendance is attributed to the council's ability to change the music of the mass in selected services and make a concerted effort to understand the importance of music taste of the Hip Hop generation.

This attention to detail regarding the music of the mass seems to have become of vast importance to Black Catholics nationwide. In 1987, a new hymnal entitled *Lead Me Guide Me: The African American Catholic Hymnal* was introduced and received very well at my childhood church. This new hymnal was formulated with the Black Catholic congregation in mind and included hymns and spirituals arranged and composed by African American composers. In an article titled "African American Sacred Music in Catholic Worship," Fr. John Adamski, Pastor of Our Lady of Lourdes Catholic Church in Atlanta, Georgia, explains, "African American music seems to have a quality of engaging people in ways different from much of Catholic church music today. Perhaps it's the rhythmic difference that contributes to making the music feel accessible."[11] I believe the understanding of making the church service accessible to the congregant of the Hip Hop generation is the overall concept that has proven successful for the world of Black Catholicism. This has been proven by my small southeast Texas Catholic church, which is still alive and in full service to all of its congregants.

However, churches of other Afro-European denominations have not enjoyed the same level of congregational security. Sadly, many churches belonging to the Afro-European tradition have been forced to close their doors. The scenarios of these churches seem similar: Their church services have not undergone any alterations for several years. The children of the congregants go to other churches once they are of age. The hardworking leaders of the church are lost to illness or death. Once the leaders of the church die, the church dies. A Philadelphia newspaper offered the following report on the Reeve Memorial Presbyterian Church, a Black-congregated Presbyterian church in west Philadelphia:

> Reeve Memorial Presbyterian Church, an 85-year-old church—a congregation with no Sunday school, an eight-member choir, and attendance averaging 40— will hold its last service June 26. Its struggle to survive amid shifting demographics is a familiar one to urban churches. Three other area Presbyterian churches—Seventh United and Hermon, both in Frankford, and Melrose-Carmel in Cheltenham—have closed this year.[12]

The tradition of the Afro-European church should prove to be extremely important to all Blacks, as the Afro-European church tradition marked the beginning of Black Church history in the United States. But for any organization to continue to live, it must maintain growth and functional development. Last year, twenty-three historically Black United Methodist churches closed their doors. Now, there are slightly fewer than twenty-three hundred Black Churches in the denomination.[13] But there are pastors of Black United Methodist churches who are figuring out the keys to growth and longevity. The Reverend Ronnie Miller-Yow, pastor of Wesley Chapel United Methodist Church in Little Rock, Arkansas, changed the overall format of his Sunday-morning services. By adding call- and response-styled preaching and contemporary worship music to his church service, Wesley Chapel has seen its average attendance climb from about 30 to almost 200;

since Miller-Yow became pastor in 2003, the church has added 152 members. Most have been students from neighboring Philander Smith College, a historically Black United Methodist college, where Miller-Yow is chaplain. Pastor Miller-Yow explains, "The secret to our success is that you can't put new wine in old skins, we've created a space for traditional worship and contemporary worship."[14]

This concept of creating space for the young congregant seems to be the unifying theme for prospering Afro-European churches of the twenty-first century. The loyalty given to the original format of the Afro-European church service seems to create a sense of pride for many purists of these Black congregations and does not need to be completely abandoned. Perhaps the success of these churches lies in their ability to compromise. Most of them offer two services: one in which their traditional formats are celebrated and another where the congregants, with local Hip Hop stations preset in their car radios, can lift their hands and worship in a space free of restriction. The Hip Hop generation has proven that it demands to express its own unique form of worshiping God, and many of us loyal to Afro-European churches have answered their requests for inclusion. Organizations such as the Black Methodists for Church Renewal and the National Black Presbyterian Caucus work feverishly to promote new ideas to ensure that the future sustainers of their congregations are allowed the opportunity to be involved in the innovation of their churches. Rather than remaining loyal to the music and order of service traditions of the founding fathers of the Afro-European church, the leaders of modern-day Afro-European churches that are experiencing growth seem to remain true to the original unifying mission of the Black Church. This mission historically held that the Black Church should serve as a beacon of light to its communities, a safe place that allows the congregants the space to perform within their God-given purpose and the opportunity to worship in a space void of discrimination. The Afro-European churches that remain full on Sunday mornings have welcomed and accommodated every generation, including those belonging to Hip Hop culture.

NOTES

1. Evelyn Brooks Higginbotham, *Righteous Discontent: The Women's Movement in the Black Baptist Church, 1880–1920* (Cambridge, MA: Harvard University Press, 1993).

2. C. Eric Lincoln and Lawrence H. Mamiya, *The Black Church in the African-American Experience* (Durham, NC: Duke University Press, 1990).

3. Henry H. Mitchell, *Black Church Beginnings: The Long Hidden Realities of the First Years* (Grand Rapids, MI: Eerdmans, 2004), 85.

4. *Philadelphia Inquirer* (January 22, 1998), 13. Karl E. Johnson Jr. and Joseph A. Romeo, "Jehu Jones (1786–1852): The First African American Lutheran Minister," *Lutheran Quarterly* 10 (1996): 425–43.

5. Oralandar Brand-Williams, "Michigan's First Black Lutheran Church Started in Detroit Homes," *Detroit News* (February 23, 2010), http://wwrn.org/articles/32746/.

6. Absalom Jones biography, http://biography.jrank.org/pages/2755/Jones-Absalom.html.

7. St. Augustine Catholic Church, http://www.staugustineCatholicchurch-neworleans.org/hist-sum.htm.

8. The Introit is sung during the entrance of the priest and the Holy Bible. It is usually a verse from a psalm. The Gradual is sung after the first reading of scripture; it is used as a response to the scripture. The Alleluia is sung before the reading of the Gospel, a scripture of the New Testament. The Communion Verse is sung before communion is distributed and is usually the text of New Testament Scripture.

9. The Gloria is a song of celebration sung before the opening prayer. The Credo is sung using the text of the Apostles' Creed, a statement of Christian beliefs. The Sanctus is sung during the communion ritual and is a proclamation of God's holiness. The Angus Dei is sung during the breaking of the communion bread and proclaims Jesus Christ as the Lamb of God. The following are portions of mass (those that include music are indicated with asterisks):

Introit*
Greeting
Kyrie Eleison*
Gloria*
Opening Prayer
First Reading
Responsorial Psalm*
Second Reading
Alleluia*
Gospel Reading
Homily/Sermon
Profession of Faith*
Prayer of Intercessions
Presentation of Holy Gifts/Offertory*
Prayer over the Gifts of Bread and Wine
Eucharistic Prayer
Sanctus*
Memorial Acclamation*
Doxology and Great Amen*
The Lord's Prayer*
Sign of Peace*
Breaking of Bread/Angus Dei*
Communion*
Reflection and Prayer*
Announcements
Greeting
Blessing
Dismissal
Benediction*

10. The Communion Rite is the communion service of the Catholic mass. Communion is given at every Catholic mass.

11. Kevin P. Johnson, "African American Sacred Music in Catholic Worship," Black Catholic Congress, http://www.nbccongress.org/features/print/african-american-sacred-music_pv.asp.

12. Kristin Holmes, "Congregation Begins Its Sorrowful Goodbye," *Philadelphia Inquirer*, http://articles.philly.com/2005-05-25/news/25441151_1_congregation-urban-churches-philadelphia-presbytery. Seventh United, Hermon, and Melrose-Carmel were Black

congregated Presbyterian churches in Philadelphia. In this article, a representative from the Philadelphia presbytery explains that several other Black congregated Presbyterian churches are facing closure due to an inability to attract new congregants.

13. Heather Hahn, "Church Lacks Racial Diversity, Officials Say," United Methodist Church, http://www.umc.org/site/apps/nlnet/content3.aspx?c=lwL4KnN1LtH&b=2789393&ct=8662595

14. Hahn, "Church Lacks Racial Diversity."

REFERENCES

Absalom Jones Biography. http://biography.jrank.org/pages/2755/Jones-Absalom.html.
Hahn, Heather. "Church Lacks Racial Diversity, Officials Say." United Methodist Church. http://www.umc.org/site/apps/nlnet/content3.aspx?c=lwL4KnN1LtH&b=2789393&ct=8662595.
Higginbotham, Evelyn Brooks. *Righteous Discontent: The Women's Movement in the Black Baptist Church, 1880–1920.* Cambridge, MA: Harvard University Press, 1993.
Holmes, Kristin. "Congregation Begins Its Sorrowful Goodbye." *Philadelphia Inquirer.* http://articles.philly.com/2005-05-25/news/25441151_1_congregation-urban-churches-philadelphia-presbytery.
Johnson, Karl E., Jr., and Joseph A. Romeo. "Jehu Jones (1786–1852): The First African American Lutheran Minister." *Lutheran Quarterly* 10 (1996): 425–43.
Johnson, Kevin. "African American Sacred Music in Catholic Worship." National Black Catholic Congress. http://www.nbccongress.org/features/print/african-american-sacred-music_pv.asp.
Lead Me Guide Me: The African American Catholic Hymnal. Chicago: GIA Publications, Inc., 1987.
Lincoln, C. Eric, and Lawrence H. Mamiya. *The Black Church in the African-American Experience.* Durham, NC: Duke University Press, 1990.
Mitchell, Henry H. *Black Church Beginnings: The Long Hidden Realties of the First Years.* Grand Rapids, MI: Eerdmans, 2004.
Southern, Eileen. *The Music of Black Americans: A History.* 2nd ed. New York: W. W. Norton & Company, 1983.
St. Augustine Catholic Church. http://www.staugustineCatholicchurch-neworleans.org/hist-sum.htm.
Williams-Brand, Oralandar. "Michigan's First Black Lutheran Church Started in Detroit Homes." *Detroit News,* February 23, 2010. http://wwrn.org/articles/32746/.

Part III

Gospel Rap, Holy Hip Hop, and the Hip Hop Matrix

Chapter Twelve

Beats, Rhymes and Bibles: An Introduction to Gospel Hip Hop

Josef Sorett

For many people it seems counterintuitive to examine Hip Hop music and culture for anything of religious significance. Reverend Calvin Butts's steamrolling of rap CDs in 1994 has been etched into America's consciousness as representative of the general posture of religious communities to this now global cultural phenomenon.[1] Nonetheless, like other black musical forms before it, religion and spirituality have been pervasive throughout Hip Hop since its emergence roughly thirty years ago. Of black diasporic musics, Paul Gilroy accurately asserts that they are, "facilitated by a common fund of urban experiences, by the effect of similar but by no means identical forms of racial segregation, as well as by the memory of slavery, a legacy of Africanisms, and a stock of religious experiences."[2]

With regards to Hip Hop, perhaps the most obvious religious ingredient in that stock has been Islam, which in various forms—Sunni, Nation of Islam, and Five Percenter—has been ubiquitous.[3] Chuck D, Rakim, Ice Cube, Nas, Busta Rhymes, Mos Def and many others have expressed allegiances to these traditions.[4] Beyond Islam, Hip Hop historians will never forget the neo-nationalist, afrocentric mysticism invoked by groups such as X-Clan, who called listeners to look, "to the East."[5] During the mid-nineties there was the conscious, eclectic, backpacker spirituality of De La Soul, A Tribe Called Quest and others affiliated with the Native Tongues collective. Moreover, countless fans have witnessed the evolution of the indomitable KRS-One from his Boogie Down Productions, *Criminal Minded* days to his 2002 *Spiritually Minded* album which included the track "Lord, Live Within My Heart." Recently, critics have decried the apparent Hip Hop fundamentalism advocated by KRS and his Temple of Hip Hop.[6] Much more could be said of the spiritual ponderings of numerous other artists, including Lauryn Hill,

Tupac, Biggie, Scarface, and Trick Daddy. Yet KRS's own progression and his later use of traditional Christian language, marks a broader pattern in Hip Hop music.

Christianity has always had an overt presence in rap music—some may remember "Son of the King" on MC Hammer's debut album[7] —but it has emerged more forcefully in recent years. Hip Hop devotees have witnessed shouts out to Creflo Dollar by Mase, Outkast and 50 Cent, DMX's angst-filled prayers, and the Grammy Award-winning "Jesus Walks." None of which took place without controversy. Take the latter example, which also earned Kanye West a nomination from gospel music's Stellar Awards. After much debate within Christian music circles, and scrutiny of West's broader career trajectory, the nomination was revoked.[8] However, outside of these quarters "Jesus Walks" was widely celebrated on major radio stations and popular video shows, and it elevated spirits (and bodies) in nightclubs across the nation. But for every mainstream success there are thousands of other artists grinding it out in the underground.[9] Enter here the largely overlooked, but thriving nonetheless, sub-genre now referred to as Gospel Hip Hop.

To be sure, rap music is not something that was quickly welcomed into black churches, i.e. Rev. Butt's steamroller. Such reticence is shaped largely by a "politics of respectability" that deems much of Hip Hop's aesthetic profane—what Imani Perry refers to as its "rough and funky" quality.[10] As with Gospel-Blues in the early twentieth century and the R&B-inflected sound of contemporary Gospel music of the next generation, the church's response to Hip Hop has been rife with complicated negotiations. While Gospel-Blues had Thomas Dorsey and contemporary Gospel had Tremaine Hawkins, Gospel Hip Hop has Stephen Wiley, the unsung original Christian MC.[11] In 1985, six years after the release of "Rapper's Delight,"[12] Wiley debuted with "Bible Break," the first commercially-released Christian rap song.[13] Distributed to Christian markets across the country, the single's biggest contribution was its ability to teach children the books of the Bible through employing rudimentary rhythms (this author can still recite the song almost verbatim). Although not as artistically gifted as Dorsey or Hawkins, perhaps the many educators who now use rap as a pedagogical device ought to give Wiley his due.

On his fourth album, *Get Real,* Wiley would articulate the hermeneutic that defined early Christian rap. Wiley and many of his contemporaries were African American youth ministers who opted to preach over sub-par Hip Hop beats rather than the customary Hammond B3. That their tracks were inferior was justifiable because, as Wiley rapped, "It's not the beat, but it's the Word that sets the people free. So, give me the Word!"[14] This strategic privileging of content over form buttressed the arguments of Christian rappers against congregations who were often resistant to a sound associated with ghetto-dwelling, gangster-ized youth.[15] In effect, like two generations of black religious musicians before them, Christian rappers consecrated a popular "secular" form by anointing their rhythms with sacred text, positing an exilic—in this world, but not of it—ethic in relation to the larger Hip Hop community.[16]

With the exception of its explicitly Christian lyrics, much of Gospel Hip Hop has mirrored the stars and styles of its secular counterpart. Shortly after Wiley, Michael Peace commanded attention with a raw vocal aesthetic that aspired to the status of an early LL Cool J. The three man group P.I.D. (Preachers in Disguise) donned all black—with the addition of clergy collars—a la Run-D.M.C. before Reverend Run and Darryl McDaniels were *Down with the King*.[17] At times, such imitations rang more untrue than others, as was the case with The Rapsures, whose visual presentation was reminiscent more of a Motown quintet than the Furious Five.[18] Sadly, Gospel Hip Hop even has its own patron saint in the late Danny "D-Boy" Rodriguez, an MC who in 1989 was killed during a drive-by shooting while ministering in the streets of Dallas, TX.[19] By the early 1990s, west coast "gangsta' rap" had taken over the mainstream Hip Hop scene, and Gospel Gangstas emerged as the Christian rap group of choice. In fact, the group's core members were themselves ex-O.G.s using rap to lure teenagers away from gang life. Hundreds of lesser known groups appeared over the next decade; and today, twenty one years post-"Bible Break," Gospel Hip Hop has come into its own. With Philadelphia's Cross Movement arguably the cream of the crop, many Christian rappers now display quality lyricism and strong music production to match.

At the intersections of Hip Hop and evangelism is where some of Gospel Hip Hop's most exciting work gets done. One cannot discount the ministry-motivation driving the music. However, the current shape of Gospel Hip Hop is as complex as the broader culture from which it takes cues. As its own cottage industry it encompasses the four elements typically invoked in definitions of Hip Hop (MC-ing, Breaking, DJ-ing and Graffiti) and the commercial opportunities attendant to each. Such complexity is best captured at Rapfest, an annual event held in South Bronx—the site most frequently credited as the birthplace of Hip Hop.[20] Rapfest is a block party/outreach event that attracts performers that vary in race, gender, denomination, and geography, often traveling from as far as Texas and Puerto Rico. Along with a stage show, vendor booths are set up where consumers, converts and critics buy and sell CDs and DVDs, clothing, magazines and more—all oriented by a Hip Hop Christology.[21]

While Rapfest is possibly the oldest and biggest of its kind, now in its eleventh year, similar events have sprung up all over the country, and these are outnumbered by a host of local church-based Hip Hop ministries that meet more regularly. Flavor Fest is another popular annual event held in Tampa, FL. Flavor Fest's host, Crossover Community Church,[22] is also one of the first wholly-Hip Hop churches, where worship includes breaking, graffiti, and DJ-ing; and the pastor, Tommy Kyllonen, aka Urban D(isciple), is both preacher and MC. Kyllonen made headlines earlier this year by simultaneously signing a book, CD and movie deal.[23] And while enthusiasts await the release of his trilogy, the movement already has its handbook: *The Hip-Hop Church*.[24] Coauthored by Efrem Smith and Phil Jackson, both pastors of Hip Hop congregations, the book might be described as Hip Hop meets *The Purpose Driven Life*.[25]

Across this growing commercial backdrop, Holy Hip Hoppers express a range of understandings of the import of the Gospel on their craft. As stated earlier, the ministry-motif is a recurring theme, and much of the language of Gospel Hip Hop evinces a traditional Christian theology (i.e. heaven/hell, sin/salvation, angels/demons, etc). Yet for some, faith does not translate into outright Jesus-talk. The Nashville-based rap group GRITS, for example, opts for a more open language of parables, injecting social critique into their lyrics toward the broader end of transformation.[26] Gospel Hip Hop artists can be mapped across a fault line that delineates the pull of artistic and religious commitments.

At a prayer meeting prior to the 2002 Kingdom Come outreach in the Queensbridge Housing Project, the event's convener, Minister David Dean, aka Chosen, voiced several sentiments that are shared by much of the Gospel Hip Hop community. First, Dean argued that it addresses two under-represented demographics in black churches: men and young people.[27] Second, he framed the still-marginal status of Gospel Hip Hop artists as a critique of conspicuous commercialism on the part of mainstream rappers and prosperity preachers alike.[28] Lastly, Dean pointed to Kingdom Come as evidence of the Gospel's ability to heal Hip Hop's strongest vices, noting that many artists in attendance at Kingdom Come had ministered just weeks before in the Bronx at Rapfest. For Dean, this reciprocity symbolically redeemed the early Hip Hop beef, circa 1987, between the Bronx's Boogie Down Productions and Queensbridge's MC Shan, during which KRS One declared, "The 'Bridge Is Over.'"[29]

Does Gospel Hip Hop possess the power to atone for the sins of Hip Hop and the Church? Most likely not; but the verdict is not in yet. In the meantime it is certainly a growing force, as myriad churches—including storefronts, mainline and megas and crossing racial-cultural boundaries—have developed Hip Hop ministries.[30] If controversy is any sign of longevity, Gospel Hip Hop even has its own institutionalized critic par excellence in Minister G. Craige Lewis, founder of EX Ministries, who is committed to saving youth from the most recent instantiation of "the devil's music."[31] Yet for scores of Christian Hip Hop loyalists, Gospel plus Hip Hop presents the possibility of rebuilding bridges within the Church and in the larger world it is called to serve, all to a beat.[32]

An earlier version of this chapter was published under the same title in The African American Pulpit *(Winter 2006–2007): 12–16.*

NOTES

1. Mel Tarpley. "Rappin' About Rap," *New York Amsterdam News* (September 23, 1995).

2. Paul Gilroy. *The Black Atlantic: Modernity and Double Consciousness.* Cambridge, MA: Harvard University Press, 1993, 80.

3. Felicia M. Miyakawa. *Five Percenter Rap: God Hop's Music, Message and Black Muslim Mission.* Bloomington: Indiana University Press, 2005.

4. Charise Cheney. "Representin' God: Rap, Religion and the Politics of a Culture," *The North Star: A Journal of African American Religious History.* Vol. 3, No. 1 (http://northstar.vassar.edu/volume3/cheney.html)

5. X-Clan. *To the East, Blackwards.* 4th and Broadway Records, 1990.

6. Boogie Down Productions. *Criminal Minded.* B-Boy Records, 1987; KRS One. *Spiritually Minded.* Koch Records, 2002. http://www.templeofhiphop.org; Adisa Banjoko. "The Weakness of 'Being Hip Hop'" in *Lyrical Swords, Volume II: Westside Rebellion.* San Jose, CA: YinSumi Press, 2005, 45–46.

7. MC Hammer. "Son of the King," *Let's Get it Started.* Capitol Records, 1988.

8. The Stellar Awards recognizes excellence within the Gospel music industry. Although his nomination was later revoked, West did receive invitations from churches to perform at their youth services. See Natalie Hopkinson. "Rap Gets Religion, But Is It Gospel," *Washington Post* (September 24, 2004).

9. Imani Perry. *Prophets of the Hood: Politics and Poetics in Hip Hop.* Durham, NC: Duke University Press, 2004, 202–203.

10. Evelyn Brooks Higginbotham. *Righteous Discontent: The Women's Movement in the Black Baptist Church, 1880–1920.* Cambridge, MA: Harvard University Press, 1993, 185–229; Perry. *Prophets of the Hood,* 4; Teresa L. Reed. *The Holy Profane: Religion in Black Popular Music.* Lexington, KY: University Press of Kentucky, 2003.

11. Michael W. Harris. *The Rise of Gospel Blues: The Music of Thomas Dorsey in the Urban Church.* New York: Oxford University Press, 1992; Guthrie P. Ramsey. *Race Music: Black Cultures from Bebop to Hip Hop.* Berkeley: University of California Press, 2003.

12. The Sugar Hill Gang. *Rapper's Delight.* Sugar Hill Records, 1979. "Rapper's Delight" is credited as being the commercially released rap song.

13. Wiley. "Bible Break." Interestingly enough, at the time Wiley was a member of the crusade team at Kenneth Hagin's Rhema Bible Church in Broken Arrow, OK, where black parishioners are few and far between. Wiley later served as an assistant pastor/youth minister at the predominantly black Crenshaw Christian Center in Los Angeles, CA, under Frederick K.C. Price. Both churches are rooted in the now prominent Word of Faith movement.

14. Stephen Wiley. "Gimme' Da' Word" on *Get Real.* Brentwood Music, 1989.

15. Robin D.G. Kelley. *Race Rebels: Culture, Politics and the Black Working Class.* New York: The Free Press, 1994, 183–227.

16. Wallace D. Best. *Passionately Human, No Less Divine: Religion and Culture in Black Chicago, 1915–1952.* Princeton, NJ: Princeton University Press, 2005; Cheryl J. Sanders. *Saints in Exile: The Holiness-Pentecostal Experience in African American Religion and Culture.* New York: Oxford University Press, 1996.

17. Run-D.M.C. *Down with the King.* Profile Records, 1993.

18. On the cover to their only album, *Loud, Proud and Born Again* (1990), the group is featured wearing matching suits and neckties. Grandmaster Flash and the Furious were an early rap group that recorded classic songs, including "The Message" (1982).

19. See http://www.christianmusicarchive.com; http://www.wikipedia.com lists Rodriguez as having died in 1991.

20. Tricia Rose. *Black Noise: Rap Music and Black Culture in Contemporary America.* Middletown, CT: Wesleyan University Press, 1998; Jeff Chang. *Can't Stop, Won't Stop: A History of the Hip-Hop Generation.* New York: St. Martin's Press, 2005.

21. Jerma A. Jackson. *Singing in My Soul: Black Gospel Music in a Secular Age* (Chapel Hill: University of North Carolina Press, 2004). Jackson illustrates the impact of commerce on the shaping of gospel music in a manner that is helpful for thinking about Gospel Hip Hop.

22. See http://www.crossoverchurch.org and http://www.flavorfest.org.

23. Kyllonen's book, CD, and DVD are all titled: *Unorthodox . . . Where Hip-Hop Meets the Church: Poised To Make History*: Grand Rapids, MI: Zondervan, forthcoming. For more information see http://www.thegospelzone.com

24. Efrem Smith and Phil Jackson. *The Hip-Hop Church: Connecting with the Movement Shaping the Culture.* Downers Grove, IL: Intervarsity Press, 2005.

25. Rick Warren. *The Purpose Driven Life: What On Earth Am I Here For?* Grand Rapids, MI: Zondervan, 2002.

26. Charlie Braxton. "Rhyme and Reason: Up-and-coming local duo GRITS are Christians, and they're rappers—but don't peg them as Christian rappers." *Nashville Scene* magazine (October 24, 2002).

27. C. Eric Lincoln and Lawrence Mamiya. *The Black Church in the African American Experience.* Durham, NC: Duke University Press, 1990, 382–384.

28. Dean's criticism resonates with similar critiques of the influence of commercialism on mainstream Hip Hop raised by "secular" underground artists; but Dean also draws from a clear religious motivation.

29. Boogie Down Productions. "The Bridge Is Over" on *Criminal Minded.* B-Boy Records, 1987. Minister David Dean's comments are paraphrased from *The Yolanda Show*, Brooklyn Cable Access Television, Summer 2002.

30. There are too many churches that sponsor Hip Hop ministries to name even a significant portion of them here.

31. See http://www.exministries.com. For a discussion of "the devil's music" see Teresa L. Reed, *The Holy Profane*, 89–112.

32. Anthony B. Pinn. "Making a World with a Beat: Musical Expression's Relationship to Religious Identity and Experience," in *Noise and Spirit: The Religious and Spiritual Sensibilities of Rap Music*, Anthony B. Pinn, ed. New York: NYU Press, 2003.

BIBLIOGRAPHY

Banjoko, Adisa. "The Weakness of 'Being Hip Hop'" in *Lyrical Swords, Volume II: Westside Rebellion.* San Jose, CA: Yinsumi Press, 2005, 45–46.

Best, Wallace D. *Passionately Human, No Less Divine: Religion and Culture in Black Chicago, 1915–1952.* Princeton, NJ: Princeton University Press, 2005.

Bone Thugs-n-Harmony. "Tha Crossroads," *Eternal.* Ruthless Records, 1995.

Boogie Down Productions. "The Bridge Is Over," *Criminal Minded.* B-Boy Records, 1987.

Braxton, Charlie. "Rhyme and Reason: Up-and-coming local duo GRITS are Christians, and they're rappers—but don't peg them as Christian rappers." *Nashville Scene* magazine (October 24, 2002).

Chang, Jeff. *Can't Stop, Won't Stop: A History of the Hip-Hop Generation.* New York: St. Martin's Press, 2005.

Cheney, Charise. "Representin' God: Rap, Religion and the Politics of a Culture," *The North Star: A Journal of African American Religious History.* Vol. 3, No. 1.

Dean, David. As seen on *The Yolanda Show*, Brooklyn Cable Access Television, Summer 2002.

Gilroy, Paul. *The Black Atlantic: Modernity and Double Consciousness.* Cambridge, MA: Harvard University Press, 1993.

Harris, Michael W. *The Rise of Gospel Blues: The Music of Thomas Dorsey in the Urban Church.* New York: Oxford University Press, 1992.

Higginbotham, Evelyn Brooks. *Righteous Discontent: The Women's Movement in the Black Baptist Church, 1880–1920*. Cambridge, MA: Harvard University Press, 1993.
Hopkinson, Natalie. "Rap Gets Religion, But Is It Gospel," *Washington Post* (September 24, 2004).
Jackson, Jerma A. *Singing in My Soul: Black Gospel Music in a Secular Age*. Chapel Hill: University of North Carolina Press, 2004.
Kelley, Robin D. G. *Race Rebels: Culture, Politics and the Black Working Class*. New York: The Free Press, 1994.
KRS One. *Spiritually Minded*. Koch Records, 2002.
Kyllonen, Tommy. *Unorthodox . . . Where Hip-Hop Meets the Church: Poised to Make History*. Grand Rapids, MI: Zondervan, forthcoming.
Lincoln, C. Eric, and Lawrence Mamiya. *The Black Church in the African American Experience*. Durham, NC: Duke University Press, 1990.
Miyakawa, Felicia M. *Five Percenter Rap: God Hop's Music, Message and Black Muslim Mission*. Bloomington: Indiana University Press, 2005.
Perry, Imani. *Prophets of the Hood: Politics and Poetics in Hip Hop*. Durham, NC: Duke University Press, 2004.
Pinn, Anthony B. "Making a World with a Beat: Musical Expression's Relationship to Religious Identity and Experience," in *Noise and Spirit: The Religious and Spiritual Sensibilities of Rap Music*, Anthony B. Pinn, ed. New York: NYU Press, 2003.
Ramsey, Guthrie P. *Race Music: Black Cultures from Bebop to Hip Hop*. Berkeley: University of California Press, 2003.
Reed, Teresa L. *The Holy Profane: Religion in Black Popular Music*. Lexington: University Press of Kentucky, 2003.
Rose, Tricia. *Black Noise: Rap Music and Black Culture in Contemporary America*. Middletown, CT: Wesleyan University Press, 1998.
Run-D.M.C. *Down with the King*. Profile Records, 1993.
Sanders, Cheryl J. *Saints in Exile: The Holiness-Pentecostal Experience in African American Religion and Culture*. New York: Oxford University Press, 1996.
Smith, Efrem, and Phil Jackson. *The Hip-Hop Church: Connecting with the Movement Shaping the Culture*. Downers Grove, IL: Intervarsity Press, 2005.
Tarpley, Mel. "Rappin' About Rap," *New York Amsterdam News* (September 23, 1995).
Warren, Rick. *The Purpose Driven Life: What On Earth Am I Here For?* Grand Rapids, MI: Zondervan, 2002.
Wiley, Stephen. *Bible Break*. Benson Music Group, 1985.
Wiley, Stephen. "Gimme' Da' Word," *Get Real*. Brentwood Music, 1989.
X-Clan. *To the East, Blackwards*. 4th and Broadway Records, 1990.

ONLINE RESOURCES

http://www.christianmusicarchive.com
http://www.crossoverchurch.org
http://www.exministries.com
http://www.flavorfest.org
http://northstar.vassar.edu/volume3/cheney.htm
http://www.thegospelzone.com
http://www.wikipedia.com

f

Chapter Thirteen

Isn't Loving God Enough? Debating Holy Hip Hop

Cassandra Thornton

My introduction to Holy Hip Hop came through a life-changing experience at a Cross Movement CD release party in 1999. At the party, there were many youth, mostly teenagers and folks in their early twenties, like myself. I anxiously waited for the musicians to take the stage, and when they did, the whole room, especially those who never heard them, was taken by surprise at their cunning ability to rhyme about the Gospel. The crowd exploded into praise when they performed their hit song "I Am That I Am" and then grew quiet and listened attentively as the Ambassador, one of the members of the group, shared his popular heartfelt song, "Super Stars."[1] My eyes filled up with tears after that song, and the whole place became silent. As I looked around the room to see other people's reactions, many of the teens and young adults had their eyes closed and heads bowed. Some of them had friends hugging and holding them as they began to cry. It wasn't an altar call, but God had spoken to them through that rap song and convicted their hearts. This was exactly what I had been praying for: to see young people understanding the Gospel and seeking Christ for answers, for healing, and for salvation.

Feeling very overwhelmed and moved by this response, I went to sit down to meditate on all this. It made so much sense. If you want to successfully reach any culture, the best way to do so is to know and speak the language of that culture. Most of the teens and young adults at the concert, as well as in churches, are a part of the Hip Hop Culture. The language of that culture is rap. Therefore, if you communicate the Gospel through rap, these people will understand and relate to it better than your traditional pastors teaching it to them from a pulpit. The other advantage of incorporating the Gospel into rap is that you will be able to globally indoctrinate people of all ages, races, and economic classes because this is what the Hip Hop Culture is composed of. It is an international culture. As I continued to sit in my chair thinking about this, God planted a seed in my heart, mind, and soul. Since the winter of 1999, I have been promoting Holy Hip Hop concerts, teaching classes on the culture, as well as serving as a radio personality and mobile DJ.

God has made numerous provisions for me to attend conferences, concerts, and video shoots all over the country, where a large attendance of Christian rap artists and other promoters, DJs, producers, comedians, and clothing designers congregate. Over time, true friendships and divine purposes started surfacing with these various individuals. Fellowships were no longer just at events but in one another's homes and during holidays, birthdays, and other special occasions. Due to the initial lack of support from churches for Holy Hip Hop, we started supporting one another financially, through prayer, and by swapping services, and just like the early apostles, hardly any of us was left with a need (Acts 4:32–35). As the fellowship and support continued to grow within the culture, talk of coalescing under one umbrella, or movement, to show the world our unity became more frequent (John 17:22–23). During the summer of 2003, Maji, a renowned Christian producer from Detroit, created the Yuinon (pronounced "Union"), which became the vehicle for all the various Christian ministries to unify and display our uncompromising stance for holiness and truth. I joined the Yuinon in November 2003 as a mobile DJ, promoter, and freelance writer. I am also a member and Chapter Representative of the Urban Gospel Alliance, which helps to promote and give artists a platform to display their God-given talent through events.

I continue to share Christ through Hip Hop with the hope that those caught up in the culture will be saved. All my work as a mobile DJ, radio personality, and educator is out of my obedience to fulfill this God-given call and responsibility.

A BRIEF HISTORY OF HOLY HIP HOP

Holy Hip Hop and Christian rap has been in existence for more than twenty years. In its inception, people just wanted to rhyme for God; there was no formal movement. Some of these patriarchs were Stephen Wiley, Michael Peace, Dynamic Twins, LPG, Danny "D-Boy" Rodriguez (who was the first Christian rapper to become a martyr), I.D.O.L. King (In Dedication of Louis King), P.I.D. (Preachers in Disguise), and S.F.C. (Soldiers for Christ).

After these patriarchs, the first generation of Christian rappers emerged on the scene in the 1990s, which included Gospel Gangstaz, Urban Disciple, T-Bone, A-1 Swift, Prime Minister, and the CMCs. Most of these groups were pretty evangelistic and helped set the stage for the second generation, which brought the Holy Hip Hop movement, an organized evangelistic movement to reach those in the Hip Hop Culture. This happened around the mid-1990s. Some of these ministries include Cross Movement, Mark J, Elle Roc, Remnant Militia, and New Breed.

Some of the most notable ministries within the third generation include Bang Theory, Flavor Alliance, I.D.O.L. King, Lamp Mode Recordings, Much Luv Records, Reach Records, and the Yuinon.

According to I.D.O.L. King, Holy Hip Hop is defined as "the voice of a generation set apart to glorify God, reach the lost, and edify the saints."[2]

I.D.O.L. King has also put together some guidelines by which we can understand, appreciate, create, and critique Holy Hip Hop music:

> 1. Does each song teach, rebuke, correct, equip, and/or train an individual in righteousness? (2 Timothy 3:16)
> 2. When a person feels perplexed by the things they face daily, can they find themselves singing one of these songs to be edified, encouraged, and inspired to carry on?
> 3. When listening to these songs, ask yourself, do they convey the hope of salvation Jesus Christ offers to all men?
> At the end of each CD, if you can answer yes to any of these questions, Holy Hip-Hop's mission has been accomplished.[3]

THE ARGUMENTS AND PRESUPPOSITIONS AGAINST HOLY HIP HOP

The biggest adversaries of Holy Hip Hop are ignorance and "ministries" that propagate their personal disbeliefs by passing them as biblical truth. These so-called ministries prey on and take advantage of churches who likely would not have embraced Holy Hip Hop at first glance, because it challenges their traditional religious customs. These "ministries" have capitalized on spreading, not the truth, but myths and fables that uninformed itching ears desire to hear (2 Timothy 4:3–4). One such "ministry" is EX Ministries, founded by Elder G. Craige Lewis. EX Ministries has put up quite a fight against Holy Hip Hop and caused discord and division in the body of Christ. While it is the popular belief that this "ministry" has grown because of the "truth" it has been spreading regarding Hip Hop, it has actually been growing because of the slanderous remarks that they have made toward popular Christian and secular artists. One of the marketing tactics that the secular music industry employs to promote an album or artist is slandering. The artist or label will make a demeaning remark about another top-selling artist or label to attract the attention of the fans of that other artist/label as well as the media. This same tactic has been used by EX Ministries. By slandering popular Christian and secular artists, whether intentionally or not, it has gained international awareness. My motive for mentioning this ministry is not to slander or demean it but to dispel the lies and myths it has been spreading. The Bible tells us in 2 Timothy 3:16,

> All Scripture is God-breathed and is useful for teaching, rebuking, correcting and training in righteousness, so that the man of God may be thoroughly equipped for every good work. (New International Version)

Given this passage, I examine and weigh the validity of the theories and arguments that EX Ministries has made against Holy Hip Hop, not with my opinion, but with the indisputable word of God.

EX MINISTRIES THEORY AND ARGUMENTS

The prevalent and controversial theory that EX Ministries has been teaching about Hip Hop is the following:

> The spirit of hip-hop is a demonic force, birthed in Hell, and sent with a mission to deceive, glorify sin, and take control of the minds of our people, thus giving Satan complete control of an entire generation. And it's all done through music![4]

Given this presupposition, Ex Ministries has created and taught several misleading arguments about Holy Hip Hop, which I aim to rebut using the Bible, real-life scenarios, and actual occurrences. It should be noted for future reference that as Christians, we are not wise to indulge ourselves in meaningless conversations and gossips such as this because the outcome is not fruitful and beneficial to the body of Christ. The Bible makes this point clear in several scriptures:

> As I urged you when I went into Macedonia, stay there in Ephesus so that you may command certain men not to teach false doctrines any longer nor to devote themselves to myths and endless genealogies. These promote controversies rather than God's work—which is by faith. The goal of this command is love, which comes from a pure heart and a good conscience and a sincere faith. Some have wandered away from these and turned to meaningless talk. They want to be teachers of the law, but they do not know what they are talking about or what they so confidently affirm. (1 Timothy 1:3–7, New International Version)

> Who is wise and understanding among you? Let him show it by his good life, by deeds done in the humility that comes from wisdom. But if you harbor bitter envy and selfish ambition in your hearts, do not boast about it or deny

the truth. Such "wisdom" does not come down from heaven but is earthly, unspiritual, of the devil. For where you have envy and selfish ambition, there you find disorder and every evil practice. But the wisdom that comes from heaven is first of all pure; then peace-loving, considerate, submissive, full of mercy and good fruit, impartial and sincere. (James 3:13–17, New International Version)

Don't have anything to do with foolish and stupid arguments, because you know they produce quarrels. And the Lord's servant must not quarrel; instead, he must be kind to everyone, able to teach, not resentful. Those who oppose him he must gently instruct, in the hope that God will grant them repentance leading them to a knowledge of the truth, and that they will come to their senses and escape from the trap of the devil, who has taken them captive to do his will. (2 Timothy 2:23–26, New International Version)

With that established, let's examine these arguments to dispel the lies and bring unity back to the body of Christ.

Argument 1

Rap is entertainment, not ministry. Even though there is a level of ministry found in Christian music, it's the beat and the melody that's the draw. So, when it's time to draw men to Christ, the music should not be used to do it, but the Spirit of God will do it through an effective preacher. [5]

Rebuttal 1

They overcame [Satan] by the blood of the Lamb and by the word of their testimony: they did not love their lives so much as to shrink from death. (Revelation 12:11, New International Version)

To a nonbeliever, the Bible is just a theory. Nevertheless, we understand the Bible to be a collection of testimonies of believers, Christians, which validates that what the Bible says is true and still practical and relevant in today's times. Our testimonies are a powerful tool because they cannot be discredited, regardless of how much science and logic one may present. It's just like the story in John 9:1–34. In brief, a man was born blind. Jesus healed him, and the Pharisees refused to believe it. The man's response to them was "One thing I do know. I was blind but now I see!"

Christian rap and Holy Hip Hop contain the testimonies and stories of believers and their transformation from darkness to light, which demonstrates the power and evidence of God. The songs and other expressions establish a relational connection with the nonbelievers, giving them faith to believe that God can save and change them. Scripture is also referenced in Christian rap, and Hebrews 4:12 tells us,

> For the word of God is living and active. Sharper than any double-edged
> sword, it penetrates even to dividing soul and spirit, joints and marrow; it
> judges the thoughts and attitudes of the heart. (New International Version)

Because of the scriptural content in Christian rap, the Spirit of God can use
the music to challenge the thoughts and attitudes of the listener and convict
his or her heart, which may ultimately lead one to repentance and a
relationship with God. Whether this decision is made or not, we can have
peace knowing that God's word will never return void (Isaiah 55:11).

Finally, when believers are at a concert or an outreach and hear these
Christian rap songs, it reminds them of God's unfailing love and His grace
and mercy, which compels them to praise and worship Him. This kind of
praise and worship ushers in the presence of God and allows the nonbelievers
in the same room or vicinity to have a personal encounter with God. They
can also feel His presence. This is normally when deliverance and salvation
take place for a nonbeliever at a Holy Hip Hop event. It is for these
aforementioned reasons that Christian rap is ministry.

Argument 2

> We have collected information from various sources to show you how active
> the enemy has been in the music industry. But don't take our word for it. Open
> your eyes. Pick up a current issue of *Vibe* or *Source* magazine. *Jet* or *Ebony*.
> Or just watch a video show on BET. You will see that everything that hip hop
> glorifies is negative and against the word of God. There is no exception. Hip
> hop is a culture and lifestyle from Hell![6]

Rebuttal 2

I have also collected information from various sources to show how active
Christ has been in using His people to reach those in the secular music
industry, as well as the urban car industry. Two Christian rap artists, Corey
Red and Precise, appeared in the June 2002 issue of *Black Men* magazine,
which featured on the cover a half-naked picture of Ashanti (an R&B singer
and actress). Some of the articles in this magazine included "Ashanti
Unwrapped," "Does Size Matter?" "What You Need to Know about Her
Orgasm," and "Corey Red & Precise Spit Prophetic." How's that for a
lineup? Their article appears in the middle of the magazine after the featured
article on Ashanti. Only God could orchestrate something like this. The four-
page interview, which includes a photo shoot of them, starts off with the
writer, Marcus Blassingame, giving a brief bio of who Corey Red and
Precise are, describing them as skilled and phenomenal MCs who always rep
(represent) Christ!

The first question Red and Precise are asked by *Black Men* magazine is why do they think the Hip Hop community or world wants to hear them rap about Christ and against the content that is driving the recording industry? Red responds by saying that God can use all the trash (manure) to fertilize the ground for the good that is to come.

When asked about their ultimate goal, they respond emphatically that they are here to glorify Jesus and to save souls!

The Lord presented these two Christian rappers the opportunity to be interviewed by a major magazine, and recognizing this rare opportunity to be exposed to a large secular audience, they didn't compromise and talk about how tight their lyrics are; rather, they chose to talk about the things of God: who Christ is and the hope we can have in Him. Interestingly enough, their stance to always represent Jesus in their rhymes is what caught *Black Men* magazine's attention, more than anything else, to interview them.

Vibe magazine in its April 2005 issue, which featured on the cover a black-and-white picture of 50 Cent (a secular rap artist), interviewed the leaders of Christ Tabernacle in Queens, which has a popular Hip Hop ministry. This article, called "Breath, Stretch, Pray," was unique in that it had more pictures than words. *Vibe* showed six full-color pages of youth worshipping, praying, and crying out to God, which was a good idea to do since words could not express what it captured in these pictures. The last picture of the article shows a long line of youth and explains that they often wait up to three hours to attend an 8:00 pm service.

Another good example of Hip Hop being used as ministry is the Holy Rollerz Christian Car Club.[7] Tricked-out cars with shiny, spinning rims form a big part of the Hip Hop Culture. Holy Rollerz seeks to evangelize to those caught up in this aspect of the culture. An excerpt from the bio on its website reads,

> We will strive to promote the love of the Lord in an area where He has rarely before been given the glory. Many car clubs tolerate drinking, illegal racing, profanity, and sexual promiscuity. WE DO NOT. We are trying to give young car enthusiasts a club that neither promotes nor tolerates any of these things.[8]

Holy Rollerz has ten chapters nationwide. It is known by the secular industry for attending car shows in tricked-out vehicles and evangelizing to the people there. At the 2005 Nopi Nationals (a popular car show), it handed out five hundred Bibles over two days.[9] What were the attendees' reactions? They ran up asking for more copies to give to their friends and family members.

God has truly blessed this car club for its willingness to go out and be His witnesses to an industry that wants nothing to do with Him. This car club has now been featured on the first DVD documentary on the history of street racing and the whole urban car scene. The DVD is called the *R Generation* and can be purchased in stores nationwide.[10] The chapter that interviews Holy Rollerz is called "Holy Horsepower." In this chapter, Brian Wood, one of the founders, shares his testimony on how he always loved cars and how he used to break into them. He talks about being sent to prison at the age of eighteen and joining the skinheads while in there. Before leaving prison, he decided that he was going to change and do something with his life, and so he gave his life to Christ. When he was released, he started the Holy Rollerz Car Club. The interview on the DVD follows the car club to church and shows its members worshipping there and later shows them at one of the car shows. In the video, Brian explains,

> It's not all about the cars. The cars are the common bond that brought us together, but they're not the most important things. These are our hobbies and this is our passion but this is not what makes who we are. What makes who we are, is who we are in Christ. We believe in a higher power and that's what makes us different from the other clubs out there.

The chapter on the DVD concludes with the group members praying and asking God to use them to be His witnesses. These are just a few examples of how Hip Hop can be used to glorify God.

Argument 3

> Kanye West is packing out church altars when he makes his appeal for salvation, even [though] his music promotes sin, sex, and violence. How is he any different than a Holy hip-hopper? They are both using hip-hop to reach the youth right? He is positive right? The one thing I can appreciate about Kanye West is that he is true to what he does. He is not trying to change hip-hop into something holy. He knows that it's all just hip-hop.[11]

Rebuttal 3

The main difference between the Christian rapper and the secular rapper, such as Kanye West, is whether they have a relationship with God. The Bible says in Matthew 12:34, "For out of the abundance of the heart the mouth speaks." The Christian rapper is going to rhyme about things that glorify God, whereas the secular rapper is going to glorify things that please the flesh and the world. Matthew 7:21–23 says,

> Not everyone who says to me, "Lord, Lord," will enter the kingdom of heaven, but only he who does the will of my Father who is in heaven. Many will say to me on that day, "Lord, Lord, did we not prophesy in your name, and in your name drive out demons and perform many miracles?" Then I will tell them plainly, "I never knew you. Away from me, you evildoers!" (New International Version)

You don't have to be a Christian to preach the Gospel or to produce a Christian album or song. Anybody can preach, sing, or rap it and successfully lead folks to Christ because the power is in the Word and in His name alone, not yours. Even Satan quotes scripture in the Bible. However, what profit is there to lead thousands to Christ, only for you to lose your soul and go to hell? This is what God was saying in Matthew 7:21. This is the fate that's in store for those who do things for God (regardless of how great) but don't have a personal relationship with Him. Kanye West's song "Jesus Walks" sincerely touched the lives of thousands of people, and it did lead some of them to Christ. However, if he does not have a personal relationship with God, he will not be walking with Jesus on judgment day.

BE YE TRANSFORMED BY THE RENEWING OF YOUR CLOTHES?

Although Romans 12:2 teaches us to be transformed by the renewing of our minds, there is another popular argument that a few pastors have brought to my attention. They believe that your maturity and sanctification in Christ is shown by the way you dress. If you don't look a certain way, then they cannot take you seriously as a minister.

This is another religious teaching that Satan has been using for years to keep the body of Christ divided. Your urban clothing is not a force field that keeps you from hearing, understanding, and maturing in the things of God. When it comes to worship, the Bible says, "God is spirit, and his worshipers must worship in spirit and in truth" (John 4:24). Therefore, it doesn't matter whether you're wearing a three-piece suit and gator shoes or a throwback jersey with baggy jeans and Timbs. Naturally, I'm not approving of Christian ladies coming to church in miniskirts. We should dress in a modest way that won't tempt people to lust after us. However, it is the role of the Holy Spirit to bring the conviction, the convincing, and the empowering ability to change—not the pastor and the saints. Their job is to give the believer the word and to lead by example. Your personal preference and "biblical" reasoning of proper dress attire will only last for a season in the minds of believers, but when the Spirit teaches and convicts their hearts, it will change them for a lifetime.

We live in a society that teaches us that we can change who we are or at least disguise who we are by changing our outer appearance. Therefore, if the church tells you to start dressing differently because you are a new creation in Christ, be aware that this is a carnal mentality. Isn't this what criminals do? When criminals have to appear in court, they dress modestly to trick people into thinking that they're innocent, law-abiding citizens. They may look innocent on the outside, but deep down inside, in their hearts, they're criminals. It's the same with Christians. What good is it to dress like a devoted and obedient Christian if you are not one in your heart? This is why David said in Psalm 51:10, after committing adultery with Bathsheba, "Create in me a clean heart, O God, and renew a steadfast spirit within me." By today's religious standards of spiritual maturity, we would have considered David to be a strong and mature man of God, sort of like a Bishop, because he had the look. However, he was really an adulterer because he was one in his heart. Matthew 5:28 says, "But I tell you that anyone who looks at a woman lustfully has already committed adultery with her in his heart." As we continue to grow in Christ, the Holy Spirit will teach us how to dress and conduct ourselves and change our hearts.

There are eternally detrimental consequences if we continue to teach the religious practice of having the look but not the heart and lifestyle of a Christian. For us believers, we will not mature in our walk with God. For the world, the biggest adverse outcome has been the creation of the R&B genre. You probably heard the popular saying: there wouldn't be R&B if it wasn't for Gospel. For the most part, it's true. Most of your R&B singers came out of the church. They had the religion and church look but not the relationship and word in their heart. Their move from the church to the secular R&B industry was done out of a biblical ignorance to the scriptures, as well as to a lack of mature godly examples to show them that you can't love both the world and Christ. The Bible makes this point clear in the following scriptures:

> You adulterous people, don't you know that friendship with the world is hatred toward God? Anyone who chooses to be a friend of the world becomes an enemy of God. (James 4:4, New International Version)

> Do not love the world or anything in the world. If anyone loves the world, the love of the Father is not in him. For everything in the world—the cravings of sinful man, the lust of his eyes and the boasting of what he has and does—comes not from the Father but from the world. (1 John 2:15–16, New International Version)

Bobby Herring, whose Christian rap name is Tre9, is the CEO of Much Luv Records. In June 2006, at his annual Texas Holy Hip Hop Awards, he held a panel discussion with two secular artists (Lil Keke and Big Mike), along with a couple of Christian rap artists.[12] After much debate about doing both secular and gospel music, it was discovered that no one had ever showed these secular artists scriptures like the ones I just mentioned, which they were receptive to.

Another example of artists making the wrong choice out of a lack of mature godly counsel and biblical ignorance can be found in the new VH1 reality series *The Salt-N-Pepa Show*. Salt-N-Pepa was a very popular all female rap group in the mid-1980s. The group consisted of Cheryl "Salt" James (now known as Cheryl Wray), Sandy "Pepa" Denton, and their DJ Spinderella. The group broke up in 2002 after Salt left for personal reasons, including accepting Christ as her Savior. In the first episode of the show, Salt and Pepa are meeting up for the first time in years to discuss performing as a group again. Pepa, although bitter at Salt for walking away from the group, still wants to perform with her, but Salt is not into performing anymore. Salt's biggest challenge is trying to figure out how to perform again without compromising. When Salt consults her prayer group as to what she should do, one of the members of the group tells her with sincere intentions:

> You can still do this Cheryl. It's not 10 years ago, and you can go out there, and be on stage, and touch so many lives, and still have that comfort zone of the good place you still are now. I know you can do it. We know you can do it. [13]

Unfortunately, this was poor advice, and I wish I could have been there to share with Salt the truth of God's word, which would have liberated her from having to feel obligated to be a part of this group again. Throughout the whole first episode, God was convicting her heart about being a part of the group again. She even told Pepa after one of their rehearsals, "I don't even want to do this. Period. The fact that I'm here is a compromise." [14] If I could have been there to provide some advice to Salt, the scripture I would have shared with her is 2 Corinthians 6:14–15, 17:

> Do not be yoked together with unbelievers. For what do righteousness and wickedness have in common? Or what fellowship can light have with darkness? What harmony is there between Christ and Belial? What does a believer have in common with an unbeliever? Therefore come out from them and be separate says the Lord. (New International Version)

My prayer for Salt and other former secular artists who have surrendered their lives to Christ is that they will meet mature, knowledgeable, and obedient Christians whom they can be accountable to and who can also disciple them. I pray that they will recognize and obey the Holy Spirit when it is convicting their hearts about doing something.

EFFECTIVELY USING HOLY HIP HOP AND CHRISTIAN RAP TO REACH OTHERS

Dr. Don Elligan is a clinical psychologist in Boston and Chicago who was searching for an effective way to connect to his troubled and disturbed clients that are a part of the Hip Hop culture. He developed a program and wrote a book about it, called *Rap Therapy*.[15] The definition that he gives of rap therapy is "utilizing a child's interest in rap music to communicate important lessons in life."[16] In this book, I found three interesting points and discoveries that Dr. Elligan expounded on that are applicable to gaining an understanding of how to use Christian rap to reach and teach people about Jesus and salvation.

> We often take for granted that to young people lyrics are simply lyrics. Useless mumblings or jibber jabber as opposed to intimate and sensitive expressions of reality from their perspectives.
>
> Reaching young people where they are can create a better working relationship that will be ultimately beneficial in a multitude of ways.
>
> Many young people have been led astray by harmful messages within Hip Hop, it may be the case that healthy messages within Hip Hop will lead them back!

Christian rap and Holy Hip Hop are forms of rap therapy, utilizing a person's interest in rap to communicate the Gospel. With the three statements in mind, let's go over a couple of steps on how you can use Christian rap to communicate the Gospel effectively.

First, find out what rap music your youth or friends are listening to and listen to it discerningly. This will give you a glimpse into the real areas they are struggling and dealing with and not some mythical Hip Hop demon. You might want to do this in a group setting for accountability. The Yuinon has a "Di-Section" column on its website that shows the contradictions between what various secular artists talk about in their songs and what the Bible teaches. You can use this as a resource to teach people.

Second, now that you know what they're struggling with, use the word of God to correct it (2 Timothy 3:16); use Christian rap to enforce and validate it (Revelations 12:11); and use prayer to destroy it.

ADVICE TO CHRISTIAN RAPPERS

I'm often asked by upcoming Christian rappers what advice I might share that will assist them to be effective ministers of Christ on the mic. My first answer is to know the word of God thoroughly, to be able to explain it to others, and know how to pray. You should spend more time studying the Bible than writing your raps. How can you talk about something you don't know? In regard to prayer, it has the power to destroy demonic influences and change situations.

My second piece of advice is to learn to cope and to accept rejection in a positive way. The Gospel has never been a popular message, and the world is going to hate you because it hates Christ. Allow God to take you through trials of being rejected so that you can gain perseverance in this area. He wants you to endure when you are rejected for His namesake.

My last piece of advice is that being the best rapper is not required. In the world, your skills need to be tight to survive, but it's not like that in Christian rap. While it is important to perfect your craft, especially if you want to sell your music, you don't have to be the top dog. People's salvation and deliverance do depend, not on your skills or ability to rhyme, but on the power and anointing of God. I have seen both seasoned and unseasoned rappers lead many to Christ. While their skill levels are comparatively different, the one thing they have in common is a thorough knowledge of the word of God, and they can communicate it well to their audiences.

A CHARGE TO THE CHURCH

My charge to the church is the following: First, spend more time teaching the essentials of the Christian faith and making disciples, rather than talking about myths and endless genealogies, such as the origins of Hip Hop, which promotes controversy (1 Timothy 1:4). Second, become accountability partners with the artists in your church and equip them so that they are able to share their faith effectively to the world. Finally, stop spreading the lies and teachings that Holy Hip Hop is not of God and that it can't be used as ministry, just because it challenges your traditional personal preference. People can come to know Christ through Holy Hip Hop ministries, as evidenced in this chapter.

CONCLUSION: ISN'T LOVING GOD ENOUGH?

When I was in high school, I used to struggle with listening to secular music, especially as a young believer in Christ. This type of music wasn't allowed in my Christian home, but I still heard a lot of it at school and other people's houses. As I started growing closer to God by reading my word and spending time in prayer, I began to love the things that He loves and hate the things that He hates. My spirit started becoming sensitive and offended by some of the music I was hearing. These secular songs were approving and encouraging acts that Jesus hated: sexual immorality, lust, pride, and the love of money, to name a few. I eventually stopped listening to secular music because the lyrics in the songs were grieving my spirit to the point that I couldn't relax while listening to it anymore.

It didn't take me having to know the origins of Hip Hop to stop listening to this music. Loving God alone was enough. This should be the same for every Christian. The Bible says in Mark 12:30 that the greatest commandment is

> Love the Lord your God with all your heart and with all your soul and with all your mind and with all your strength. (New International Version)

One of the reasons that this commandment is the greatest is that loving the Lord, with all that is within you, will keep you from sinning. How is that possible? Because loving God is obeying God (John 14:15). We show God how much we love Him by obeying Him.

Hosea 4:6 says, "My people are destroyed for lack of knowledge." We, as a body of Christ, have spent too much time being distracted by all sorts of foolish talk and pointless arguments that have caused division. As a result of this, many churches today are powerless and ineffective because they know nothing about the God they claim to be serving, nor is there any unity that shows the power of His love. We need to get back to studying the elementary truths of God's word all over again (Hebrews 5:12), making disciples, and loving one another unconditionally just as He loves us. My final verse and prayer to conclude this chapter is Jesus's prayer in John 17:23:

> May they be brought to complete unity to let the world know that you sent me and have loved them even as you have loved me.

NOTES

1. Both "I Am That I Am" and "Super Stars" are on the Cross Movement's 1999 DMG release, *House of Representatives*.

2. Official website of I.D.O.L. King, http://www.idolking.org/index2.html. Opening statement on home page is titled "True Holy Hip Hop" and was composed by C. O. Scott and copyrighted in 2002.

3. I.D.O.L. King, http://www.idolking.org/index2.html .

4. Although if we could quickly cite Elder G. Craige Lewis's self-published book *The Truth behind Hip Hop* (Longwood, FL: Xulon Press, 2009), the evidence of this "ministry" is best revealed by the numerous Facebook and MySpace posts, blogs, and other social media outlets that transmit Elder Lewis's prose.

5. Lewis, *The Truth behind Hip Hop*, 170–71.

6. Paraphrase of a principal argument made on numerous DVDs and articulated on a number of social media, blog, and Internet sites.

7. The Holy Rollerz Christian Car Club operates out of Kennesaw, Georgia, and was founded in 1999.

8. http://www.holyrollerz.org/.

9. Nopi Nationals is an annual national car show (since 1991) sponsored by Nopi Custom and Performance Auto Parts.

10. Thomas Trail, dir., *R-Generation: What Drives You?* (BBF Media, 2004).

11. Lewis, *The Truth behind Hip Hop*, 158.

12. The Texas Holy Hip Hop Awards, founded in 2002, expanded over a few years and by 2007 emerged as the All Eyes on Me Achievement Awards. For information view, see http://www.dasouth.com/awards/index.php.

13. Episode 1 ("Pushin' It") of *The Salt-N-Pepa Show* debuted on VH1, October 14, 2007. The show is produced by Left/Right Inc.

14. Episode 1 ("Pushin' It") of *The Salt-N-Pepa Show*.

15. Don Elligan, *Rap Therapy: A Practical Guide for Communicating with Youth and Young Adults through Rap Music* (New York: Dafina Books, 2004).

16. Elligan, *Rap Therapy*.

Chapter Fourteen

Five Theses on the Globalization of Thug Life and 21st Century Missions

Kenneth D. Johnson

Contemporary missions to youth of African descent in the Global City face an alternative and oppositional culture that is hostile to the Gospel witness. [1] That culture is now embedded in the ideology and style of Thug Life, a subcategory of hip hop music and lifestyle that first developed among impoverished and alienated inner city African American and Puerto Rican youths in the 1970s.

The use of new media, communications technologies, new methods and systems of influence, psychographic marketing, and other devices have packaged, disseminated and globalized Thug Life as an alternative and oppositional cultural system that has morphed into a way of life that has some of the characteristics of a *religio-cultural system* with its own *weltanschauung*. [2] Contemporary missions must develop a credible and stylistically up-to-date Christian apologetic to engage the world-and-life view of Thug Life held by youths of African descent in the inner cities of the First and Third Worlds in order to reach them with the Gospel *kerygma*.

This essay is meant as a start of a more extensive discussion within the missions community as to how the Globalization of Thug Life in youth culture occurred, and why it is important to understand this phenomenon's implications for 21st Century Missions. [3] We begin with a brief overview of the rise of Thug Life in its origins as a variant of hip hop music in the United States, and then present five theses about modern media and communications and the presence of Thug Life in the context of global youth culture, and how missions can address this cultural challenge to its Gospel witness.

ORIGINS OF HIP HOP MUSIC

The musical form known as hip hop developed among African American and Puerto Rican youths in the impoverished neighborhoods of New York City in the 1970s. It drew upon the contemporary Black American musical forms such as R&B (Rhythm & Blues) and the various Soul music genres that had their expressions located in particular cities such as Philadelphia, Memphis, Detroit, Minneapolis, and Chicago. Also, new forms of spoken word poetry with musical accompaniment that arose during the Black Arts Movement and the Puerto Rican Movement of the 1970s influenced Hip-Hop's use of rhyming phrases called "rap" that were set to background music provided by portable phonograph turntables. Athletic urban dance forms known as "break-dancing" also developed concurrently with the music. The use of rhythm and syncopated percussion beats, and the minimizing of melody, along with the insertion of snippets of earlier R&B and Soul music tracks and other ambient sounds completed the basic structure of hip hop music. [4]

HIP HOP'S MALEVOLENT TURN

Hip hop music evolved into more sophisticated musicianship in the 1980s as it grew from a localized New York urban youth phenomenon to a national music form among African American and some Latino youths, all in the inner cities of the United States. Other racial and ethnic groups such as Asian Americans and Euro Americans, often from middle class suburbs, joined the new musical movement. Most hip hop music was party music, with some of it also containing social messages protesting against the drug trade, police brutality, poverty and generalized government injustice.

In 1988, the Los Angeles group N.W.A. released its album *Straight Outta Compton* that is generally regarded as the turn towards a more malevolent social vision in hip hop music known as *gangsta rap*. This variant of hip hop had lyrics paying tribute to the glories of gang life among youths who were engaged in criminally violent and predatory responses to perceived injustices on the part of the white American power structure, although many victims of this gang violence were in fact fellow residents in African American neighborhoods. In the music, the prime targets were gang rivals, and the agents of state authority in Los Angeles such as local police, who were despised due to their numerous documented incidents of police brutality, corruption, collusion with the crack cocaine drug addiction epidemic, and general disrespect for residents in African American neighborhoods.

Other hip hop artists soon followed with lyrics of withering social criticism mixed with a lionization of Black male criminality, especially as expressed in the form of gang affiliation, attempts to affirm manhood in the guise of misogyny, and the frequent recourse to gun violence to express a will-to-power over others in the neighborhoods, whether the residents were part of the despised white power structure or not. As the music began to be identified by and its artists signed up with the major record labels and distributors in Hollywood and New York City, the emphasis shifted towards portraying gang members (and in real life, the hip hop artists imitating them) seeking wealth, power, and the sexual favors of women by any means necessary, including violence, even if this contributed to neighborhood decline.[5]

TUPAC SHAKUR AND "THUG LIFE"

The artists who followed this lifestyle amassed conspicuous wealth in the form of expensive cars, clothing, and jewelry ("bling-bling") and saw this as their just reward for entrepreneurship. These artists had little or no regard for the negative social messaging that this new malevolent type of hip hop music delivered to impressionable inner city youths. Tupac Shakur (b. 1971–d. 1996) was a hip hop artist who at various times was literate and socially conscious in his rap lyrics, but was also willing to excuse and glorify the criminal lifestyles of gang and inner city street culture. He became and remains a sympathetic figure to millions of youths nationally and worldwide. Shakur was an early casualty to the fatal street-inspired murders that occurred among some rap artists in the 1990s.

It was Tupac Shakur who aptly described the world-view and lifestyle of this newer hip hop music as "Thug Life." He recorded a record album and formed a rap group of the same name, and had the phrase tattooed prominently on his body in allegiance to its moral system and ideals.[6]

TRANSMISSION OF THUG LIFE

Many other hip hop artists now embrace Thug Life as their personal world-and-life view as well as their form of artistic expression in music and music videos. With the help of the mostly white-owned multinational media conglomerates, this music, visual culture and material fashions have been transmitted to youths of all social classes in the United States and in many nations across the globe, who often see these musical forms as a means to create their own local oppositional cultures and give vent to both adolescent rebellion as well as legitimate sociopolitical protest.

A notable factor is the rise of an oppositional culture of Thug Life among youths in African descent in the impoverished inner cities of the developed First World, including the inner cities of Toronto, London, and Paris. In addition, youths of different racial or ethnic backgrounds have adopted elements of the Hip-Hop/Thug Life musical forms for protest purposes, such as those in Romania, Palestine, Egypt, Bolivia, and Jamaica (concurrent with its own indigenous protest music) among other places in the Third World.

GLOBALIZATION OF THUG LIFE

We assert that Thug Life is becoming globalized as part of a new global youth culture. This global youth culture is simultaneously driven by the financial lusts of multinational capitalism and the yearnings of youths in various parts of the world for a new mode of expressing their protests against injustice, as well as these youths' enthrallment with the crass materialist culture and narcissism of the developed West represented in this form of entertainment.[7] There is deep irony in the notion that while America has become the primary engine of global youth culture, Black American music in the form of hip hop serves as the cultural rocket fuel for that engine. This growing oppositional culture of Thug Life contains a vision of reality and life that is in many ways hostile to the values of the Gospel, and contains elements that resist the *kerygmatic* command leading to repentance, *metanoia*, faith, divine reconciliation, and the fruits of repentance in the living of a righteous life that God approves of.

THE FIVE THESES

We now set forth the following *Five Theses on the Globalization of Thug Life* for consideration by contemporary missioners hoping they might create a credible, morally compelling and culturally engaging apologetic for affected youths, so that barriers to the reception of the Gospel witness might be removed, and that upon the delivery of the *kerygma*, some of these youths might respond in a salvific manner.

Thesis One

The rise of globalization, new communications technologies, and cultural transmission through media and marketing systems has created a new set of "Roman Roads" to deliver the message of the Gospel.

Unlike in the late 19th century during the renewal of the modern missions movement, today the presence of new communications technologies such as the internet, new methods of media data storage like compact disks (CDs), iPods and other ways of transmitting both music and visual images accompanying it have accelerated the transmission of contemporary Western entertainment forms to inner city youths in the First World, and among youths in some cities of the Third World. The new entertainment forms are sometimes controversial, as witnessed by the reactions of many in the Islamic world and Muslims in the developed world who object to the overthrow of traditional moral norms by the new entertainment with what they see as subversive cultural values of Western cultural imperialism and its moral degeneracy.

Like the world of the Apostle Paul in Christianity's first century, contemporary media forms, like the message of early Christianity, are primarily delivered to people in cities. The strategic location of urban environments, with many peoples, cultures and value systems rubbing up against each other, create cultural interactions and sometimes cultural borrowings that can later result in changes to individuals' self awareness and functioning in their own life-worlds. This occurred when the Apostle Paul and others carried the Gospel message to the cities of Asia Minor in the Roman Empire. Similar venues exist today in cities throughout the globe as populations previously isolated in the countryside or separated by national boundaries, are now pushed together as a result of internal displacement, natural catastrophes, war refugee status, or simple economic necessity as people search for safety, work and wealth in cities.[8]

The opening of new economic markets and the use of electronic communications are now the equivalent of the "Roman roads" that the Apostles used to spread the Gospel. In a way, this is an old phenomenon in that at various times in history there have been episodes of "local globalization" that connected the then-known societies in various places and eras into local imperial systems.[9] The distinctive opportunity today is the soon-to-be prospect of a total integration of and connection with nearly all the world's cultures for the first time, with these cultures linked in two-way communication, giving and receiving worldviews and material culture among them, linked together by modern communications technology and consuming a common media diet.

In the context of modern media communication, contemporary methods of consumer marketing, including some that have been adapted from psychological influence and propaganda techniques, have been fused to entertainment production methods in order to create an entire worldview and lifestyle experience packaged as part of the consumption process of the new entertainment products. Western societies, especially the United States, were the experimental sites where these techniques were developed, deployed, and further refined as a profit-making tool for the culture industry, as represented by the large multinational media entertainment corporations. [10]

The new avenues of cultural communication are not restricted to corporate-produced media. These avenues are also open to the communication of the Gospel. Early media missionary efforts in the use of radio, and current use of television satellite technology can now yield to "narrowcasting" using the Internet to deliver podcasts and video streams to reach specific populations with the Gospel message. However, as the secular entertainment forms have already reached many target populations with their messages, missioners must run harder and faster to craft alternative and culturally aware messages that utilize the idioms and styles of various global youth cultures, and that directly and indirectly engage with and confront the ideology of Thug Life, even while preserving the Gospel's essential content. This requires acknowledging that Thug Life now serves for many youths as a world-and-life view akin to a religious system that now stands as a barrier against the life transforming power of the Gospel. Further delay by missionaries will only strengthen Thug Life's grip on the hearts and minds of youths who are looking for ways to meet their needs for justice and material security, even while their spiritual hungers go unmet.

Thesis Two

Youth Culture increasingly drives the world's consumer consumption and will continue to do so, and American culture is youth culture's dominant form today.

A new phenomenon is present in the developed Western nations with the rise of a consumer cohort among youths who wield billions of dollars in spending power. This fact has not been lost on the corporate sector which each day continues to test and refine new ways to sell consumer goods and services to a cohort of youths aged 5 to 18. The marketing techniques not only sell things, but also subtly acclimate and develop notions of taste and consumer preferences that often conform to the corporate manufactured youth-targeted consumer products and services. [11]

This relation between Western youths flush with cash and the corporations chasing after them is a process held in tension similar to that of a Hellenistic dialectic, in that youths often change their consumer preferences without regard to the previous psychological conditioning deployed by the corporate marketers. To keep up, modern corporations hire consumer research firms to be on a continuous search for new social and cultural trends developed by youths, in order to be the first to align themselves with new youth preferences in clothing, music, language and style in order to secure profitable production of new consumer products and services and to quickly discard those that youths have rendered obsolete and "uncool."[12]

There are important exceptions to the Western domination of the production and dissemination drive in youth culture. For example, in much of Asia, Japan (which could also arguably be considered Western) wields great influence through its export of youth-oriented media products such as music, video and animation, and clothing styles in countries like China, South Korea and Singapore. The Arab world, while deeply infiltrated by Western youth media, also partakes of media aimed towards adolescents developed in the more technologically advanced Gulf states, as well as Egypt which has long been the standard setter of media products produced in the Arabic language. Iran, whose culture is Islamic with roots in Persian, not Arab culture, has a rising cohort of adolescents and young adults who chafe at the cultural restrictions of their Islamic regime and who in secret eagerly consume Western media.

The high proportion of youths under the age of 18 in the Third World, with continued high birth rates exceeding replacement needs in some places like sub-Saharan Africa, clearly reveal future consumer markets for global capital. It is the hope of corporations that these youths and their nations will eventually experience modernization and economic growth, and open markets and openness to Western media. These businesses know that brand loyalty is often developed early in life, and that modest investments now can reap a continuous flow of profit from a loyal customer base as it matures into adulthood and continues along the human lifecycle. More sophisticated media producers, such as MTV, Inc., have gone beyond exporting Western media products and have instead created media production units that are specific to local and national youth cultures in order to fuse the best of Western technological and media production and marketing techniques with the national youth cultures' music and style in order to capture the attention and brand loyalty of these Third World youths.[13]

The products of American youth culture, and especially its musical forms, are the currently dominant cultural exports to those youth in the Third World who can afford to partake of them. Now that a majority of the world's population, including the world's young people, lives in cities, they constitute a perfect captive audience that are easily and efficiently reached at low cost by corporate producers.[14] As these costs continue to plummet, and as barriers to entry in the media marketplace are reduced further, similar opportunities for cultural production and dissemination exist for Gospel missioners to repackage and proclaim the Gospel in media forms that engage the new grammar of the media-savvy youths in the cities of the Third World.

Thesis Three

The increasing spread and reception of a variant of American Hip Hop Culture, "Thug Life," has now become globalized, especially among youths of African descent, and has thereby become a global driver of youth culture.

The music, style, and lifestyle/ideology of Thug Life has now left American shores and arrived among youths of African descent elsewhere in the globe. It has begun to shape these youths' identity and motivate them to develop an oppositional culture in their own societies.

Unlike traditional societies which gave deference to adult authority and adopted strong group social controls upon personal behavior, the new society of cities that afford residents more anonymity and dilute the tight group cohesion of village and small kin groups, now give space for youths to create their own social identity in defiance of parents' and guardians' previous ways of living.

This phenomenon is less pronounced in Third World cities due to the recent nature of internal migrations from countryside to city and the lingering retention of traditional notions of adult authority. However, in the inner cities of developed countries outside the United States, youths of African descent, whether born in those countries or of recent immigrant heritage, are adopting the habits of Thug Life with its associated harms.

During 2005 in Toronto, Canada, several Afro-Caribbean communities experienced a rolling series of murders and gun attacks perpetrated by youth gangs. These gangs were composed largely of Black youths, with a mixture of Canadian-born and recent immigrant Caribbean youths. This was shocking to the adults in the community because the families of the delinquent youth, while perhaps experiencing elements of racial discrimination, had not experienced poverty comparable to that of gang-infested neighborhoods in the United States.

Furthermore, the married mother-father family unit is present to a much greater degree among Afro-Canadians, many of whom are in the middle class. Finally, Canadians of all classes and racial groups tend to be quite law-abiding and gun violence in that country has been extremely low. What was the change that led to the violence?

It was discerned by external experts as well as local pastoral leaders that the lack of effective parental guidance, especially on the part of fathers who were otherwise present in the home but ineffective in parenting, and the rise of attitudes and lifestyles associated with Thug Life created the atmosphere for gang activity and the subsequent violence. Of this situation, Boston youth violence expert the Reverend Eugene F. Rivers III noted in public remarks in Toronto that "You can reduce crime by making sound investments on the prevention side so you're not paying disproportionately on the law enforcement side."[15] He also held Christian churches to account for their retreat from engagement with youth culture, stating, "The black churches have failed. We failed to take the message into the streets. Now the streets have come and brought their messages into the church. The churches must now mobilize to engage this generation of young people, which heretofore we had ignored."[16]

As the role of responsible adults with conventional values diminishes in the daily lives of youths, the vacuum is replaced by the new ethical system of Thug Life. This system lionizes a consumerist lifestyle, displaces older value systems and resists Gospel values of peace and an attitude of moderation toward material possessions. Some theologians like Cornel West in the American context, believe that Thug Life and a culture of violence indicates the presence of nihilism in communities of African descent, at least in developed countries. As West notes, this

> [n]ihilism is to be understood here not as a philosophic doctrine that there are no rational grounds for legitimate standards or authority; it is far more, the lived experience of coping with a life of horrifying meaninglessness, hopelessness, and (most important) lovelessness. The frightening result is a numbing detachment from others and a self-destructive disposition toward the world. Life without meaning, hope, and love breeds a coldhearted, mean-spirited outlook that destroys both the individual and others.[17]

While Cornel West was discussing the plight of inner city African American communities and the saturation of violence that characterized them in the 1990s, his statement could easily apply to the ideology of Thug Life as practiced by inner city Black youths in other developed countries today.

Yet another example of Thug Life and Black-on-Black crime exists in England. Significant numbers of Afro-British youths, whether born in Britain or to recent immigrants from the Caribbean, have been enticed to enter a gang culture of hedonism and violence in a number of tough cities such as London, Brixton, and Birmingham. Gun trafficking of weapons obtained through middlemen who in turn obtained the firearms from the conflicts in Eastern Europe is now pervasive among certain Black youths who use them for intimidation and crime and as part of a preexisting illegal drug trade. Many of these youths are disproportionately represented among those who receive Anti-Social Behavior Orders (ASBOs) that curtail their neighborhood movements and associations with other suspected gang members. While meant by the government as a more humane alternative than jail time for juvenile offenders, it has now become a badge of honor to accumulate numerous ASBOs as a way of gaining higher street credibility as a rebel against state authority.[18] Black Britons certainly endure some racial discrimination, and their children suffer from poor schools and diminished employment opportunity. Poverty and its harmful fruits, such as drug abuse, are present, although not as severely as in African American communities. The music of Thug Life speaks to Afro-British youths' alienation and soothes the wounded manhood of adolescent Black males, even while still failing to galvanize these youths into a movement for effective political action within the British system. Their parents seem to be unaware of their young people's new norms, and otherwise have few answers for them. As in the United States, the breakdown of the married nuclear family or failure of such families to form at all result in many Afro-British boys lacking positive male role models while their single mothers struggle to rear them alone. In 2002, fifty percent of Afro-Caribbean mothers in Britain under age 35 had never married, five times the non-marriage rate of white Britons.[19]

Space does not permit a detailed discussion of the uprisings of youths and young adults of Black African, North African/Arab and other racial origins in the *banlieues* of Paris in 2005 to protest racial and ethnic discrimination, anti-Muslim bigotry and persistent poverty, and educational exclusion and joblessness engendered by the French state and tolerated in French society. Television coverage included a few individuals who were creating French variants of gangsta rap that expressed youth rage. However, it seems Thug Life, even without a direct and linear importation from America, still dwells among some impoverished French youths of color. On this point, Sorbonne professor and Bank of France economist Guy Milliere noted that

> Twenty years ago, there were much less Muslims in France, and they were doing their best to become French Muslims. It is not the case anymore. Muslims in France now are regarded with fear and suspicion because many young Muslims choose to live a thug life (fifty per cent of the inmates in the French jails are Muslim). Fear and suspicion have a basis in reality. The young Muslims that do not choose to live a thug life consider themselves members of the Arab-Muslim community more than they consider themselves as French citizens. Or when they say they are French citizens, they add very often: "we are French citizens, so the French government has to show more respect for Islam and the Arab world."[20]

The foregoing examples demonstrate the influence of Thug Life among youths of African descent in some of the developed nations as they challenge both prevailing forms of civil society as well as government authority. Can an alternative cultural apologetic provide credible and engaging alternatives for these young people?

Thesis Four

The cultural production called Thug Life must not only be considered as a mere fad, nor as just another musical genre, or an object for analysis by Cultural Studies, but must also be examined as a religious system with its own Weltanschauung, and which must be approached as an alternative religio-cultural system for the purpose of contemporary mission efforts.

Could missiology's analytic tools applicable to other religions have any value in analyzing the claims of Thug Life? It depends on the definition of religion. Some scholars prefer a rigorous definition of religion crafted to clearly distinguish it from worldview.[21] However, if we view Thug Life as an emergent religio-cultural phenomenon, we can use a more flexible definition. University of Chicago theologian Dwight N. Hopkins has offered the following criteria of a religion:

> Religion is a system of beliefs and practices comprised of a god (which is the object of one's faith), a faith (which is a belief in a desired power greater than oneself), a religious leadership (which determines the path of belief), religious institutions (which facilitate the ongoing organization of the religion). Religion also has a theological anthropology (which defines what it means to be human), values (which set the standards to which the religion subscribes), a theology (which is the theoretical justification of the faith), and revelation (which is the diverse ways that the god manifests itself in and to the world).[22]

Thug Life has some of Hopkins' elements, although these are not grounded in a notion of sacrality. Some rap artists maintain a generic belief in God, as do the youths who listen to the music produced. Likewise, the notion of a higher power is ambiguously present to provide support in time of extreme life-and-death peril, but at other times remote enough so that the higher power does not criticize or get involved with the Thug Life adherent's daily living. The dance clubs provide the secular temples for the new faith, and the gangs provide the hierarchical social organization that provides an alternative to both faith communities and the nuclear family. Hedonism and the nihilism that Cornel West described are the bases for its theological anthropology, and its values include gang loyalty and solidarity, and a "no snitchin'" policy that intimidates witnesses from testifying in court to assist police or crime victims. Thug Life does not have a theology, but it does offer the "is" of hostile street life over the "ought" of society's morality as its theoretical self-justification for its own belief system.[23] Finally, revelation would be the one area that Thug Life is lacking, since in the end it has a materialist ideology with no active role for a God, even though some of its artists do make appeals to God or Allah in order to justify some of the choices that people make for their own survival against their rivals. A God-concept is sometimes present but underdeveloped as a source of revelation in gangsta rap or in the lifestyle of Thug Life.

Thug Life also has its own ethical code, analogous to what sociologist Elijah Anderson has described as the "code of the street" instead of society's "code of the citizen."[24] Thug Life's street ethics permit and even encourage interpersonal violence as a first resort to conflict resolution, and the strong male assertiveness in street life carries over into highly structured gender relations with an ever-present misogyny indifferent to the needs of women and girls. The worldview of Thug Life is not entirely amoral; its advocates still use the moral notions of rightness and wrongness, even though they disagree about the specific content of just and unjust acts. In this way, those that engage in the lifestyle are well aware of but suppress their self awareness of the moral paradox of those who protest wrong acts done against them but who nevertheless are not morally clean themselves in that they also commit harm against others. Or as the Apostle Paul in Romans 2:1 notes, "Therefore you have no excuse, whoever you are, when you judge others; for in passing judgment on another you condemn yourself, because you, the judge, are doing the very same things."[25]

But as a cultural system or worldview, Thug Life does provide some psychic benefits to its adherents. It affords its young followers the opportunity to be heard, and to gain a sense of personal identity, racial and ethnic identity formation, and a sense of family solidarity that is often lacking in their own households and natural families. The street norms that Thug Life propagates claim to help its devotees avoid victimization on the street, or at least the feeling of being a potential victim. Finally, the musical medium of rap performances can be enacted anywhere like a secular liturgy by youths even at the most basic economic levels using simple, low cost, improvised musical instruments and the human voice, affording them the opportunity to tell their personal stories and thereby gain personal significance and a feeling of personal efficacy, even if their music never reaches beyond their own neighborhoods. Nearly all the basic things that religion provides in the non-supernatural realm, Thug Life offers, packaged in a readily understood and culturally engaging idiom, without any accountability to a divine being.

Thesis Five

Thug Life dwells primarily in cities, and provides an operating life script for urban youths in global cities of immense size and diversity. Mission's efforts to engage urban youths must include an apologetic that confronts the claims of Thug Life with credible alternatives, even while using some of Thug Life's stylistic forms as a medium to transmit the salvific content and lifestyle options of the Gospel.

Thug Life today is primarily an urban youth phenomenon. It began with Black and Brown youths in the United States, and has migrated to various nations across the globe and has been utilized by other racial and ethnic youths to advance their own local concerns for justice, and as a lifestyle alternative to that of their own traditional societies. While space does not permit a rigorous cross-national comparative study of Thug Life's migration to countries like Romania in the former Soviet Bloc, or in the Muslim world among Asians or Arabs, or even in other Third World countries in Africa or Latin America, the initial effects among excluded urban youths of African descent in other Western developed countries points a future research path to trace the global evolution of the Thug Life religio-cultural phenomenon.

In the meantime, as missioners attempt re-evangelization of youths in the West, they run the risk of a head-on collision with the cultural dominance of the Thug Life ideology and its daily practices among alienated young people resulting in a failure of successful evangelization. There is an opportunity to do a trial run of sorts to find new ways to formulate an apologetics for urban youth evangelization in the developed world that if successful, could later be used in the cities of the Third World with appropriate modifications to counter and defeat the religio-cultural influence of Thug Life when it arrives.

How to begin? Missioners' first step should be to acknowledge that Thug Life accurately identifies areas of real need, even though its responses might be unacceptable from a Gospel perspective. For example, the displacement and overthrow of male dominance in these societies might have been a just response to the claims of women. But the liquidation of the male role has led to an infantilization of men and a revolt of males against adult maturity and responsible behavior towards women, especially in the establishment of monogamous and healthy marriages and development of married family life as the environment for child rearing and socialization.[26]

Structural changes in the economy demanding higher levels of education as the minimum passport for entry to gainful employment has left a generation of youths and young male adults behind, unable to join in the rest of society's material gains and to fulfill at least part of the male provider role that many women in the inner city still expect. Due to broken families and lack of effective socialization by fathers as authority figures working in concert with their mothers, young urban males, and increasingly young urban females, yield themselves to negative male peer influences in a desperate search for identity, security, and instruction on how to survive and get one's needs met in a hostile society. The previous buffering effects of the trinity of home, school and church have been dissolved, with none of these institutions offering credible and engaging alternative lifestyles on a consistent basis that meet youths' needs for material security and advancement and to satisfy their need to belong to something greater than themselves. Thug Life offers youths a seductive, but ultimately self-defeating set of choices that eventually result in harm. Bold evangelization can expose these inadequate choices in favor of alternatives rooted in the Gospel.

The second step for missioners to break the hold of Thug Life is to openly acknowledge the truth of Thug Life's social criticism, confess the Church's indifference and lack of prophetic witness and action, and begin to show how the Gospel themes speak directly to the need for personal salvation and transformation, and the prophetic confrontation that the Gospel demands against the powers and principalities of the age in the social realm. Thug Life offers a radical critique of the exclusion and injustice that youths perceive regarding institutions of civil society and government, especially police misconduct. However, this critique is internally flawed in that it rarely extends to the underlying secular materialism that is a product of capitalism as we know it today, and which has exacerbated the state of economic exclusion and amorality that dominates the life of the inner cities of the developed world. Thug Life's young adherents are complicit in this problem, since they deeply value a sensate and materialist culture and the prospect of becoming rich, by any means necessary. This also explains why the Cultural Left in the developed world, especially in the United States, has been unable despite years of effort, to effectively mobilize in any sustained way the millions of young people and their consumer power toward serious political action.[27] Somehow, the Left has been unable to capture the hearts and minds of this generation for its agenda, much less fight effectively the corporate media and culture industries and their hold on the minds and identities of affected youths.[28]

Mission efforts could harness the rap music idiom itself by supporting skilled youths to provide their artistic visions of an alternate social reality in the inner cities based on the predisposition to peace that characterizes the person and work of Jesus Christ. Any number of themes that rap music discusses today can be addressed from a Gospel perspective, and missioners and the churches that send them must find ways to financially support the development of alternative cultural and musical products that can compete on their technical merits with anything that secular media can produce. Such an approach is no different from the work of the Apostles as they inculturated the Gospel *kerygma* and post-conversion lifestyle teachings into the idioms of the various ethno-cultural groups they reached throughout the Roman Empire. Since then, at its best, mission has found ways to use existing cultural forms as vehicles for the Gospel, even while guarding against syncretism or subversion of the core Christian message. Suitably updated for our century, missioners can use similar approaches to reach urban youths in the grip of Thug Life.

The third step for missioners to reach affected urban youth is to personally model the behavior and lifestyle associated with the Gospel in ways that are culturally engaging to the youths, and engage in the daily personal life coach mentoring of young people. Thug Life thrives in the absence of responsible, mature adults in the neighborhoods. Few missioners would think of going on the mission field without learning the customs and folkways of the people groups they intend to serve. Yet too many existing youth ministries in the developed world use worn-out methods and culturally unattractive modes of interaction with young people, and fail to maintain a daily adult presence in the roughest neighborhoods where they can be seen and heard.

As noted earlier, young people are highly attuned and acclimated to modern media consumer culture, with its emphasis on the visual, the aural, high concept design and function, and the continuous excitement of the new. This is a challenge that some churches and parachurch agencies have attempted to meet in the form of more contemporary worship and narrative expositions of the Gospel's teaching. That is good, but still insufficient. Missioners must not only master the current cultural forms that youths partake of, but must also begin to find ways to influence and reshape the youths' taste and lifestyle preferences, with the same or greater level of determination and precision of the corporate conglomerates' marketing teams. Christian mission, whether using its own methods or selectively borrowing from contemporary secular techniques, must approach urban youth culture with a high level of analytical rigor, so that with the empowerment of the Holy Spirit in the salvation and ongoing sanctification of urban youths, these young people can have their minds and cultural preferences and lifestyles renewed steadily on a daily basis, in order to counter the Thug Life culture.

Finally, as a fourth step, missioners must find ways through narrative as well as Socratic reasoning to engage youths' own natural reason to test and falsify the value claims of Thug Life. The internal contradictions of the Thug Life worldview can be logically discerned, and through the use of narrative and youths' recounting of and reflection upon their own personal experiences, young people can reason for themselves, and even apply retroactive empirical tests to discern whether the claims of Thug Life are consistently true as a coherent system of thought and way of life.

Sophisticated apologetic methods are routinely used to defend the truth claims of the Gospel and used in evangelization work and in imparting the implications of the Gospel to new adherents to anchor their understanding and practice of their new faith. A similar rigorous approach that is youth friendly and packaged in an appropriate way can be used with young people for evangelization and post-conversion catechesis. The common doctrinal emphases of orthodox Christian teaching can be shown to relate to youths' own lived experiences, if we are willing to do the hard work of cultural translation to engage young people's emotions and thinking.

CONCLUSION

It is time for missioners to reconsider how they will retool themselves and their presentation of the enduring content of the Gospel to a new generation shaped by a global and secular media culture.

This discussion has begun in the inner cities in the United States among some African American churches as they consider the plight of Black young people ensnared in the deadly coils of the Thug Life ideology and lifestyle, even while these churches continue to slip into irrelevancy and ineffective witness among these inner city youths. This situation is also ironic in that many of the affected youths would be happy to embrace alternatives to Thug Life, but find the churches indifferent to their condition, or lacking any morally or culturally credible alternatives or leadership that provide life affirming messages while delivering prophetic condemnation of the hypocrisy and continuing acts of systemic racism, poverty, and corrupt social institutions. Without the bold honesty that characterized the ancient Gospel witness of the first Christians, these youths will not transfer their allegiance to the risen Christ in a manner that leads to salvation.

The situation with the youths outside of the United States who have adopted Thug Life is no different. This youth population constitutes the base of most future adherents to Christianity.[29] If the New Testament is to be taken at its word, many of these youths may experience a Christ-less eternity with all the implied harms that arise as a consequence. Modern missioners empowered by and in obedience to the Triune God, will need to embrace the risks of serious cultural work to develop new methods of evangelization of these young people. As part of this task, missioners must exercise the courage to preach and teach the whole truth of the Gospel and its implications for individual morality and lifestyles and the just and right ordering of society. These ministers of the Gospel have the high privilege in the 21st century of being God's co-laborers in a search-and-rescue mission to find, engage, and save these lost youth in the name of Jesus Christ.

An earlier version of this chapter was published under the same title in the Antioch Agenda: Essays on the Restorative Church in Honor of Orlando E. Costas *(Kashmere Gate, Delhi: Indian Society for Promoting Christian Knowledge, 2007).*

NOTES

1. The term "oppositional culture" seems to have first entered the academic literature in education studies about African American student underachievement, particularly by the education scholar John Ogbu in his *Black American Students in an Affluent Suburb: A Study of Academic Disengagement* (Lawrence Erlbaum Associates Inc., 2003). While his specific conclusions about Black underachievers rejecting educational attainment due to "acting white" have largely been disproved, the term has been expanded for use to describe any set of behaviors or worldviews that deviate from the cultural mainstream. This is the sense in which sociologist Elijah Anderson uses the term in his ethnographic study of a Black Philadelphia inner city neighborhood, *Code of the Street: Decency, Violence, and the Moral Life of the Inner City* (W. W. Norton; 1st edition, 1999). The idea of group deviation from society's norms as a form of cultural resistance was theorized earlier by structural-functionalist sociologist Robert K. Merton in his *Social Theory and Social Structure* (The Free Press, 1956).

2. Philosophical theologian Paul Tillich had a very expansive definition of "religion as the heart of culture" that seemed to include the notion of worldview in his *Theology of Culture* (Oxford University Press, 1959). We can begin with this as a working definition of religion and then further sharpen our definition when we examine this question in detail under Thesis Four.

3. The phrase "Globalization of Thug Life" was coined by Kenneth D. Johnson and first appeared in print in an interview with this author in the article "Hip-Hop Martyrs: Youth, Violence and Transformation" by Episcopal priest Pat McCaughan in *The Witness* (Volume 86, Number 5/6, May-June 2003, online at http://www.thewitness.org/archive/mayjune2003/hiphop.html).

4. Of necessity this description of Hip-Hop's origins is compressed. For a comprehensive discussion, see Nelson George's *Hip Hop America* (Penguin Books, 2005).

5. Cultural critic Norman Kelley noted in his *The Head Negro in Charge Syndrome* (Nation Books, 2004) that as of 2004, "Most independent rap record labels are partially owned by one of the five major labels—Time Warner, Sony Music, Bertelsmann Music Group, Vivendi/Universal, [and] EMI . . ." (p. 141).

6. Tupac Shakur's album on his own record label was *Thug Life: Volume 1*, Out Da Gutta Records, released on September 26, 1994. It was later re-released by Interscope Records, a subsidiary of Time Warner, with many of its songs removed due to the rising public criticism of gangsta rap music.

7. Narcissism here is not only excessive self-love (egoism), but also the inability of persons to distinguish between their own personal identity and the social status and consumer products they constantly seek to acquire. See Christopher Lasch, *The Culture of Narcissism: American Life in an Age of Diminishing Expectations* (W.W. Norton, 1979), especially pp. 31–50.

8. Trends in cross-border migration for economic reasons affect youths in the Third World directly. See the United Nations Population Fund's report *Moving Young: State of World Population 2006: Youth Supplement* (United Nations Population Fund, 2006) that tells the individual stories of migrating youths and relate these to the underlying social conditions that led to this.

9. The Egyptian, Babylonian, Assyrian, Persian, Greek, and Roman empires served in this way. Islamic empires such as the Mughal dynasties in India, the Caliphate in Iran and surrounding countries, and the Ottoman Empire are other examples. The various kingdoms and imperial systems in Europe from the Middle Ages to the Enlightenment, and the imperial expansion of Britain, France, and Belgium among other powers in the "scramble for Africa" from the 1880s to 1914 (the start of World War I) also created new communications links and cultural exposures.

10. Cultural historian Stuart Ewen describes this marketing process in *All Consuming Images: The Politics of Style in Contemporary Culture* (Harper, 1990). Rebecca Piirto describes the new field of psychographics for consumer marketing in *Beyond Mind Games: The Marketing Power of Psychographics* (American Demographics Books, 1991).

11. We are indebted to lay media critic and Bible teacher Matthew D. LeBlanc of the First Baptist Church of Los Altos, California, for the rudiments of a yet-to-be-published media theory to explain how youths' tastes for sordid media products are developed. Media companies selling Thug Life products say they are not responsible for their debased moral content and that it is simply what the youths want to buy. But these companies are too modest, since they do not acknowledge their role in the initial production, marketing, and distribution of these products to youths who initially did not request them, thereby shaping and directing the youths' new notions of artistic taste and style. This in turn motivated youths to buy more of the companies' records and music videos with the negative content, which then reinforced the youths' tastes that the companies previously developed. Thus, *a reinforcing and reciprocal exchange process is established between youth consumers and corporate producers*, to be broken only when youths tire of the current media products and shift to new musical and lifestyle choices outside the gaze of the corporate marketing experts.

12. On January 21, 2001, the Public Broadcasting System's *Frontline* documentary program produced "The Merchants of Cool" which documented corporate America's efforts to market consumer products to teenagers. The show is available online along with interview transcripts at http://www.pbs.org/wgbh/pages/frontline/shows/cool/.

13. MTV International Networks, Inc. foreign divisions include MTV India, MTV Brazil, and MTV China. MTV also delivers programs to immigrant populations in the United States, and has recently formed MTV Desi (http://www.mtvDesi.com) to market its programs to the Indian diaspora in America. MTV is owned by another large media conglomerate, Viacom, Inc.

14. According to the United Nations Population Fund report *Urbanization: A Majority in Cities* (United Nations Population Fund, 15 December 2005, accessed on January 24, 2007, at http://www.unfpa.org/pds/urbanization.htm), "In 2007, for the first time in history, more than 50 per cent of the world's population will be living in cities. By 2030 this percentage will go beyond two thirds, with more than 90 per cent of urban population growth taking place in developing countries. During the next 25 years, the UN Human Settlements Programme (UN-Habitat) estimates that the number of urban residents will increase by more than 2 billion people, while the rural population will decline by about 20 million, and by 2030, all regions of the world will have urban majorities."

15. From the *CTV News with Lloyd Robertson* website, "'Boston Miracle' pioneer offers Toronto help," January 9, 2006, accessed on January 24, 2007 at http://www.ctv.ca/servlet/ArticleNews/story/CTVNews/20060108/eugene_rivers_060108/20060109?hub=CTVNewsAt11

16. From the Canadian Broadcasting Corporation's reporter Mary Wiens, "Reporter's Notebook: 'The Black Community has a Special Responsibility,'" January 20, 2006, accessed on January 24, 2007, at http://www.cbc.ca/toronto/features/marywiens/tenpoint.html.

17. Cornel West, *Race Matters* (Beacon Press, 1993), p. 14–15.

18. A London newspaper reported that a British Government study "did confirm that Asbos were being used disproportionately against ethnic minority groups. More than 20% of those given an Asbo were black or Asian [South Indians or Pakistanis]—two and half times more than their representation in the general population." Alan Travis, "Teenagers see Asbos as Badge of Honour," *The Guardian*, November 2, 2006. Accessed on January 24, 2007 at http://society.guardian.co.uk/youthjustice/story/0,,1937746,00.html

19. Data quoted by commentator Joseph Harker, "Rap culture has hijacked our identity," *Guardian*, March 6, 2002, accessed on January 24, 2007 at http://www.guardian.co.uk/comment/story/0,,662599,00.htm. Harker in the same article notes Afro-Britons' changed perceptions as to the greatest source of danger in their communities: "If, 10 years ago, you asked black people in inner-city areas what they most feared when walking the streets, they would probably have said it was police officers; today they'd reply that it's loud, aggressive gangs of young black boys—who may or may not be criminals, but are deliberately trying to strike terror into those around them, living up to the gangsta-rap culture which has been imported from the US since the late 1980s. 'We're from the street,' they grunt, 'we want respect' (expletives deleted).' Thug Life has now colonized inner city Black neighborhoods in Britain."

20. Milliere's remarks were given during an online symposium, "The Death of France?" moderated by Jamie Glazov at FrontPageMag.com, June 9, 2003 and accessed on January 24, 2007 at http://www.frontpagemag.com/Articles/ReadArticle.asp?ID=8268. These remarks were made well before the 2005 youth uprisings in France.

21. Missiologist Charles H. Kraft in *Anthropology for Christian Witness* (Orbis, 1996) believes that there should be a rigorous distinction between "worldview" and "religion" because of the difficulties in using the terms to describe Western societies, as he notes, "we need to decide whether it would be best to redefine religion in such a way that western science is considered a religion or to approach the matter in a different way" (p. 198). But he then says, "If we call science a religion because it functions as the core of western societies much as supernaturalism functions as the core of most other societies, we end up with a naturalistic, atheistic religion" (p. 198). Kraft believes that religion should relate to the supernatural and is but one of the "surface-level subsystems, along with politics, economics, and the rest" (p. 199) but worldview "includes no behavior at all, only the underlying assumptions on which all of a society's behavior is based" (p. 199). While useful for conventional missiology, we believe a more flexible definition is needed that can better capture the dynamic nature of religio-cultural phenomena like Thug Life.

22. Dwight N. Hopkins, "The Religion of Globalization" (*Other Journal*, Issue #5, Capitalism, January 2005, accessed on January 24, 2007, at http://www.theotherjournal.com/article.php?id=53). This definition of religion is more conducive to our efforts to analyze Thug Life.

23. Hip-Hop music as the overall genre of which Thug Life and gangsta rap is a part, does seem to have ethical and philosophical content embedded in its lyrics and lifestyle. Two philosophers, Derrick Darby (Texas A&M University) and Tommy Shelby (Harvard) have teased out these elements in their edited volume, *Hip Hop and Philosophy* (Open Court, 2005) whose essays discuss God, language and meaning, justice, power, and knowledge, among other themes.

24. Elijah Anderson, *Code of the Street: Decency, Violence, and the Moral Life of the Inner City* (W. W. Norton; 1st edition, 1999).

25. Romans 2:1, *The Holy Bible, New Revised Standard Version*.

26. Much of the current debate in Western societies about the nature of marriage and family life is a direct consequence of the changes in women's status beginning in the 1970s. For a study of and philosophical statement on current trends in marriage and family life among African Americans from a Christian perspective, see Kenneth D. Johnson and Eugene F. Rivers III, *God's Gift: A Christian Vision of Marriage and the Black Family* (Seymour Institute, 2005, and available online at http://www.amazon.com/Gods-Gift-Christian-Vision-Marriage/dp/0976571706/sr=8-1/qid=1169701872/ref=sr_1_1/105-2092392-4714055?ie=UTF8&s=books).

27. See Angela Ards, "Rhyme and Resist: Organizing the Hip-Hop Generation," *Nation*, July 26, 1999, also online as of 24 January 2007 at http://www.thenation.com/doc/19990726/19990726ards that documents how the internal contradictions of the Hip-Hop culture has frustrated the American Left's efforts to redirect Hip-Hop youths toward radical social change.

28. However, the American Left has not given up on trying to turn Hip-Hop culture into a leftwing social change agent. A special issue of the journal *Socialism and Democracy* in 2004 was devoted to essays assessing the capacity for such a cultural transformation, and discussed the implications of the age generational shift within the leadership of the African American Left for the rise of a new generation of Black activists to fuse Hip Hop with social change. It also reviewed the factors that have led to the increasing homogenization of the Hip-Hop genre as a function of corporate media control. See Yusuf Nuruddin and Victor Wallis, eds., *Socialism and Democracy*, Vol. 18, No. 2, July–December 2004.

29. Philip Jenkins' recent article, "Believing in the Global South," *First Things*, December 2006, reviews the statistical data in support of continued explosive growth of Christianity in the Third World.

150 Kenneth D. Johnson

BIBLIOGRAPHY

Anderson, Elijah. *Code of the Street: Decency, Violence, and the Moral Life of the Inner City.* New York: W. W. Norton; 1st edition, 1999.

Ards, Angela. "Rhyme and Resist: Organizing the Hip-Hop Generation." *Nation,* July 26, 1999. http://www.thenation.com/doc/19990726/19990726ards (accessed on January 24, 2007).

CTV News with Lloyd Robertson."'Boston Miracle' pioneer offers Toronto help." January 9, 2006. http://www.ctv.ca/servlet/ArticleNews/story/CTVNews/20060108/eugene_rivers_060108/20060109?hub=CTVNewsAt11 (accessed on January 24, 2007).

Darby, Derrick, and Tommy Shelby, eds. *Hip Hop and Philosophy.* Chicago: Open Court, 2005.

Ewen, Stuart. *All Consuming Images: The Politics of Style in Contemporary Culture.* New York: Harper, 1990.

George, Nelson. *Hip Hop America.* New York: Penguin Books, 2005.

Harker, Joseph."Rap culture has hijacked our identity." *Guardian,* March 6, 2002. http://www.guardian.co.uk/comment/story/0,,662599,00.htm (accessed on January 24, 2007).

Hopkins, Dwight N. "The Religion of Globalization." *Other Journal,* Issue #5 (January 2005), http://www.theotherjournal.com/article.php?id=53 (accessed on January 24, 2007).

Jenkins, Philip."Believing in the Global South." *First Things,* December 2006.

Johnson, Kenneth D., and Eugene F. Rivers III. *God's Gift: A Christian Vision of Marriage and the Black Family.* Boston: Seymour Institute, 2005. Also available online at http://www.amazon.com/Gods-Gift-Christian-Vision-Marriage/dp/0976571706/sr=8-1/qid=1169701872/ref=sr_1_1/105-2092392-4714055?ie=UTF8&s=books.

Kelley, Norman. *The Head Negro in Charge Syndrome.* New York: Nation Books, 2004.

Kraft, Charles H. *Anthropology for Christian Witness.* Maryknoll, NY: Orbis, 1996.

Lasch, Christopher. *Culture of Narcissism: American Life in an Age of Diminishing Expectations.* New York: W.W. Norton, 1991.

McCaughan, Pat. "Hip-Hop Martyrs: Youth, Violence and Transformation." *Witness,* Volume 86, Number 5/6 (May-June 2003), http://www.thewitness.org/archive/mayjune2003/hiphop.html (accessed on January 24, 2007).

Merton, Robert K. *Social Theory and Social Structure.* New York and Glencoe: The Free Press, 1957.

Milliere, Guy. "The Death of France?" *FrontPageMag.com,* June 9, 2003. http://www.frontpagemag.com/Articles/ReadArticle.asp?ID=8268 (accessed on January 24, 2007).

Nuruddin, Yusuf, and Victor Wallis, eds. "Hip-Hop, Race, and Cultural Politics." Special Issue. *Socialism and Democracy* 18, no. 2 (July–December 2004).

Ogbu, John. *Black American Students in an Affluent Suburb: A Study of Academic Disengagement.* Mahwah, NJ: Lawrence Erlbaum, 2003.

Piirto, Rebecca. *Beyond Mind Games: The Marketing Power of Psychographics.* N.p. American Demographics Books, 1991.

Public Broadcasting System."The Merchants of Cool." *Frontline,* January 21, 2001. Also online at http://www.pbs.org/wgbh/pages/frontline/shows/cool/.

Shakur, Tupac. *Thug Life: Volume 1.* 1994 by Out Da Gutta Records.

Tillich, Paul. *Theology of Culture.* New York: Oxford University Press, 1959.

Travis, Alan."Teenagers see Asbos as Badge of Honour." *Guardian,* November 2, 2006. http://society.guardian.co.uk/youthjustice/story/0,,1937746,00.html (accessed on January 24, 2007).

United Nations Population Fund. *Moving Young: State of World Population 2006. Youth Supplement.* New York: United Nations Population Fund, 2006. http://www.unfpa.org/swp/2006/moving_young_eng/introduction.html (accessed on January 24, 2007).

United Nations Population Fund. *Urbanization: A Majority in Cities.* New York: United Nations Population Fund, 2005. http://www.unfpa.org/pds/urbanization.htm (accessed on January 24, 2007).

West, Cornel. *Race Matters*. Boston: Beacon Press, 1993.
Wiens, Mary. "Reporter's Notebook: 'The Black Community has a Special Responsibility."
Canadian Broadcasting Corporation. January 20, 2006. http://www.cbc.ca/toronto/features/
marywiens/tenpoint.html (accessed on January 24, 2007).

Chapter Fifteen

Hip Hop, Theology, and the Future of the Black Church

Osagyefo Uhuru Sekou

I AIN'T NO PREACHER?

In 1994, while I was teaching students in a middle school in St. Louis, Missouri, alternative strategies to avoid gang violence, I happened upon the crime scene of a drive-by shooting of a young man who at one time attended the school. In fact, he had been killed in a drive-by a few blocks from the school. At the murder scene, I saw the lifeless body of this kid, killed by the violence that plagued the city. St. Louis has had the dubious placement as the number one city for youth homicide several times in the last two decades.

At the same time that I worked at the middle school, I served as youth minister of a local Baptist church. At the request of the young man's sister, a member of the church, I spoke at the funeral, held at another church. I opened my remarks by quoting Ice Cube, "Today was a good day."[1] In the song, Ice Cube reflects that a good day in the ghetto is evidenced by no one he knows getting shot. I talked about the young man's life. I expressed my own bewilderment and sadness at the death of yet another young Black man, but I was confident and sure that God still loved me and the attendees. And indeed, it was a good day, too, because God still loved us.

When I concluded, the audience exploded. A church with a huge population of unchurched gang members and drug dealers stood and applauded. What occurred immediately after was saddening. The pastor of the church followed me to the podium and spent the next thirty minutes trashing young people and youth culture. His words were so damning that I pushed them from my memory. I do, however, recall the sick feeling in my stomach, which I again am experiencing as I write these words.

Using the Bible as a whip, he gave those young people a serious lashing. I do remember him saying that if the police stop and beat them, they deserve it. He also referred to the police as ministers of God.

The next day at school, three of my toughest students burst into my classroom.

"Mr. Sekou, Mr. Sekou, Jimmy runnin' around here lying on you and we are going to kick his ass."

"No, no, that is not an option," I responded. My conflict resolution skills kicked in. Slowly and calmly, I queried, "What is Jimmy saying?"

"His punk ass is runnin' around telling people you a preacher. He says you preached at his cousin's funeral. And we know you ain't no mutherfuckin' preacher because . . . "

One of my defenders paused with a tear-soaked voice, and another picked up where he left off, " . . . because you love us. You don't look down on us. You let us listen to Tupac and you help us understand what he says about our lives and society. You ain't no preacher are you?"

With flattered sadness, I smiled and lied, "No, son, I ain't no preacher."

SPIRITUAL BUT NOT RELIGIOUS

One hot June afternoon on the eve of the late Tupac Shakur's birthday, we gathered in the fellowship hall of Mt. Zion Baptist Church in Newark, New Jersey. The hall was suited for about two hundred people, but well over five hundred crammed into the space. Cameras and reporters swarmed and hovered as Hip Hop artists, young movement activists, and celebrities alike gave selective interviews and posed for photojournalists and daunting fans. Reporters seemed stunned at the fact that the words "Hip Hop" and "politics" were being used in the same sentence. The occasion was the National Hip Hop Political Convention.[2]

In the midst of the pivotal presidential election of 2004, six thousand or more youth activists, organizers, Hip Hop authors and journalists, and a few clergy gathered to contemplate the role of Hip Hop in American politics. The opening event of the convention at Mt. Zion Baptist sought to bridge the infamous generation gap. With the war in Iraq, expanding prison industrial complex, crumbling public schools, and a palpable breach between the Civil Rights and the Hip Hop generations, an intergenerational dialogue kicked off three days of intense debate concerning the political future of our generation and, ultimately, our democracy. Moderated by a youth pastor and movement elder, the dialogue included movement veteran Dr. Ron Daniels, the Reverend Dr. Michael Eric Dyson, and me. I began my talk with a harsh criticism of the very institution that was hosting us, the same institution that gave me my voice—the Black Church. I laid bare the level of mistrust engendered by some Black Church leaders and lamented the fact that a number of churches in our communities are led by commuter shepherds: self-serving pastors who drive luxury automobiles from well-manicured suburbs to impoverished inner cities for Sunday service. More often than not, the commuting clergy preach to a commuter flock: Black middle-class members of these houses of worship who do the same as their pastors.

I noted that a number of young people within the Hip Hop generation had been burned by the church. They were exposed to a number of religious traditions, such as Islam, and found at least a truth that helped them make sense of the world in their own image. Hence, I stated, "This is why a number of people in our generation say, 'I am not religious. I am . . . '" and on cue, over five hundred young people bemoaned, "spiritual."

Nearly four years later, with another major presidential election looming, I recalled this experience at another historic gathering at Harvard Divinity School. Sponsored by Harambee, the divinity school's Black student organization, the symposium was entitled "Hip Hop and Its Religious Sensibilities"—yet another pairing that puzzled both reporters and Ivy League professors who were in the audience.[3] The panel was a collection of theologians, clergy, a female Muslim divinity student, a Christian rapper/DJ, two African American studies professors, a youth practitioner, and myself. As I told the Newark story to the audience at Harvard, it on cue responded with the generational mantra "I am spiritual."

For a decade and a half, I have pondered the question of the relevance of the Black Church and its relationship to Hip Hop. In my first book, *urbansouls*, I mediated on my experiences as a youth advocate and youth minister. As a result of the book, which this chapter builds upon, I have been referred to as a "Hip Hop theologian." Equally, I am a child of the Black Church, an ordained elder in the Church of God in Christ. I love the church. It saved my life and offered me the space to explore my gifts and celebrate in the public the presentation of those gifts. Yet, this is not the experience of many of my peers.

These aforementioned experiences offer a damnable critique of the Black Church and its relationship to Hip Hop and young people. Whether the setting is an inner-city middle school, gang funeral, the nation's most famous school of religion, or a gathering of young political activists, the criticism of the Black Church remains unified. In their minds and lives, the Black Church is irrelevant to their life chances.

Moreover, there is a serious shortage of theologians or scholars of religion who attempt to craft a systematic theology or spirituality that takes the voices of youth seriously. This is in part a reaction to the lack of value attributed to poor Black and Brown youth voices in the academy, to the inability of the Black Church to relate to youth, and, above all, to the sheer lack of courage among African American religious leaders. Black clergy need to learn to sit at the feet of young folks and engage them in sustained ways. This lack of engagement is fueled by a belief among older African

Americans and younger Black folks with petite bourgeois sensibilities concerning youth. In a word, the problem with Black folks is young Black folks—à la Bill Cosby.[4]

READING THE GRAFFITI ON THE WALL

As a theologian and a clergyman, I have three perennial questions that haunt my existence: How do we end human misery? In light of said misery, how do humans make meaning for themselves in circumstances not of their choosing? And what does our contemporary situatedness (circumstances) have to teach us about meaning making? Given that religion is primarily a meaning-making activity and that humans use it to situate themselves within a broader context to face dread, death, and despair, religion must offer an eternal story in the face of a finite reality.

The foreboding gap between the Black Church and youth has lead youth to seek and create alternative spaces of meaning making. Hip Hop's saliency proves a space of meaning. How do we interpret that meaning? To achieve such an answer, one must take ontological risk that will lead to existential vertigo.

> Ontology itself can not formulate ethical precepts. It is concerned solely with what is, and we cannot possibly derive imperatives from ontology's indicatives. It does, however, allow us to catch a glimpse of what sort of ethics will assume its responsibilities when confronted with a human reality in situation.[5]

Hip Hop reflects the situation of youth and their relationship to the church and society. Hip Hop reflects the situation of youth in America. And if the Black Church is to remain relevant in the twenty-first century, it must ponder its relationship to Hip Hop, youth activism, and young people.

Treating young people as theological agents is sure to cause the same consternation that puzzled the reporters at the National Hip Hop Political Convention and the reporters and Ivy League professors seated in the audience of the forum at Harvard Divinity School. Hip Hop and theology are not typically shared in the same discourse. They are often seen as oppositional. In the preface to his book *The Parallaz View*, philosopher and cultural critic Slavoj Žižek provides a vision for blending of seemingly unrelated topics,

> A short circuit occurs when there is a faulty connection in the network— faulty, of course, from the standpoint of the network's functioning. Is not the shock of short-circuiting, therefore, one of the best metaphors for a critical

reading? Is not one of the most effective critical procedures to cross wires that do not usually touch: to take a major classic (text, author, notion), and read it in a short-circuiting way through the lens of a "mirror" author, text, conceptual apparatus ("minor" should be understood here in Deleuze's sense not "of lesser quality," but marginalized, disavowed by hegemonic ideology, or dealing with a "lower," less dignified topic)? If the minor reference is well chosen, such a procedure can lead to insights which completely shatter and undermine our common perceptions.[6]

By suggesting that young people are theological agents, the historical theological canon and the subhegemony of the Black Church on religious discourse are short-circuited. Given Hip Hop's impact on the life chances of youth, I want to position Hip Hop artists as paratheologians. The term *paratheologian* is inspired by St. Clair Drake's insightful category *paraintellectuals*. Hip Hop artists are persons outside the church and seminary who are active consumers of theological knowledge and use that knowledge for intellectual, activist, and artistic purposes.[7]

Second, I want to posit Hip Hop in part as a theology of existence, a systematic theology of ongoing critique of existence that is realized in everyday interactions and practices. Its theology of existence is partially shaped by the constraints of oppressive society and the hope experienced in said situation. This theology has a basic set of discursive coordinates that are epistemological, ontological, or ethical positions. In Hip Hop, existence is explicitly thematized and cannot be avoided by anyone serious about articulating a theological project relevant to the life and life chances of young Black people and their relationship to the Black Church.[8]

This chapter honors spiritual sensibilities of a generation by highlighting the theological and religious moments of Hip Hop. The intent of this work is to develop, not a Hip Hop theology, but rather a theological read of Hip Hop Culture as a means to help us see young people as theological agents, religious beings, and spiritual creatures.

NOTES

1. "It Was a Good Day" was released by Ice Cube in 1993 on the Priority Records release *The Predator*.

2. Founded in 2003, the National Hip Hop Political Convention was called into action to envision, adopt, and implement a political agenda of the Hip Hop generation. Eight major issues and themes drive the work of the convention: criminal justice; economic justice; educational empowerment; equality; global issues; health, wellness, and the environment; media regulations; and the organization mobilization of organizers and activists. Conventions were held in 2004, 2006, and 2008.

3. The panel was held on February 28, 2008, and moderated by Dr. Marcyliena Morgan, professor of African and African American studies and director of the Hiphop Archive at the W. E. B. DuBois Institute (Harvard University). Panelists included DJ Lady Grace, Josef Sorett, Mariama White-Hammond, Emmett G. Price III, Maryam Sharrieff, and myself.

4. On July 7, 2004, Bill Cosby spoke to an audience in Washington, DC, invited by the National Association for the Advancement of Colored People on the occasion of the fiftieth anniversary of the *Brown vs. Topeka Board of Education* Supreme Court case. In his speech, Cosby challenged many in the Black community to wake up and aid in their own self-development, self-mobilization, and self-determination. Yet, the comments were made in a derogatory and disparaging manner and led to a national frenzy that took place in mass and social media, including the most notable response by Michael Eric Dyson in the form a complete book, *Is Bill Cosby Right? Or Has the Black Middle Class Lost its Mind?* (New York: Basic Civitas, 2005).

5. Jean-Paul Sartre, *Existentialism and Human Emotions* (New York: Philosophical Library, 1957), 91.

6. Slavoj Žižek, *The Parallax View* (Cambridge, MA: MIT Press, 2006), ix.

7. Quoted in Ira E. Harrison and Faye V. Harrison, *African American Pioneers in Anthropology* (Knoxville: University of Tennessee Press, 1999), 8.

8. This idea is based on Paget Henry's "African and Afro-Caribbean Existential Philosophies," in Lewis Gordon's *Existence in Black: An Anthology of Black Existential Philosophy* (New York: Routledge, 1997), 11–36.

Chapter Sixteen

Confessions of a Hip Hop Generation Minister

Patricia Lesesne

I have two confessions. My first confession is that I deeply despise Hip Hop culture, rap music especially. The objectification of women in rap music and the manner in which material objects are celebrated as substitutes for self-worth are sickening and saddening. My second confession, however, is that five of the seven radio dials in my car are set to radio stations that claim to play the best of "today's hottest Hip Hop and R&B," and I regularly retreat into each of them. Even though I cut these sessions short when the lyrics begin to hurl hand grenades at my self-worth as a woman—and at some point they always do—I always come back, listening for that one song that is not ripe with misogyny or materialism. When I examine my attraction to and disdain for rap music more closely, I realize that the beats that accompany rap music are uniquely capable of capturing the deepest range of emotions, from intense love and intoxicating lust to blinding rage and murderous disdain. I am also drawn to rap music because the adept use of language in rap lyrics often approaches and surpasses sheer linguistic genius. I share this attraction to Hip Hop culture, rap music in particular, with our young people. At the same time, I hate what rap music reveals to us about the generation that is consumed by it. I am convinced that it reveals a deep level of disconnectedness and depravity, occasioned by their location at the vortex of social decline, urban decay, gender bias, institutionalized and internalized racial hostility, an economic ambush on working- and middle-class people, and a war on the family.

Our response must be to figure out how to transform the Black Church, an institution that is seen as dead and irrelevant to our children, into a living and breathing organism that our young people can rely on to address their disastrous moral states, as well as the desperate social conditions that give rise to them. My dilemma, however, is opening the lines of communication between my students and me so that we can identify the problems closest to their hearts and shape our institutions to address them. For me, these lines of communication are clogged with my contempt for the depravity represented in Hip Hop music and culture, on the one hand, and my students' absolute veneration of the music to the exclusion of reason and morality, on the other.

Many, maybe even most, of our children are consumed by Hip Hop culture. Hip Hop fashion, however lascivious for the women or unaffordable for the men, dictates their dress. The language of Hip Hop is their primary mode of communication. The young people with whom I work literally attempt to converse with me almost exclusively by using rap lyrics.

* * *

"Ms. Lesesne, Ms. Lesesne. Guess what?" Marcus asked me at the beginning of class.

I knew that whatever he was going to tell me did not have anything to do with the lesson that I was about to introduce. I also knew that if I didn't listen to him, then he would not focus on the lesson later.

"What, Marcus?" I responded.

He began to quote the lyrics of a rap song, "I wake up in the morning, brush my teeth, and count the money . . . " (he censored himself) and then smiled proudly as if he had just cited the elements of the periodic table by heart.[1]

I didn't know what to say, so I smiled weakly and said, "That's nice, Marcus."

He strutted to his seat with a big grin on his face and proceeded to be relentlessly disengaged from the lesson.[2]

* * *

Our young people's mimicry of Hip Hop language and fashion is not a big deal; every generation creates and enjoys harmless fads. What I am more concerned about is the extent to which they adopt the values and worldviews represented in lyrics of the songs they listen to for hours on end, day in and day out. For example, the misogyny reflected in Lil Wayne's "Over Here Hustling" is reprehensible—"I won't front for y'all. It's money over everything and b*****s under all."[3] The violence that is celebrated in "Put You on the Game" by the Game is disturbing—"I'll leave you with your vest broken, chest open, and then hop in the low-low with the tech smokin'."[4] The materialism that is exalted in the title alone of "Diamonds and Girl" is disheartening.[5] In this capitalist anthem, the rapper brags about the fact that he paid "$100,000 for the grill." The drug use that is accepted as a part of everyday life in David Banner's lyrics to "9MM" is frightening—"I'm a pill-poppin animal, syrup sipping n***a. I'm so high you couldn't reach me with a f***in antenna."[6]

Many Hip Hop generation ministers have recognized as much and are coaching the rest of us in creating a more welcoming environment. While reaching this generation must start with efforts such as welcoming gospel rap into our worship experiences and keeping a straight face as young people enter our sanctuaries with their pants sagging, I believe that reaching this generation for Jesus—the revolutionary peasant who took on the Roman empire—involves more. If the Black Church is going to get the saving knowledge of Jesus Christ to citizens, residents, and resident aliens of the Hip Hop community, it must do so by addressing the genesis of their rage and the murderous aspects of their experiences.

Marcus is being raised by an overindulgent single mother who seems to reward his mediocre academic performance with expensive clothes, shoes, and gadgets. He always has the latest in fashion and electronics but has not been working up to his academic potential since he started middle school. She rationalizes his budding sexist disposition by highlighting the lack of morals that the young women have who are enticing her son. His father is absent, and he attends a school where none of the teachers are Black and only a fraction of a percentage are male. His mother has worked her family into the outskirts of the middle-class tax bracket, but Marcus still lacks much of the social capital and respect of his peers.

His fellow students—mostly White and privileged—see him as the incarnation of the Hip Hop gods that they worship on the rap videos, in the Hip Hop magazines, and through the music that they consume obsessively. They see Marcus as cool but not intelligent. In a freestyle rap contest one day, one of his White male peers said to him without flinching, "Marcus, you don't know enough words to beat me in this contest. Besides, you're only going to rap about unintelligent things like girls and clothes." Unlike Marcus, his peers have a life and worldview outside of Hip Hop. For many of his peers, Hip Hop is a passing fancy. While Marcus is at home most summers, many of his peers are on European vacations with their families. After school, they are with their tutors, at violin lessons, or at soccer practice. Meanwhile, Marcus and his boys are hanging out in public places fulfilling Hip Hop prophecies.

My interactions with Marcus are similar to my interactions with Shawn, another young person with whom I work. Much of what I said about Marcus applies to Shawn, except that Shawn is angry.

* * *

In the middle of the lesson, Shawn yelled, "You know who it is!" from the back of the classroom.

"It's me snitches!" Liam returned the call from the front of the room. He was singing the clean version of the rap.

From there Shawn left his seat and picked up the circular top of a lab bench that had broken from the base. He turned it into a wheel on a turn table and began moving it in circular and semicircular motions as he synchronized mixing and scratching noises to each turn and half-turn. From there he walked to the front of the classroom and tagged the chalkboard with a graffiti symbol that translated into "ACE DUECE PICASSO." From head to toe, his basketball jersey, cotton undershirt, socks, sneakers, and low-riding jean shorts were a perfect symphony of black, yellow, and white, punctuated with designers' signatures and the jersey numbers of professional athletes.

* * *

Most attempts at redirecting Shawn end with him angrily informing you that you can't tell him what to do or that he *ain't gonna* do what you just told him to. Sometimes he complies temporarily. Most times there is a standoff.

Like Marcus, Shawn and his family are living on the thin ledge of the window of opportunity surrounding those with the social capital of the middle class. Shawn lives with his father, his father's girlfriend, and their new baby. Besides Shawn and the baby, Shawn's father has three other children from two other women. Shawn is the oldest, and he has not had his dad's undivided attention in years. His father does not have a college degree but works long hours at his stable blue-collar job. His is often on edge and does not have much room in his mental or emotional cache for Shawn to make the slightest misstep, however normal for a child his age. They communicate mostly by yelling at each other.

Increasingly unstable family structures, deteriorating values, ineffective postdesegregation schooling options, minimal after-school programs and extracurricular choices, increasing economic oppression (where people work more and receive less for their work), inequitable opportunities for young people to realize their potential—these are aspects of the Hip Hop generation's experiences, and these conditions cause the rage expressed in many rap lyrics. At least that's what a local youth pastor believes: He is convinced that rap music is but an outward expression of this generation's rage toward and disappointment with the generation before. He believes that Black men are the main target of this rage—absentee fathers and role models, those who are not meeting the expectations placed upon them to protect and provide. I am beginning to think that there is some credence to that. If that is the case, the Black Church must address this rage and confront the conditions that have given rise to it, if we are going to effectively cross the divide between the Black Church and the Hip Hop generation.

NOTES

1. Lyric from Gudda Gudda's 2009 release "Gettin' to the Money." Gudda Gudda is an artist signed to Lil Wayne's Young Money Entertainment.

2. All names and other identifying information have been changed or altered.

3. Lil Wayne's "Over Here Hustling" was released in 2006 from his album *Dedication*.

4. West Coast artist the Game released "Put You on the Game" on his 2005 Interscope album *The Documentary*.

5. Lil Wayne's "Diamonds and Girls" was first released on the 2007 *Heavy Rotation All-Star Compilation Volume 10*.

6. The song was first released on *The Best Thing Smokin' Volume 16* in 2007 and later released on his 2008 Universal Records album *The Greatest Story Ever Told*.

Chapter Seventeen

Spiritually Educating and Empowering a Generation: Growing Up in a Hip Hop Matrix

René Rochester

From its roots as an inner-city phenomenon to its global appeal, Hip Hop has spawned a continuing economic, political, social, and cultural movement around the world.—Emmett G. Price III[1]

The opening epigraph speaks directly to a world where Hip Hop Culture is rapidly becoming the norm. As Christian leaders concerned with educating and empowering the next generation, we must be equipped to spiritually educate, minister to, and empower youth and young adults whose "mother tongue" has been learned in the culture of Hip Hop. As facilitators of learning, we find it imperative to investigate what young people may already know and understand about biblical spirituality. It is our responsibility to continue educating and equipping ourselves to effectively communicate the foundational truths of the gospel of the kingdom of God.

This chapter wrestles through the question, what do we do if young people's existing knowledge of biblical truth is what they have learned in a song or from imitating the appearance of Holy Hip Hop? The process of thought to address this question consists of three basic constructs: the matrix, the music method, and the medium and its message.

THE MATRIX

When the word *matrix* is spoken, many people reflect back to the films that launched the careers of the Wachowski brothers. The duo directed the Matrix trilogy, starring Laurence Fishburne, Jada Pinkett Smith, and Keanu Reeves. The film series depicts a massive artificial intelligence system that has tapped into people's minds and created the illusion of a real world while using their brains and bodies for energy, tossing them away like spent batteries when they're through. Morpheus (Fishburne), however, is convinced that Neo (Reeves) is "the One" who can crack open the Matrix and bring his people to physical and psychological freedom. The premiere film has a scene where Neo is in the womb of a computer structure and then is birthed from a machine into the *matrix*. His world is now what he was born into. The generation of young people we are reaching and teaching are also born into a matrix, the social-cultural matrix of Hip Hop.

The word *matrix* refers to something within or from which something else originates, develops, or takes form.[2] Developmental psychologist Lev Vygotsky believed that individuals who are embedded in a sociocultural matrix and behavior cannot be understood outside it.[3] Their cultural context shapes their thinking, language, values, understanding of self, goals, and skills. Various anthropologists note that a person's native language, or mother tongue, is the first language learned.[4] In terms of that view, the person is called a *native speaker* of the language, although one may also be a native speaker of more than one language if all the languages are learned naturally, without formal instruction, such as through cultural immersion before puberty. Often, a child learns the basics of his or her first languages from the family; however, families today are broader than kinfolk such that "family" could mean the social context of a child's community. If a child's dominant language is Hip Hop, there may be translation difficulties as we teach and share from a biblical context.

Anthropologists define culture as everything that occurs in a society—all of the customs and practices handed down from generation to generation.[5] These contributions usually come from formal institutions, such as churches, the government, and, increasingly, the media; from mores, or standards of behavior; and from laws and conventional practices and customs.[6] Cultural immersion of most youth today comes through the medium of visual and audio communication networks. Generational learning is impacting the masses through the mass media production.

According to Vygotzgy, young people can be taken to a next level of learning and understanding with the assistance of another. A teacher or musician becomes a mediator, facilitator, and coparticipant in guiding instruction.[7] Vygotzgy points out the significance of the teacher and musician. In many cases, the musician, through the means of media production, has become one of the most influential teachers of the day. Referencing the opening epigraph, the statement informs us of the ongoing influence of Hip Hop Culture throughout the world.

THE MUSIC

According to a number of resources (far too many to mention), music can be defined as organized sound. There are observable patterns to what is broadly labeled *music*, and while there are understandable cultural variations, the properties of music are the properties of sound as perceived and processed by humans. This organized sound (music) consists of changes in air pressure. The frequency, size, and complexity of those changes determine what we hear. We hear the frequency of pressure changes as changes in pitch; we hear the size of pressure changes as loudness or amplitude; and we hear the complexity of pressure changes as timbre. Timbre is the quality that gives distinction from one voice to another; it distinguishes the uniqueness of sound from different instruments.

What are we listening to? When Jesus spoke to His disciples and the crowds who followed, he often concluded a portion of instruction by saying, "He who has an ear to hear, let him hear."[8] He knew that the young men who followed Him were of the Jewish culture, that they had learned to listen to the teachings of the rabbis, and that they had been instructed, as little boys through the reading of the Psalms, to *selah*, or pause and reflectively think about what they just heard. There is evidence that all of the Psalms were sung and spoken with music in the Temple in Jerusalem. Since we are designed to respond to song and poetic movements, music has the power to tutor us through beliefs and through ways to act on those beliefs.

When our outer ears pick up sounds, receptors within absorb what is heard through the pressure of the airwaves. Differences in pressure are detected by receptors in the inner ears and from there conveyed to the brain as action potentials. Now that the brain has received a message, there will be actions based on what was heard. When Jesus began preaching and teaching after His baptism and ordination at the river Jordan, His first message was "Repent, for the kingdom of heaven is at hand."[9] This statement speaks volumes when you understand the meaning of the word. There are two words in the New Testament translated as "repentance," one of which denotes a change of mind, or a reformation of life; the other, sorrow or regret that sin has been committed.[10] In this case, the word *metanoeo* is used: the preposition *meta* means "afterward" or "after," and *noeo* means "to exercise the mind," "to consider, perceive, and understand," and "to heed."[11]

Jesus was challenging the people to think different and to respond to what they understood to be true. Although Jesus was known as a carpenter's son, He actually was the Son of God! So in His omniscient understanding of how the brain was designed by the creator of the universe, He makes a pointed statement that speaks directly to what neurologists call *action potentials*.[12] Areas of the cortex in the temporal lobe of the brain interpret action potentials as sound, language, and music. Musical activity involves nearly every region of the brain that we know about and nearly every neural subsystem. Could this be why Jesus called His disciples to love the Lord their God with their mind?[13]

How does the brain listen to music? Pages could be written discussing the anatomy and physiology of the brain from a neurological perspective, but this is not the ultimate goal of the chapter. The goal in this case is to understand thought processes, memories, emotions, and experiences that happen to take place in the anatomy of the brain. Information from the auditory cortex is transmitted to the frontal lobe, which associates the sound of music with thought and stimulates emotions and past experiences. People have stored representation of songs and the sounds of musical instruments in their long-term memory, which would confirm that music can be imagined.[14] When a song is imagined, the brain cells that are activated are identical to those used when a person actually hears music from the outside world. Brain scans have shown that the visual cortex is also stimulated so that visual patterns are imaged as well.

Are you listening? In most movie theaters, one of the last projections on the screen before the feature presentation are the words "The audience is listening," with an amplification of a chord of music played in surround sound. The audience is the group of listeners or spectators who are hearing the music being played—or in this case, digitized or scratched. Listening to music starts with the area below the cortex—the cochlear nuclei, the brain stem, the cerebellum—and then moves up the auditory cortices on both sides of the brain.

Certain characteristics of musical and language input are probably analyzed selectively by the two hemispheres of the brain. A key difference: the left hemisphere is concerned more with word distinction and speed and, in this case, tempo of the music; the right hemisphere, with distinguishing frequency, meter differences, or rhythm, a process called *spectral sensitivity*. Information from the auditory cortex is transmitted to the frontal lobe, which associates the sound of music with thought and stimulates emotions and past experiences. Compelling evidence suggests that the brain's response to music has strong biological roots.[15] The brain's ability to respond emotionally to music is connected to biology and culture. The brain has specialized areas that respond only to music, and these areas are able to stimulate the limbic system, provoking an emotional response. Many researchers believe that the ability to perceive and enjoy music is an inborn human trait. This credible evidence speaks of the omniscient God of the universe, who created mankind in His image and likeness and fashioned him to worship and praise His name. Jesus said that those who worship Him should worship in spirit and in truth.[16] If every individual has the innate ability to perceive and enjoy music, could there be a purpose for this pleasure in music?

The apostle Peter refers to this innate ability of response to praise in his letter to the gentiles who had come to believe in Jesus. Peter reminds them what Christ has done for them. Like the Jews, these Gentile Christians are a diaspora, a chosen people scattered and living as strangers in a Roman society.[17] Their task is to "be holy," set apart for the Lord's service, and to "sound the praises of him who called them out of darkness or ignorance to the things of God's kingdom and into his marvelous light."[18] In this passage we see the apostle reminding the people of who they are called to be. The medium, or messenger, Peter delivered a message to believers, who then filtered the message through former teachings they had previously heard.

THE MEDIUM AND ITS MESSAGE

If there is going to be Holy Hip Hop, there must first be a holy medium to deliver a message of truth. To those in the listening audience who know the truth of God's word, they will have a filter to process the sound coming through their ears. However, the young people who have no biblical background of truth can be stimulated by the "sound of music," and once neural arousal takes place, the neurons are ready to be involved wherever there is activity. In the previous section, I note the powerful medium of music communication, where brain research shows evidence of ear-brain pathways specifically designed for receiving music messages. Understanding music's ability to transfer emotions, moods, and passions, we as spiritual educators must take a serious look at how we are training a generation to deliver a doctrinally sound message. We also have the mandate to equip the equippers with the appropriate tools to teach a generation of listeners to heave ears to discern a message that is able to influence a behavioral response.

Effective teachers know that to teach any topic, we must first find out what students already know. Tapping students' existing knowledge base enables us to identify an entry point for introducing new knowledge. The apostle Paul refers to this line of thought in his letter to a young man, Timothy. Paul considered Timothy like a son and encouraged him to be strong in the grace that is in Christ Jesus. Timothy was being admonished that his strength came from the grace given to him from the anointed one Himself . . . Christ. Paul went on to tell him to be strong in

> the things which you have heard from me in the presence of many witnesses, these entrust to faithful men, who will be able to teach others also.[19]

The passage of scripture speaks volumes to those of us who are mentors and spiritual leaders. The admonition is for Timothy to take the things that he heard from Paul. The word used for "heard" in this text is *akuo*, meaning what you have given an audience and grown to understand. Timothy was to take this information, hold onto it, and religiously teach it to those faithful *anthropos* (human beings), men and women who can teach *didasko*—that is, hold discourse with others to instruct them. [20]

Several years ago, Memorex had a commercial that featured Ella Fitzgerald performing a short scat. In the commercial, a statement is made about the quality of Memorex, and the narrator closes with "Is it Ella, or is it Memorex?" Memorex declared that its technology reproduced a quality sound that could stand in place of the original. Current technology continues to improve mass production of music quality. With the ability to download and duplicate, many have been trained as mimic masters rather than learned students of the message of the text. Too often, when a young person has a gift to spit a rhyme or sing a song, we place him or her in front of a crowd, to reach and teach the masses. Who's teaching him or her how to walk in the Spirit and the knowledge of the truth? Jesus defines truth for us in John 17:17. "Set apart Thy servants in truth, for Thy word is truth." We teachers need to translate the word of God in a relevant way to this growing Hip Hop generation. The message of being vessels set apart for the Master's use is a foundational concept that must be communicated.

SET APART FOR SERVICE

To youth who are looking for their own style, language, and music, there is a place for the desire to be set apart, and that is "representin" God's kingdom. Jesus said that His servants are set apart or distinctly different as they allow themselves to be shaped and transformed in their thinking and living life in accordance with His word. Personal development of biblical understanding provides individuals a filter to discern what is Godly and acceptable. [21] Continual conceptual deposits of truth allow foundational levels to be processed and worked into ownership by each person. Once a foundation is laid, it will be used to mediate new information.

When there are gaps in our base-level knowledge of foundational truth, it opens up space for the deposit of other influences that may not agree with the original information. For example, a young person who is just coming to a knowledge about the triune God and being launched out too quickly will not have developed a discerning ear to the things of the Spirit of God. Incomplete learning is evident when individuals get a little bit of the Word from a music medium and there has not been the practice and use of the Word they are readily rapping about. Each individual will have to choose how to balance new information with the old.

Individual beliefs will constantly be pulled and tugged on. Confidence in one's belief system is significantly connected and affected by personal experiences, imitation of others, social persuasions, and physiological cues from stress, anxiety, and fear levels. Teachers who are aware of the persuading factors that pull on the students entrusted to their care must be prayerful and strategic in teaching foundational truths. Error is easier to discover when it is placed against the authority of the truth.[22] Once a person's senses are trained to discern between truth and error, she or he is less susceptible to conceptual error. The process of discernment enables you to make choices. If the seed of truth is sown, it is up to the Creator of the universe to bring to fruition the purposed end in the young person's life.

CONCLUSION

So what shall we say to all these things? God places different calls on different men's and women's lives to serve Him in the kingdom of God. Some people are called into the area of ministering through athletics; to others, writing; and then there is music. Those whom He calls into music ministry should be well trained with their tools and gifts. Their skills are usually developed before they answer the call into the ministry and some before they even come to Christ. As stated earlier, there are some foundational truths that all new believers need to grasp. The first ministry of a new believer is not public ministry; we are called to be ministers of reconciliation, to minister salvation to the lost, and to minister to one another as brothers and sisters, through the Word of God.

At the beginning of any ministry, including music, there needs to be a time of preparation. *Preparation* in this context means to be grounded for the call. There is an apprenticeship period that we must experience as ministers of the Gospel, a time of preparation and of learning the tools of the ministry. The first and most important thing that we learn is the Word of God. We must gain spiritual insight and understanding of God's will for our life through the study and application of His Word. Second, we must work with the Holy Spirit to develop and perfect whatever skill God has given to us. He desires a quality of excellence from us; we are to display Him before the people. During this time of preparation, we are learning how to communicate the gospel, how to grow in relationship with others, and how to minister through our gift.

When you read about the musicians in the Old Testament, they often went before the soldiers. That's frontline warfare. A lot of injuries take place on the battlefield if you're not prepared and girded properly. No matter what the all God has on your life, no matter how excited you are about it, or how much you want to please God, if you don't get grounded in the Word of God, there is going to be much difficulty. In closing, we can learn from the words of the Lord to a new, up-and-coming leader of his day, Joshua:

> This book of the law shall not depart from your mouth, but you shall meditate on it day and night, so that you may be careful to do according to all that is written in it; for then you will make your way prosperous, and then you will have success. (Joshua 1:8)

NOTES

1. This quote came from personal correspondence with the editor during the development phase of this piece.

2. Stated definition was developed in consultation with www.Dictionary.com.

3. René Van der Veer and Jaan Valsiner, eds., *Vygotsky Reader* (Hoboken, NJ: Blackwell, 2004).

4. William A. Haviland, Harald E. L. Prins, and Dana Walrath, *Cultural Anthropology: The Human Challenge*, 12th ed. (Belmont, CA: Wadsworth/Thomson Learning, 2008), 110.

5. Haviland, Prins, and Walrath, *Cultural Anthropology*, 26.

6. Jerome Bruner, *The Relevance of Education* (New York: Norton, 1971).

7. Patricia H. Miller, *Theories of Developmental Psychology* (New York: Worth, 2002 [1983]).

8. Mark 4:23.

9. Matthew 4:17.

10. This information was gathered using the Barnes' Notes through the Biblesoft electronic database (1997).

11. All Hebrew and Greek definitions come from the consultation of Biblesoft's *New Exhaustive Strong's Numbers and Concordance with Expanded Greek-Hebrew Dictionary* (1994).

12. William Pryse-Phillips, *Companion to Clinical Neurology*, 2nd ed. (New York: Oxford University Press, 2003).

13. Matthew 22:37.

14. Daniel J. Levitin, *This Is Your Brain on Music* (New York: Dutton Books, 2006).

15. David Sousa, *How the Brain Learns* (Thousand Oaks, CA: Sage, 2005).

16. John 4:23.

17. 1 Peter 1:1.

18. 1 Peter 2:9.

19. 2 Timothy 2:2.

20. Biblesoft's *New Exhaustive*.

21. Hebrews 5:14.

22. John 17:17.

Chapter Eighteen

An Invisible Institution: A Functional Approach to Religion in Sports in Wounded African American Communities

Onaje X. Offley Woodbine

Many scholars, researchers, and laypeople restrict the concept of religion to distinct "kinds" of traditions, communities, institutions, and practices. For them, religion has to do with special beliefs in transcendent entities associated with specific places, persons, and times.[1] The religious studies literature refers to this approach as a substantive interpretation of religion.[2] By specifying the essential element of religion as belief in transcendent entities, substantive interpretations of religion help us to distinguish it from other areas of human culture and practice. However, alongside this perspective, scholars of religion have conceptualized religion in a different way—less in terms of what it "is" than what is "does."[3] They write of a functional perspective: religion has to do with traditions, communities, institutions, and practices that address human suffering in the context of the "big questions" of life: who am I, whose am I (identity and affiliation); why am I here, what ought I do (meaning and purpose); what is sacred, what ought I believe or hold dear?[4] This approach to religion gives it an existential emphasis: religion is defined by the contexts and lived experiences of suffering of its practitioners—wherever, whoever, and whenever they may be. Among the liabilities of functional approaches to religion is that one may perceive religion everywhere in everything—and thus nowhere in nothing. Among the strengths of this viewpoint is that it does not narrowly restrict our attention to certain beliefs, traditions, and communities, thus leading us to fail to appreciate how strategies for addressing suffering in the context of the big questions of life have developed in a variety of forms and contexts.[5] In this article, I seek to approach sports—specifically, basketball—among urban African American youth as religion. The question I seek to answer is

"How can we come to appreciate that suffering and healing in the streets is a religious project among urban African American youth, and one that has taken on an indigenous form and expression?"[6] By doing so, we do not simply come to see sport and specifically basketball in a new way. Rather, we come to understand more fully the humanity of African American youth in the ghetto, the depth of suffering, and the needs that are met from an insider's perspective within a marginal community; we see how religion has taken on an indigenous form in the context of slavery, trauma, and persistent dehumanization.

SIGNIFICANCE OF STUDY

Past theorists of suffering urban African American youth often construed the problem as outsiders, drawing from their established traditions of inquiry. Researchers tend to refer to these "outsider" methodological approaches as etic perspectives (in contrast to emic perspectives), in which intellectuals strive to produce objective analyses of beliefs, behaviors, traditions, cultures, and communities.[7]

Etic-oriented analyses of African American plight often draw from Western positivist frameworks to determine valid, quantifiable causes of emotional and physical destruction in Black ghettos. In the natural sciences, this has sometimes led to evolutionary theories promulgating a predisposition of the Black "race" toward manual labor and away from intellectual pursuits.[8] In contrast, theorists wedded to the social sciences have sometimes rejected the explanatory power of "race" as a valid biological concept but affirm its determinative significance as a social/environmental reality. They seek to demonstrate measurable ways that racist social structures and institutions adversely determine the consciousness and behavior of Black people.[9]

Ironically, while theorists of the natural and social sciences may debate the causes of Black suffering, methodologically, both groups usually share an etic point of view. Specifically, these opponents often share the propensity to reduce African American people's consciousness to measureable quantities associated with the concept "race." In doing so, they establish "race" as the central fact of African American existence. While there are obvious benefits to this circumscribed point of view, what may be less obvious are its limitations. Particularly, by specifying "race" as *the* analytic point of departure, these theorists reinforce the historical tendency of outsiders to simplify, homogenize, and subjugate complex African American youth in the ghetto.

To amplify this methodological limitation, I draw from W. E. B. DuBois's eloquent description of the devastating social/existential consequences of wielding dominant "outsider" perspectives to explain African American youth's suffering.[10] Specifically, DuBois chronicles ways that "outsiders" inevitably carry forward false stereotypes that reinforce African American social and psychological invisibility.[11] In the absence of alternative perspectives, Black folk often internalize these dominant "outsider" perspectives as normative (i.e., internalized racism). This often leads to self-annihilation among Black people ("living within a veil"), who may repress more authentic dimensions of self from public view to survive in an extremely harmful world.[12] The sickening consequence is that over time Black folk may be unable and unwilling to express the truer matters of their hearts and indigenous traditions, for fear of further desecration.[13] Indeed, one of the most effective ways that oppressed people conceal more genuine elements of themselves from oppressors is to at some level cease to be aware that these elements even exist within their own traditions.

In this sense, etic/emic hermeneutic distinctions, amplified by DuBois's social/existential analysis, help us acknowledge how the legacy of slavery and racism reinforces our conspiratorial participation in the annihilation of more authentic elements of African American life. This failure leads to the continued invisibility of the humanity of African Americans and the dismissal of valuable indigenous wisdom traditions to envision solutions.[14] To address our failure in empathy, I turn to an emic approach in this article, analyzing street sports traditions in terms that may be meaningful to African American athletes themselves, to help all of us deftly symbolize more latent but astonishingly present matters of their hearts expressed in basketball.[15]

In the interest of advancing this emic perspective, I explicate contrasting etic theories in the literature on Black athletes and society. These models serve to illustrate strengths and weaknesses of etic methods and provide entrée into reinterpreting Black basketball traditions of the ghetto in a new light.

In studies of race and sport, three etic models proliferate the literature. The first set denies "race" as a valid explanatory category to elucidate the role that sports play in the plight of African Americans. Perceiving "race" as a false biological concept, these scholars assert that when it is applied to African American athletes in any way, it serves to reinforce acerbic stereotypes associated with slavery. CBS sportscaster Jimmy "the Greek" Snyder, in a 1988 interview, portrayed the most infamous example of this acrid racial thinking in sports. He snidely remarked that African Americans dominate sports because slave owners mated their "big black to his big black woman so that he could have a big black kid."[16] Snyder's comments, grounded in a popular form of biological determinism, define the essential ideas of the second set of models. The second set interprets Black dominance in sports and negative racial disparities in other social arenas, such as employment and education, as a natural genetic outcome of slavery.[17] In contrast to both of these, a third set of models rejects genetic theories of "race" but highlights "race" as a social/environmental reality for the purposes of understanding sports' role in African American oppression.[18] African Americans' need to survive and adapt in a racially restrictive environment, not their innate traits, has led them to "fixate" on "prominent black athletes . . . and, this, in turn has stunted intellectual, social and economic development in the black community."[19]

William Rhoden advances one of the best examples of this third etic approach to the role of sports in Black plight. He traces mechanisms of a hegemonic sports "conveyer belt" system, from White corporate elites to college recruiters and local basketball programs in the ghetto, illustrating how Black athletic labor is cheaply bought and sold by a White majority.[20] Rhoden convincingly demonstrates the resiliency of racism in American sports and its traumatic impact on Black America. However, in signaling racial/economic oppression to be his analytic point of departure, Rhoden implicitly dismisses the cultural agency of African American athletes themselves.

This omission gives the false impression that African American athletes are the sum of their genes and/or environment, and it ignores elements of Black consciousness and culture, irreducible to deterministic frameworks. In particular, these etic models dismiss the fact that African Americans have always tended to engage their suffering and healing in religious and spiritual terms.[21] Currently, very few academicians, with the exception of John Edgar Wideman and Scott Brooks,[22] have sought to ground African American sports in the communal, spiritual values of Black history and culture. This gap in our ideas requires the development of an alternative approach.

To reinterpret Black athletes in the ghetto as initiators of indigenous basketball wisdom traditions that address "big questions" in the context of suffering, I draw from narrative accounts of their lived experiences. These accounts supply a "felt sense" for deeper kinds of resources, meanings, and practices that Black athletes express that are indigenous to the ghetto.[23] This "felt sense" will justify use of interdisciplinary tools in studies of the function of religion to symbolize their experiences more deeply in terms that scholars, religious leaders, and laypersons appreciate, understand, and will further develop.

VIGNETTE 1

C.J. is an African American male in his mid-twenties. He was born and raised in a predominately poor and Black inner city in the Northeast. At the time I interviewed him, he had been to prison twice for a total of four years for illegal possession of a firearm and illegal substances. Upon his release from prison, he felt conflicted between living a dangerous life of crime in the streets and pursuing his dream to play professional basketball.

In our interview, he often commented that the network of basketball elders, community gyms, and local leagues in his neighborhood kept him safe and showed him love, but guns and drugs were also a part of his everyday struggle living in the ghetto. He seemed overwhelmed and felt as though he could only be a basketball player, drug dealer, or gang member.[24] There were no other options for a poor Black male.[25] These three life options even operated while he was in prison, where he found that what kept him hoping and living were the prison basketball games in which he could demonstrate his humanity and gifts with others. After some conversation about these topics, I finally asked him to put into words the lived experience of actually playing basketball: "If you could put words to how you experience playing on the court, what words would you give to it?" His gut-wrenching response overwhelmed and awed me and, I must tell you, deeply saddened me:

> Ah, man, playing. I can remember playing one day. I had a game. My cousin, he had passed away, my favorite cousin you know? I wrote a book about him when I was younger and he had got shot and he had passed away and I was down. I was down and I was miserable but I was like "what am I going to do? I got a game today?" So I went to the game. I mean it's funny because I'm not going to say I didn't want to play. I still wanted to play basketball, but I had that on my mind. You know, and that was serious, you know? Because most people, something like that would have happened they wouldn't even go to a game but I still had love for the game and before he passed I know he had love for the game too. So I go into the game, I had the sad face on and I don't know what it was you know? I just played and I know I wasn't playing as hard as I use to play but everything was just, everything was going in man. Everything and I wasn't shooting the ball hard as I used to, dribbling it hard but I never got stripped. I don't know why. Usually somebody just come take the ball right out of my hand but it was just the love of the game I had and I believe my cousin was there with me still. And there's so much people go through when they're playing in the city. You know, there's people who come to the game and they're alright, you know? They had a good day, a good regular day but they come to play. But there's people, you know, they come on the court, they have issues you know? Some people, they done been through some things but they know basketball is going to take them there, you know, take their mind off of it. And for the most part I seen people, like, they just came from the

streets, something happened, or something happen in the house and they're putting up 40, 50 points, like letting it all out, you know? Like "dag, what happened to you today," you know? So just life man, like that's why you have so many tough players in the city right now because man, they done been through some things man and everything's not good.

In this narrative, C.J. comments that he felt compelled to play basketball on the day that his cousin was murdered, because of the love they shared through the medium of "the game." Grieving and seeking to restore his cousin's love, he entered the game with a deeply introspective demeanor, and in this egoless state of consciousness, he seemed to surrender his ability to control the outcome of his actions. Despite his effortlessness, no one could take the ball from him, and the ball just kept going into the basket. C.J. recognizes the coincidence of his lack of will and the orderly movement of the ball as a sign of his cousin's spiritual presence, and he experiences this meaningful coincidence as the restoration of a love bond forged in the space of the game, which transcends the brokenness of death.

Moreover, he comments that basketball is used as a medium of spiritual reconnection and healing across African American inner-city communities. Most play basketball, he feels, because the game will "take them there" beyond the restrictive modes of existence they are forced to live and suffer everyday in the ghetto. He attributes African American athletes' ability to score an outrageous number of points in street basketball games as a sign of their willingness to explore the deepest wounds of their hearts on hallowed basketball grounds, where they feel safe enough and loved enough to "let it all out" and use their bodies and emotional outbursts to testify to a self-worth and purpose that cannot be broken, imprisoned, or destroyed by persistent cultural trauma. In this narrative, C.J. begins to show us how basketball may function as an indigenous religious tradition of healing in Black lives, addressing the "big questions" in the midst of unimaginable loss and suffering in the streets.

VIGNETTE 2

Remarkably, this next illustration, as told by Chris Paul, has deep resonances with the lived experience of C.J. When he was in high school, Paul, currently an All-Star African American NBA player, discovered that his biggest basketball fan and best friend, his grandfather Papa Chilly, had been murdered. Distraught and grieving, Paul sought some way to mourn and restore the love that he and his grandfather shared through "the game" of basketball.

Much like C.J., Paul wondered how he could play in his next game without his grandfather, and yet he somehow felt he needed to play to find his missing grandfather. Unlike C.J., however, Paul had a mentor, his aunt, who recognized his need to work through his suffering and healing through the medium of basketball. To meet this need, his aunt insightfully suggested to Paul that he try to score sixty-one points in his next game, for every year of his grandfather's life. Deeply compelled to do it by some inner feeling but also troubled by the possibility of failure, Paul thought "there was no way" he could score that many points nor the exact number. However, in the next game, when Paul stepped onto the court, all he could think about was his love for his grandfather, and something moved him to use the space of the game as an ultimate sign of his grandfather's continued presence in his life beyond death. Consider Paul's lived experience:

> This is one of the times that I just felt there's no way that . . . I don't care what kind of defense you play, who you put in front of me. There's no way you are going to stop me from getting to that goal. The whole game I was just thinking about my Grandad, just thinking, you know, he's in heaven, he's watching this game, he's watching this game. Every time somebody hits me to the floor, he's up there jumping out of his seat getting angry. And as the course of the game went on, I said "I can do this."

Amazingly, as the game progressed, word began to spread throughout the crowd of Paul's mission to score sixty-one points for his grandfather. In this moment it seemed that everyone joined in Paul's precarious position, placing such meaning and weight on an outcome determined by the whim and twirl of a basketball floating through the air.[26] Of this shared communal experience of instability, his mother states,

> Then towards the end when we got to, um, fifty-six [points], they turned around, one of the kids turned around and said "Ms. Paul, he only needs five," and that's when I started to get nervous, 'cause I really wanted him to achieve it at that point.

Then with about two minutes left on the game clock and Paul with fifty-nine points, he takes the ball to the right side of the basket, jumps past defenders, and hangs in the air for what seems an eternity and finally releases the ball into the basket: sixty-one points! He then immediately fell to the floor, slain by the astonishing quality of the moment:

> And I laid it up and I got fouled and it went in, and I just, I laid there for a second and was just overwhelmed 'cause I knew that at this moment in time this is something I will never forget. It felt like I could have just died and went to heaven right there. It felt like my purpose for being here was almost over. . . . I just looked at my Dad and started crying.

Indeed, the entire community, including his dad, was emotionally torn asunder by the moment. His dad shares,

> It's just like everything came out of him. He just walked over to me and gave me a hug and just fell in my arms and that's when I just . . . it just tore me up, you know, 'cause of what he had just done.

Seeking to embody his grandfather's gift of purpose, spirit, and wisdom, Paul continues to do everything in his power to become a vessel of his grandfather's message of love and responsibility to others. Of their continued relationship, Paul testifies,

> "I'm thankful for my Grandad and I'll never forget him, ever." [27]

While there are similarities between C.J.'s experience and Paul's narrative—a uniform,[28] a bounded sacred space,[29] introspection and ego displacement,[30] discovery of a higher purpose, mourning a loving relationship, symbolic interpretation of basketball objects or icons, bodily rhythm and movement, expression of powerful emotions, spontaneity, and feeling of communion with a spiritual presence—there are some notable differences as well. In Paul's case, raised in a middle-class Black community, he consciously designed this rite of healing in detail with the participation of his community. His aunt suggested the process, and his parents, teammates, and interested persons fully participated in and validated his heroic mission[31] to relive the life, death, and restoration of his grandfather's presence in his life. Second, Paul articulated his experience of dying and going to heaven, in explicitly Christian language at high school age, which suggests that his higher education level and participation in a historically religious community that nurtured his sensibilities and identity.

These differences are important for two reasons: First, they help us to appreciate the important role of the community's participation in basketball healing rites;[32] second, they suggest that higher education level and economic status do not determine the religious significance of Black basketball healing rites in African American communities. However, higher socioeconomic status may facilitate African Americans with more conceptual and material resources to actualize the potential of this tradition to truly serve the community's effort to heal wounds in its midst.

VIGNETTE 3

In this third and final narrative—John Edgar Wideman, an internationally acclaimed writer, National Book Award finalist, and Brown University Professor—testifies that he too went to the basketball court to address wounds in the context of the "big questions" of life. Born in Pittsburgh, Pennsylvania, in a low-income African American ghetto, Wideman would later graduate from Penn University as an All-Ivy League basketball forward and become only the second African American to win a Rhodes scholarship. In light of all these achievements, however, in his autobiographical work *Hoop Roots*, Wideman affirms that his journey toward self-realization began on the basketball court. Consider his experience of playing the game in Pittsburgh streets:

> We went to the court to find our missing fathers. We didn't find them but we found a game and the game served us as a daddy of sorts. We formed families of men and boys, male clans ruled and disciplined by the game's demands, its hard, distant, implacable gaze, its rare, maybe loving embrace of us: the game taught us to respect it and respect ourselves and other players. Playing the game provided sanctuary, refuge from a hostile world. (p. 2)

Much like C.J. and Paul, Wideman went to the basketball court to restore his relationship with missing elders, with community, and with himself despite the dehumanizing forces in his life. And as in the previous two narratives, not only did Wideman find refuge, love, and belonging with his peers and elders in this world, but he sometimes entered into sacred time with an Other world, surrendering his false self-centeredness in the service of something more.[33] These moments on the court had the power to "take him there," to supply techniques to "die and go to heaven" and rediscover his purpose through "the game" despite hegemonic forces.

> Learned about time as I was learning about the game. Because the game is time. Not time out from the real business of life. Not simply play time. Like good gospel music, the game brings time, tells time, announces the good news that there is Great Time beyond clock time and this superabundance, this sphere where you can be larger than you are, belongs to nobody. It's too vast. Everlasting. Elsewhere. Yet you can go there. It's in your hands. White people nor nobody else owns it. It's waiting for you to claim it. The game conjures Great Time.[34] (p. 56)

Indeed, all of the narratives speak to the game of basketball as a compelling tradition that supports African American ability to conjure an Other reality beyond death, despair, and racism to repair an anti-Black world. As a lived tradition indigenous to the ghetto, basketball functions as a religious institution, providing a set of tools—sanctuaries, symbols and icons, community elders and mentors, ego-displacing practices, ecstatic experiences, belonging, and ultimate purpose—for African Americans to transform death into life in the streets. These data necessitate the use of tools in the study of the function of religion to symbolize African Americans' experiences more fully, to diagnose and treat their suffering more ably.

ANALYSIS OF AFRICAN AMERICAN INDIGENOUS BASKETBALL TRADITIONS: TOOLS IN THE STUDY OF THE FUNCTION OF RELIGION

Given the lived testimony of African American athletes, I suggest reinterpreting African American grassroots basketball traditions as religious communities indigenous to the ghetto. In particular, C.J., Paul, and Wideman utilize "the game" to address problems of pain, loss, and despair in the context of bigger questions: why am I here, what ought I do (meaning and purpose); who am I, whose am I (identity and affiliation); what is sacred, what ought I to believe or hold dear?[35]

Addressing these deeper problems and questions in the midst of suffering and the need for healing lies at the center of religious traditions around the world.[36] Given that human beings are finite, limited, and vulnerable to physiological instability, religion's capacity to point to the existence of other worlds with the power to stabilize, redeem, and restore human life through ritual techniques is critical.[37] Religions and their ritual practices provide a set of tools for human beings to surrender false, illusory, and painful aspects of existence to struggle toward deeper connections with truth, power, and wellness.[38]

Moreover, that healing techniques reside at the center of religion has promoted religion's central role in African American history and culture.[39] For persons of African descent, who are dealing with the terror of living in an anti-Black world, religion's promise of an Other world has provided a sense of self-worth, power, and hope that was otherwise missing.[40] To promote Black survival, rituals have played a critical role across the African Diaspora, providing a set of nondiscursive bodily techniques (rhythm, ecstatic experience, and song) to displace ego wounds related to slavery, loss, and systemic racial abuse to rediscover connections to something greater in themselves and the world.[41] Establishing loving associations of elders, mentors, and extended families, religions in the African Diaspora have maintained communities of refuge that have collectively "approved, acknowledged, and confirmed" their suffering and healing in the service of spirit.[42] In this sense, African American communities have supported the healing efficacy of Black rituals by holding sacred spaces safe enough to encourage unscripted dimensions of self to be expressed, shared, and remembered.[43] In summary, we might conceptualize religions in the African Diaspora, of which Black basketball in ghettos has become a member, as primarily practical traditions of "healing, ritual, and community" for those seeking "refuge, elevation . . . liberation" in an anti-Black world.[44] In this chapter, it has been my purpose to exercise paradigms in Black religious thought and the social sciences to guide scholars, religious leaders, and laypeople in more empathic appreciation of Black athletes' voices and their indigenous traditions as religious so that in the future we may reenvision a theoretical model that illuminates and mends the pain of the ghetto more deeply.

"Invisible institution" is a phrase borrowed from Albert J. Raboteau's classic text Slave Religion: The "Invisible Institution" in the Antebellum South *(New York: Oxford University Press, 1978).*

NOTES

1. Chris R. Schlauch, *Faithful Companioning: How Pastoral Counseling Heals* (Minneapolis, MN: Augsburg Fortress, 1995).
2. Peter L. Berger, *Pyramids of Sacrifice: Political Ethics and Social Change* (New York: Penguin, 1977).
3. Walter H. Capps, *Religious Studies: The Making of a Discipline* (Minneapolis, MN: Fortress Press, 2000).
4. Carl Gustav Jung, *Psychology and Religion* (New Haven, CT: Yale University Press, 1960); Erich Fromm, *Psychoanalysis and Religion* (New Haven, CT: Yale University Press, 1950); Erik H. Erikson, *Young Man Luther: A Study in Psychoanalysis and History* (New York: Norton, 1958); Meredith B. McGuire, *Religion, the Social Context* (Florence, KY: Wadsworth, 1981); Nancey Murphy, *Reasoning and Rhetoric in Religion* (Valley Forge, PA: Trinity Press International, 1994); Schlauch, *Faithful Companioning*; Anthony B. Pinn, *Varieties of African American Religious Experience* (Minneapolis, MN: Augsburg Fortress, 1998); Peter R. Gathje and David Oki Ahearn, *Doing Right and Being Good: Catholic and Protestant Readings in Christian Ethics* (Collegeville, MI: Michael Glazier Books, 2005).
5. In the last twenty years, Black religious thought has transitioned from church-centered, theological interpretations of African American religion to inquiring about the varieties of concrete manifestations of Black religion that arise in multiple contexts. For example, Anthony Pinn, in *Noise and Spirit: The Religious and Spiritual Sensibilities of Rap Music* (New York: New York University Press, 2003), argues that the dominant role of the Black Church in African American struggle has led to the marginalization of the varieties of African American religious expressions and the undue homogenization of Black religious life. Instead he employs an interpretive style bent on "the uncovering and revitalizing of religion outside of the confines of a long-standing but ineffectual theological tradition." He calls this interpretive commitment "nitty-gritty hermeneutics," a term that connotes the "rough edges" of Black religious experience in the ghetto. For Pinn, nitty-gritty hermeneutics ensures that "only a religiosity that participates in and affirms the cultural life of the community and speaks plainly to pressing issues without paying tribute to unproven theological assertions . . . is in keeping with the meaning of religion." See Pinn, *Varieties of African American Religious Experience*.

6. According to the US Department of Justice, Bureau of Justice Statistics, from 1976 to 2005, Black people were the victims and perpetrators of homicides 46% and 52% of the time in America, respectively, even though they make up only about 13% of the population. Even though nationally the homicide rate is decreasing in Boston and other major urban centers, African American male homicide rates for youth between the ages of fourteen and twenty-four have increased 78% between 2000 and 2007. James Fox, James Alan, and Larc L. Swatt, "The Recent Surge in Homicides Involving Young Black Males and Guns: Time to Reinvest in Prevention and Crime Control," Northeastern University, December 2008, http:// www.jfox.neu.edu/Documents/ Fox%20Swatt%20Homicide%20Report%20Dec%2029%202008.pdf.   About   50%   of incarcerated prisoners in America are African American. One scholar writes that community harm is so staggering in Black ghettos that the term "continuous traumatic stress syndrome" is an accurate diagnostic descriptor of everyday life. See Geoffrey Canada, *Fist Stick Knife Gun: A Personal History of Violence in America* (Boston: Beacon Press, 2005), x–xi.

7. Marvin Harris, *Cows, Pigs, Wars and Witches: The Riddles of Culture* (New York: Random House, 1974); William Divale and Marvin Harris, "Population, Warfare, and the Male Supremacist Complex," *American Anthropologist* 78 (1976): 521–38; Robert Feleppa, "On Reproducing Social Reality: A Reply to Harrison," *Philosophy of the Social Sciences* 16, no. 1 (1986): 89–99; Thomas N. Headland, Kenneth L. Pike, and Marvin Harris, *Emics and Etics: The Insider/Outsider Debate* (Stoughton, WI: Books on Demand, 1990).

8. Richard J. Herrnstein and Charles Murray, *The Bell Curve: Intelligence and Class Structure in American Life* (New York: Free Press, 1994).

9. Kenneth B. Clark, *Dark Ghetto: Dilemmas of Social Power* (New York: Harper & Row, 1965); Hussein Abdilahi Bulhan, *Frantz Fanon and the Psychology of Oppression* (New York: Plenum Press, 1985); Amos N. Wilson, *Black-on-Black Violence: The Psychodynamics of Black Self-annihilation in Service of White Domination* (Brooklyn, NY: Afrikan World Infosystems, 1991); Joy Degruy Leary, *Post Traumatic Slave Syndrome: America's Legacy of Enduring Injury and Healing* (Milwaukie, OR: Uptone Press); Elijah Anderson, ed., *Against the Wall: Poor, Young, Black and Male* (Philadelphia: University of Pennsylvania Press, 2008).

10. W. E. B. DuBois, *The Souls of Black Folk* (Chicago: A. C. McClurg, 1903).

11. Ralph Ellison accomplishes a similar feat in *Invisible Man* (New York: Random House, 1953). Also helpful is D. W. Stinson's "Negotiating Sociocultural Discourses: The Counter-storytelling of Academically (and Mathematically) Successful African-American Male Students," *American Educational Research Journal* 45 (2008): 975–1010.

12. On this point, Howard Thurman eloquently writes, "There are few things more devastating than to have it burned into you that you do not count and that no provisions are made for the literal protection of your person. The threat of violence is ever present, and there is no way to determine precisely when it may come crashing down upon you. . . . The underprivileged in any society are the victims of a perpetual war of nerves. . . . Fear, then, becomes the safety device with which the oppressed surround themselves in order to give some measure of protection from complete nervous collapse. How to achieve this? In the first place, they make their bodies commit to memory ways of behaving that will tend to reduce their exposure to violence." See *Jesus and the Disinherited* (Abingdon Press, 1949), 39–40.

13. Na'im Akbar, *Breaking the Chains of Psychological Slavery* (Tallahassee, FL: Mind Productions & Associates, 1996).

14. To draw an analogy, Black medical doctors at the Black Barbershop Health Outreach Program have sought to address major health disparities for Black men who are not engaged by the dominant White male middle-class doctor-patient medical model. Scholars and doctors around the country are increasing Black male trust in hospitals by asking Black barbershop workers to encourage hospital visits. Using an emic approach, these doctors identified a powerful internal resource and institution that would have been dismissed by dominant medical approaches, and they are saving lives. See http://www.blackbarbershop.org/.

15. See *Emics and Etics: The Insider/Outsider Debate*, ed. Thomas N. Headland, Marvin Harris, and Kenneth L. Pike (Sage), 1990. Another helpful text is H. Samy Alim, "'The Nattie Ain't No Punk City': Emic Views of Hip Hop Cultures," *Callaloo* 29 (2006): 969–90.

16. Jon Entine, *Taboo: Sports and Why We're Afraid to Talk about It* (New York: Perseus Books, 2000), 72.

17. See Robert M. Malina, "Growth and Physical Performance of American Negro and White Children," *Clinical Pediatrics* 8 (1969): 476–83; see Martin Kane, "An Assessment of Black Is Best," *Sports Illustrated*, January 18, 1971.

18. "(1) The NBA's campaign to improve its own marketability and profits through mass media (Andrews, 2006; Cole & Andrews 1996; McDonald & Andrews, 2001; Wilson & Sparks, 1996); (2) the historical and contemporary racism and discrimination that blocked alternative pathways to mobility but celebrated sports as a possibility for African Americans to achieve the American Dream (Anderson, 1990; Eitzen, 2006; Hartmann, 2000; Smith, 2008; Wilson, 1996; and (3) racist assumptions that Black athletes are naturally superior athletes in sports like basketball (Carrington, 2001; Entine, 1999; Hoberman, 1997) . . . shape the context within which young Black males, even those of limited skill and ability, aspire to hoop dreams in disproportionate numbers (May 2008)." Reuben A. Buford May, "The Good and Bad of It All: Professional Black Male Basketball Players as Role Models for Young Black Male Basketball Players," *Sociology of Sport* 26 (2009): 443–61.

19. See John Hoberman, *Darwin's Athletes: How Sport Has Damaged Black America and Preserved the Myth of Race* (Mariner Books, 1997), 6. "The sports fixation is a direct result of the exclusion of blacks from every cognitive elite of the past century and the resulting starvation for 'race heroes'; it has always been a defensive response to the assault on black intelligence, which continues to this day. That is why the sports syndrome has made athleticism the signature achievement of black America, the reigning symbol of black 'genius.'" Also see Harry Edwards, "Sport within the Veil: The Triumphs, Tragedies and Challenges of Afro-American Involvement," *Annals of the American Academy of Political and Social Science* 445 (1979): 116–27; Richard Lapchick, *Broken Promises: Racism in American Sports* (St. Martins Press, 1984); William C. Rhoden, *Forty Million Dollar Slaves: The Rise, Fall, and Redemption of the Black Athlete* (Crown Publishers, 2006).

20. The Black Coaches Association former chairman describes the process of exploiting urban Black athletes: "How tough is it to buy an inner-city kid? Buy him some shoes, take him to dinner, get him some nice clothes, maybe a car. You become his best friend, and he gets hooked like a junkie. . . . Then you control the product. The secret is controlling the product early. It's just like slavery. . . . The kids benefit from the system—at least a few lucky ones—with education and money, but what they often lose is any identification with the black community" (Rhoden, *Forty Million Dollar Slaves*, 178). Also, Richard Lapchick confirms: "We expect dedication and loyalty to the team, hard work, honesty, discipline, character building, and a commitment to winning through excellence and not through destruction of the opposition. Our coaches are to be philosophers and teachers of virtues and nurturers of their athletes, both on and off the court. The truth is very different. 'Winning isn't everything, it's the only thing,' is a reality. Winning at all costs is the philosophy most coaches believe in, no matter what pieties they may utter. Alumni and boosters pay coaches, players, and families of players. Athletes disregard academics and dream of incomes far beyond their ability. Faculties shrug their shoulders while college presidents say they can't expect athletes to take academics as seriously as other students. Sanctions for violations are rare and selective. Ultimately, it pays to cheat. It is a system gone mad. Win at all costs, at any cost" (*Broken Promises*, 164).

21. On this point, C. Eric Lincoln writes, "Beyond its purely religious function, as critical as that function has been, the black church in its historical role as lyceum, conservatory, forum, social service center, political academy and financial institution, has been and is for black Americans the mother of our culture, the champion of our freedom, the hallmark of our civilization." *The Black Experience in Religion* (Garden City, NY: Anchor Press, 1974), 5. DuBois, *The Souls of Black Folk*; Long 1974; West 1993; Pinn, *Noise and Spirit*. C. Eric Lincoln, *The Black Experience in Religion* (Garden City, NY: Anchor Press, 1974), 5. DuBois, *The Souls of Black Folk*. Charles Long, "Perspectives for a Study of Afro-American Religion in the United States," *History of Religions* 11 (1971): 54–66.

22. Scott N. Brooks, "Fighting like a Ballplayer: Basketball as a Strategy against Social Disorganization," in *Against the Wall: Poor, Young, Black, and Male*, ed. Elijah Anderson (University of Pennsylvania Press, 2008). John Edgar Wideman, *Hoop Roots* (Boston: Houghton Mifflin, 2001).

23. Eugene Gendlin, *Experiencing and the Creation of Meaning: A Philosophical and Psychological Approach to the Subjective* (Northwestern University Press, 1997).

24. In this respect, C.J. echoed leading rapper Biggie Smalls, who rhymed in his song "Things Done Changed": "If I wasn't in the rap game / I'd probably have a key knee deep in the crack game / Because the streets is a short stop / Either you're slingin' crack rock or you got a wicked jumpshot."

25. Anderson, *Against the Wall*.

26. See Pee Wee Kirkland's introduction to *Soul of the Game: The Voices and Images of Street Basketball* (Workman Publishing Company, 1997). Writing about the communal effect of street basketball games on low-income Black communities in New York City, Kirkland exclaims, "The streets were crowded for five blocks. People would watch from the highway overpass; people would hang from trees. Some would use binoculars to watch from the projects. . . . Addicts be sittin' there, forget they had habits. When the game was over people, people didn't know where they parked their cars. And the most amazing thing was, there were no police. There were never any real problems, because people had too much respect for the game" (p. 4).

27. ESPN, SportsCenter Flashback, "Chris Paul Pays Tribute to His Grandfather," May 8, 2008.

28. A uniform signifies the loss of worldly identity or the ego in the service of a larger goal. A uniform, like a mask or body painting, hides the identity of the individual, freeing the person to share parts of the self that are normally guarded or protected in everyday life.

29. Reinterpreting basketball courts as religious sanctuaries is further justified by other primary sources. Consider, for example, that in Harlem, New York City, Rucker Basketball Park is universally known as "the mecca of street basketball," where anyone who seeks to become an inner-city basketball legend, including NBA players, must make a pilgrimage to perform and pay homage to past legends. Also reflect on the fact that in Bedford-Stuyvesant, Brooklyn, a basketball court is approached with such reverence that African American athletes refer to it as "the soul in the hole," "given its name because it sits in a sunken depression below street level. . . . Before you could even step into this hole . . . you had to earn your 'soul' on the surrounding courts of Bed-Stuy" (Huet, *Soul of the Game*). Indeed, basketball courts often function as sacred spaces or the centers of Black athletes' lives. Mircea Eliade's definition of sacred space may help us to appreciate basketball courts as mediums of soul: "(a) a sacred place constitutes a break in homogeneity of space; (b) this break is symbolized by an opening by which passage from one cosmic region to another is made possible (from heaven to earth and vice versa; from earth to the underworld); (c) communication with heaven is expressed by one or another of certain images, all of which refer to the axis mundi: pillar, ladder, mountain, tree, vine, etc.; (d) around this cosmic axis lies the world (= our world), hence the axis is located 'in the middle,' at the navel of the earth'; it is the Center of the World." Mircea Eliade, *The Sacred and the Profane: The Nature of Religion* (Harcourt, 1959), 37.

30. Clevis Headley describes ego displacement as the key to efficacious ritual for persons in the African Diaspora because it leads to deeper connections with parts of self and world that are otherwise bracketed. He derives his theory of ego displacement from the religious cosmologies of the African Diaspora: "Ego reconciliation, ego repair, requires the displacing of the ego or rather the deflating of the ego through spiritually sanctioned rituals. Ego displacement essentially connects individuals to the world of spirit; it enables them to gain knowledge of their Okra, the ancestors and deities. The most convenient solution for the ego and what it excludes is for the ego to 'let go of its self-positing and centering activities and surrender to the correctives and directives of the deities and ancestors.' Contact with the spirit world requires a bracketing of the everyday ego, and this suspension of the everyday ego makes it possible for an individual to remain receptive to what is inaccessible through the senses." See Clevis Headley, "Egological Investigations: A Comparative Study of African Existentialism and Western Existentialism," *CLR James Journal* 10 (2004): 73–105.

31. For an analysis of ritual as a heroic endeavor, see Joseph Campbell, *The Hero with a Thousand Faces* (Bolligen Foundation, 1949).

32. See Victor Turner, "Liminality and Communitas," in *The Ritual Process: Structure and Anti-Structure* (Chicago: Aldine, 1969).

33. William James, *The Varieties of Religious Experience* (Longmans, Green and Co., 1902).

34. President Barack Obama notes in almost identical language in *Dreams from My Father* (New York: Broadway, 1995), "At least on the basketball court I could find a community of sorts, with an inner life all its own. It was there that I would make my closest white friends, on turf where blackness couldn't be a disadvantage." See Alexander Wolff, "The Audacity of Hoops: How Basketball Helped Shape Obama," *Sports Illustrated*, January 20, 2009.

35. Jung, *Psychology and Religion*; Fromm, *Psychoanalysis and Religion*; Erikson, *Young Man Luther*; McGuire, *Religion, the Social Context*; Murphy, *Reasoning and Rhetoric in Religion*; Pinn, *Varieties of African American Religious Experience*; Gathje and Oki Ahearn, *Doing Right and Being Good*.

36. See Schlauch, *Faithful Companioning*; Malidoma Some, *The Healing Wisdom of Africa* (Putnam, 1999); *Religion and Healing in America*, ed. Linda Barnes and Susan S. Sered (Oxford University Press, 2004).

37. Malidoma Some, *Ritual: Power, Healing and Community* (Penguin, 1997).

38. Some, *Ritual*.

39. DuBois, *The Souls of Black Folk*; Raboteau, *Slave Religion*; Charles H. Long, "Perspectives for a Study of Afro-American Religion in the United States," *History of Religions* 11 (1971): 54–66; Cornel West, *Race Matters* (Beacon Press, 1993); Anthony Pinn, *Terror and Triumph: The Nature of Black Religion* (Fortress Press, 2003).

40. DuBois, *The Souls of Black Folk*; Raboteau, *Slave Religion*; Long, "Perspectives for a Study"; West, *Race Matters*; Pinn, *Terror and Triumph*.

41. See Joseph Murphy, *Working the Spirit: Ceremonies of the African Diaspora* (Beacon Press, 1994); Dwayne Tunstall, "Africana Existential Philosophy of Education," *Philosophical Studies in Education* 39 (2008): 46–55; Headley, "Egological Investigations."

42. Some, *The Healing Wisdom of Africa*.

43. Schlauch, *Faithful Companioning*; Some, *The Healing Wisdom of Africa*.

44. Peter R. Gathje, "Teaching African American Religions as Learning to Resist Racism," in *Teaching African American Religions*, ed. Carolyn M. Jones and Theodore Louis Trost (Oxford Scholarship Online, 2006), 193–208.

Chapter Nineteen

"To Serve the Present Age": A Benediction

Emmett G. Price III

To serve the present age,
My calling to fulfill;
O may it all my powers engage
To do my Master's will!
—Charles Wesley [1]

We give thanks that over the centuries of systematic oppression, social ostracism, political disenfranchisement, and economic disparity, the displaced descendants of African soil never lost the hope of the fulfillment of faith. They were transported from the shores of the Gold Coast, through the oceans and seas, in exchange for gold and onto distant lands where the blazing golden sun watched as sons were robbed of mothers and daughters were robbed of fathers. Yet, they never lost the promise of your divine presence. In the midst of their suffering, they birthed the Black Church, an assemblage of expressions of faith, all connected by the reality of their displacement.

We thank you for the prophetic wisdom of our ancestors, who learned to tarry in the brush arbors and hush harbors where they "[Waded] in the Water" to "Steal Away" while awaiting the promised "Great Day." [2] Your grace and mercy kept us alive. Your distribution of giftedness and talents, along with angels and sympathetic Samaritans, gave us the strength to "sing your song in a strange land." [3]

When we couldn't understand what we did "To Be So Black and Blue," we danced, painted, sculpted, wrote plays, composed music, authored novels . . . with each building upon another as a collective prayer for freedom. [4] In those moments when we lost our direction, we sang "A Change Is Gonna Come" and danced "Revelations." [5] In our moments of frustration, we revisited our "Dream Deferred" and studied "Why the Caged Bird Sings."[6] We even assembled our artistic expressions to not only proclaim but also exclaim our breaking point through Hip Hop in "The Message."[7]

You heard our moans, groans, cries, wails, and guttural laments . . . you felt the urgency and intentionality of our musings . . . you understood our unique dancing, poetic metaphors, double entendres, and other creative devices that allowed our masked messages to reach you and only you when others deemed us intellectually inferior, incompatible, and incompetent.

Your omnipotent, omniscience, and sovereignty allowed us to receive the power of your presence and discard fear in exchange for truth and wisdom to feast on the fruits of your love. You have challenged us over the generations to be good stewards of your love, joy, peace, patience, kindness, goodness, faithfulness, gentleness, and self-control.[8] In times when we have failed (and there have been many), you granted us the possibility of repentance.

So it is in that reality of repentance that we invoke your presence over all your creation around the world and beyond. Help us, O Lord, to heed the words of your servant Isabella Baumfree, who challenged the church to not be so religious that we are no earthly good.[9] Help us, Dear Lord, to spread love, not hate; to seek your peace, not our war. Help us, O Lord, to nurture and develop our youth and not neglect and destroy them.

Help us, Dear Lord, to restore dignity, pride, honor, and the pursuit of righteousness in the hearts and minds of all of your children across the globe and beyond so that we will emerge blameless, courageous, and ready to receive your healing and reconciliation. Help us, O Lord, to understand the power of freedom and to realize that power in our local, regional, national, and global communities. Help us, Dear Lord, to be more vigilant toward the needs, concerns, and desires of all generations so that we will not repeat the errors of our collective pasts.

In the memory of all of the saints who dreamed of tomorrow's hope and lived for today's faith, we ask you to restore the justice, equality, liberty, and peace across the world and beyond—the same justice, equality, liberty, and peace that you once prepared in a garden called Eden.

This is our prayer for this present age.

Amen.

NOTES

1. The opening epigraph is the second verse to Charles Wesley's hymn "A Charge to Keep I Have," published in 1762. Wesley (1707–1788) is considered one of the great leaders of the Methodist movement, along with his older brother John. Charles composed lyrics to over six thousand published and unpublished hymns.

2. These three African American spirituals, as part of the Black Sacred Music tradition, remain exemplary songs of faith, courage, and hope centuries later. Although no author is credited for "Wade in the Water," numerous arrangements and recordings have been attributed to a number of individuals. Similarly, "Steal Away" (also referred to as "Steal Away to Jesus") has been documented without author, although recent research proposes that the author might be a Choctaw freedman named Wallace Willis (written before 1862); see Francis Banks's "Narrative" from *The WPA Oklahoma Slave Narratives*, edited by T. Lindsay Baker and Julie P. Baker (US Work Projects Administration) and published by the University of Oklahoma Press in 1996.

3. A reference to the question posed by exiles in Psalm 137:4 as they inquired of God how they might retain the power, presence, and proclamation of their faith through their traditional, indigenous songs so far away from home.

4. Often mislabeled as "Black and Blue," Louis Armstrong's 1955 composition was actually titled "What Did I Do to Be So Black and Blue," which, according to the lyrics, was a clear and personal commentary on racism in America during the 1950s.

5. "A Change Is Gonna Come" was written by Sam Cooke in 1963 and recorded on the RCA Victor label as a cry for the end to racism in the United States. The song would emerge as one of the great soundtracks of the Civil Rights Movement and subsequent freedom movements. "Revelations" refers to the most noted signature work by the Alvin Ailey Dance Theater. First produced on January 31, 1960, the choreographic work presents the sounds, sentiments, and movements of faith as a narrative from slavery to the present.

6. "Dream Deferred" is a reference to Langston Hughes's book-length suite of poems under the title *Montage of a Dream Deferred* (New York: Holt, 1951), which served as a post–World War II cry for justice, equality, and freedom not only for Harlem but for all Black communities suffering under the hand of oppression, hatred, and injustice. Maya Angelou's *I Know Why the Caged Bird Sings* (New York: Bantam, 1983) is a personal narrative of triumph and perseverance that served as a symbolic penchant for hope and possibility of ostracized and undervalued populations of people.

7. Featuring a hook that exclaims, "Don't push me 'cause I'm close to the edge, I'm tryin' not to lose my head," this Hip Hop classic by Grandmaster Flash and the Furious Five was recorded in 1982 on the Sugar Hill Records label and emerged as an early Hip Hop hit record.

8. These nine attributes of Christian Living are found in the Apostle Paul's letter to the Galatians in Galatians 5:22–23 in the Holy Bible.

9. Isabella Baumfree (circa 1797–1883) was best known as Sojourner Truth, the nineteenth-century emancipated slave who emerged as a leading abolitionist, suffragist, and woman's rights activist. Her famous quote "Religion without humanity is a poor human stuff" was quoted in *The Narrative of Sojourner Truth: A Bondswoman of Olden Time, Emancipated by the New York Legislature in the Early Part of the Present Century*, written by Olive Gilbert and Frances W. Titus and published in 1875. "A Memorial Chapter, Giving Particulars of Her Last Sickness and Death" was added in a 1883 publication of the book. The quote is found in the later addition within the added memorial chapter.

Selected Bibliography

Asante, M. K., Jr. *It's Bigger Than Hip-Hop: The Rise of the Post Hip-Hop Generation*. New York: St. Martin's Press, 2008.

Bolden, Rev. C. Nickerson. *Bridging the Gulf: Understanding and Ministering to Hip-Hop Youth*. Frederick, MD: PublishAmerica, 2008.

Boyd, Todd. *Am I Black Enough for You? Popular Culture from the 'Hood and Beyond*. Bloomington: Indiana University Press, 1997.

———. *The New H.N.I.C. (Head Niggas in Charge): The Death of Civil Rights and the Reign of Hip Hop*. New York: New York University Press, 2004.

Browne, Saideh Page. *Can Hip-Hop Be Holy?* GS Publishing Group, 2007.

Bynoe, Yvonne. *Encyclopedia of Rap and Hip Hop Culture*. Westport, CT: Greenwood Press, 2006.

———. *Stand and Deliver: Political Activism, Leadership, and Hip Hop Culture*. Brooklyn, NY: Soft Skull Press, 2004.

Carruthers, Iva E., Frederick D. Haynes III, and Jeremiah A. Wright Jr. *Blow the Trumpet in Zion: Global Vision and Action for the 21st-Century Black Church*. Minneapolis, MN: Fortress Press, 2005.

Chang, Jeff. *Can't Stop, Won't Stop: A History of the Hip-Hop Generation*. New York: St. Martin's Press, 2005.

Chuck D. *Fight the Power: Rap, Race, and Reality*. New York: Delacorte Press, 1997.

Cole, Johnnetta B., and Beverly Guy-Sheftall. *Gender Talk: The Struggle for Women's Equality in African American Communities*. New York: One World/Ballantine, 2003.

Coleman, Will. *Tribal Talk: Black Theology, Hermeneutics, and African/American Ways of "Telling the Story."* University Park: Penn State University Press, 1999.

Collins, Patricia Hill. *From Black Power to Hip-Hop: Racism, Nationalism, and Feminism*. Philadelphia: Temple University Press, 2006.

Cone, James H. *Black Theology and Black Power*. New York: Seabury Press, 1969.

Conyers, James L. *African American Jazz and Rap: Social and Philosophical Examinations of Black Expressive Behavior*. Jefferson, NC: McFarland, 2001.

Darby, Derrick, and Tommie Shelby, eds. *Hip-Hop and Philosophy: Rhyme 2 Reason*. Chicago: Open Court, 2005.

Dolce, Eric, J. *Jesus and Jigga: Where Hip Hop Meets Scripture*. Crown Oak Press, 2007.

Douglas, Kelly Brown. *The Black Christ*. Maryknoll, NY: Orbis Books, 1993.

Dyson, Michael Eric. *Between God and Gangsta Rap: Bearing Witness to Black Culture*. New York: Oxford University Press, 1996.

———. *Holler If You Hear Me: Searching For Tupac Shakur*. New York: Basic Civitas Books, 2001.

———. *Is Bill Cosby Right? Or Has the Black Middle Class Lost Its Mind?* New York: Basic Civitas Books, 2005.

———. *Race Rules: Navigating the Color Line*. New York: Vintage Books, 1997.

Elligan, Don. *Rap Therapy: A Practical Guide for Communicating with Youth and Young Adults Through Rap Music*. New York: Kensington, 2004.

Eure, Joseph D. *Nation Conscious Rap*. New York: PC International Press, 1991.

Floyd, Samuel A., Jr., ed. *The Power of Black Music: Interpreting Its History from Africa to the United States.* New York: Oxford University Press, 1995.

Forbes, Bruce, and Jeffrey Mahan. *Religion and Popular Culture in America.* Berkeley: University of California Press, 2005.

Forman, Murray. *The 'Hood Comes First: Race, Space, and Place in Rap and Hip Hop.* Middletown, CT: Wesleyan University Press, 2002.

Frazier, E. Franklin. *The Negro Church in America.* New York: Schocken Books, 1974.

Gee, Alex, and John Teter. *Jesus and the Hip-Hop Prophets: Spiritual Insights from Lauryn Hill and Tupac Shakur.* Downers Grove, IL: InterVarsity Press, 2003.

George, Nelson. *Hip Hop America.* New York: Viking, 1998.

Gibbs, Eddie. *ChurchNext: Quantum Changes in How We Do Ministry.* Downers Grove, IL: InterVarsity Press, 2000.

Gutierrez, Eric. *Disciples of the Streets: The Promise of a Hip Hop Church.* New York: Seabury Books, 2008.

Hinds, Selwyn Seyfu. *Gunshots in My Cook-Up: Bits and Bites from a Hip Hop Caribbean Life.* New York: Atria Books, 2002.

HipHopEMass.org. *The Hip Hop Prayer Book with Holy Bible Stories.* New York: Church Publishing, 2006.

Hodge, Daniel White. *The Soul of Hip Hop: Rims, Timbs and a Cultural Theology.* Downers Grove, IL: InterVarsity Press, 2010.

Howerton, Mike. *The Relevant Church: A New Vision for Communities of Faith.* Orlando, FL: Relevant Media Group, 2004.

Jackson, Robert, and James Williams. *The Last Black Mecca, Hip Hop: A Black Cultural Awareness Phenomena and Its Impact on the African American Community.* Chicago: Research Associates, 1994.

Keyes, Cheryl L. *Rap Music and Street Consciousness.* Urbana: University of Illinois Press, 2004.

Kirk-Duggan, Cheryl, and Marlon F. Hall. *Wake Up: Hip-Hop Christianity and the Black Church.* Nashville, TN: Abingdon Press, 2011.

Kitwana, Bakari. *The Hip-Hop Generation: Young Blacks and the Crisis in African American Culture.* New York: Basic Civitas Books, 2002.

———. *The Rap on Gangsta Rap: Who Run It? Gangsta Rap and Visions of Black Violence.* Chicago: Third World Press, 1994.

———. *Why White Kids Love Hip-Hop: Wankstas, Wiggers, Wannabes, and the Reality of Race in America.* New York: BasicCivitas Books, 2005.

Knight, Michael Muhammad. *The Five Percenters: Islam, Hip-Hop and the Gods of New York.* New York: Oneworld, 2008.

KRS-One. *The Gospel of Hip Hop: The First Instrument.* Brooklyn, NY: PowerHouse Books, 2009.

Kyllonen, Tommy (aka Urban D.). *Un.orthodox: Church, Hip-Hop, Culture.* Grand Rapids, MI: Zondervan, 2007.

Lewis, G. Craige. *The Truth behind Hip-Hop.* Longwood, FL: Xulon Press, 2009.

Lincoln, C. Eric. *The Black Church Since Frazier.* New York: Schocken Books, 1974.

Lincoln, C. Eric, and Lawrence H. Mamiya. *The Black Church in the African American Experience.* Durham, NC: Duke University Press, 1990.

Lynch, Gordon. *Understanding Theology and Popular Culture.* Hoboken, NJ: Wiley-Blackwell, 2005.

Madlock, Rev. Prell. *The Hip-Hop Kingdom Upclose and Revealed.* Longwood, FL: Xulon Press, 2010.

Mazur, Eric, and Kate McCarthy, eds. *God in the Details: American Religion in Popular Culture.* New York: Routledge, 2001.

McWhorter, John H. *All about the Beat: Why Hip-Hop Can't Save Black America.* New York: Gotham Books, 2008.

Mitchell, Henry H. *Black Church: The Long-Hidden Realities of the First Years.* Grand Rapids, MI: William B. Eerdmans, 2004.

Mitchell, Mykel. *WORD: For Everybody Who Thought Christianity Was for Suckas*. New York: NAL Trade, 2005.

Miyakawa, Felicia M. *Five Percenter Rap: God Hop's Music, Message, and Black Muslim Mission*. Bloomington: Indiana University Press, 2005.

Neal, Mark Anthony. *Songs in the Key of Black Life: A Rhythm and Blues Nation*. New York: Routledge, 2003.

———. *Soul Babies: Black Popular Culture and the Post-soul Aesthetic*. New York: Routledge, 2002.

Neal, Mark Anthony, and Murray Forman, eds. *That's the Joint! The Hip-Hop Studies Reader*. New York: Routledge, 2004.

Ogbar, Jeffrey Ogbonna Green. *Hip-Hop Revolution: The Politics of Rap*. Lawrence: University Press of Kansas, 2007.

Perry, Imani. *Prophets of the Hood: Politics and Poetics in Hip Hop*. Durham, NC: Duke University Press, 2004.

Pinn, Anthony B. *The Black Church in the Post–Civil Rights Era*. Maryknoll, NY: Orbis Books, 2002.

———. *Noise and Spirit: The Religious and Spiritual Sensibilities of Rap Music*. New York: New York University Press, 2003.

Pitts, Walter F., Jr. *Old Ship of Zion: The Afro-Baptist Ritual in the African Diaspora*. New York: Oxford University Press, 1993.

Pollard, Deborah Smith. *When the Church Becomes Your Party: Contemporary Gospel Music*. Detroit, MI: Wayne State University Press, 2008.

Pough, Gwendolyn D. *Check It While I Wreck It: Black Womanhood, Hip-Hop Culture, and the Public Sphere*. Boston: Northeastern University Press, 2004.

Price, Emmett G., III. *Hip Hop Culture*. Santa Barbara, CA: ABC-CLIO, 2006.

Price, Emmett G., III, Tammy L. Kernodle, and Horace J. Maxile. *Encyclopedia of African American Music*. Santa Barbara, CA: Greenwood, 2011.

Ramsey, Guthrie P. *Race Music: Black Cultures from Bebop to Hip-Hop*. Berkeley: University of California Press, 2003.

Reed, Teresa L. *The Holy Profane: Religion in Black Popular Music*. Lexington: University Press of Kentucky, 2003.

Robbins, Duffy. *This Way to Youth Ministry—Companion Guide: Readings, Case Studies, Resources to Begin the Journey*. Grand Rapids, MI: Zondervan, 2004.

Rose, Tricia. *Black Noise: Rap Music and Black Culture in Contemporary America*. Hanover, NH: Wesleyan University Press, 1994.

———. *The Hip Hop Wars: What We Talk about When We Talk about Hip-Hop*. New York: Basic Civitas Books, 2008.

Saunders, Rev. Joseph. *The Church in the Age of Hip Hop*. Ada, OK: Desktop Prepress Services, 2009.

Sekou, Rev. Osagyefo Uhuru. *Urban Souls*. St. Louis, MO: Urban Press, 2001.

Shomari, Hashim A. *From the Underground: Hip Hop Culture as an Agent of Social Change*. Fanwood, NJ: X-Factor, 1995.

Smith, Efrem, and Phil Jackson. *The Hip-Hop Church: Connecting with the Movement Shaping Our Culture*. Downers Grove, IL: InterVarsity Press, 2005.

Smitherman, Geneva. *Black Talk: Words and Phrases from the Hood to the Amen Corner*. Boston: Mariner Books, 1994.

Southern, Eileen. *The Music of Black Americans: A History*. 3rd ed. New York: Norton, 1997.

Spady, James G. *Street Conscious Rap*. Philadelphia: Black History Museum, UMUM/LOH Pub., 1999.

Spencer, Jon Michael. *The Emergency of Black and the Emergence of Rap*. Durham, NC: Duke University Press, 1991.

Stephens, Benjamin, III, and Ralph C. Watkins. *From Jay-Z to Jesus: Reaching and Teaching Young Adults in the Black Church*. Valley Forge, PA: Judson Press, 2009.

Sylan, Robin. *Traces of the Spirit: The Religious Dimensions of Popular Music*. New York: New York University Press, 2002.

Trent, Rev. Earl D., Jr. *A Challenge to the Black Church*. Chicago: African American Images, 2004.

Watkins, Ralph C. *The Gospel Remix: Reaching the Hip Hop Generation*. Valley Forge, PA: Judson Press, 2006.

Watkins, S. Craig. *Hip Hop Matters: Politics, Pop Culture, and the Struggle for the Soul of a Movement*. Boston: Beacon Press, 2005.

———. *Representing: Hip Hop Culture and the Production of Black Cinema*. Chicago: University of Chicago Press, 1999.

West, Cornel. *Race Matters*. New York: Vintage Books, 1994.

Whalum, Dr. Kenneth T., Jr. *Hip-Hop Is Not Our Enemy!* Bloomington, IN: AuthorHouse, 2010.

Williams, Saul. *The Dead Emcee Scrolls: The Lost Teachings of Hip-Hop*. New York: MTV Press, 2006.

Wilson, Claudia Marie. *Hip Hop Church: A Study in Liturgical Inculturation*. Evanston, IL: Seabury-Western Theological Seminary, 2006.

Woodson, Carter G. *The History of the Negro Church*. Washington, DC: Associated Publishers, 1990.

Index

2 Live Crew, 39, 42n1
"9MM", 160
50 Cent, 72, 108, 121
50 Cent and G Unit, 9

A-1 Swift, 116
African American Episcopal
    Denomination, xi, xiii
African American Episcopal Zion, xi
African Episcopal Church of St. Thomas,
    xiii
The African Peoples Party, 6
AIDS, 18, 43
Ali, Muhammad, 7
Allen, Bishop Richard, xiii
AllHipHop.com, 72, 80n19
Ambassador, 41. *See also* Cross Movement
Anderson, Elijah, 142
Angelou, Maya, 7
Apostolic Assemblies, xi. *See also* The
    Black Church, Denominations of
Ashanti, 120

Bad Boy Records, 39, 68
Badu, Erykah, 8
Baker, Ella, 6
Baltimore, MD, 48
Bang Theory, 117
Banks, Lloyd, 69
Banner, David, 160
Baptist, 95
Baraka, Amiri, 7
Barr, Jason A., Jr., xv
Basketball, 173, 175, 177, 178, 179, 180,
    181, 182, 185n18
Baumfree, Isabella. *See* Sojourner Truth
Beal, Francis, 6

"Beamer, Benz or Bentley", 69
Beastie Boys, 36
Belt, Cynthia B., xvii, 205
Bertha, Mase, 9, 39, 41, 108
Bethel African Methodist Episcopal, xiii
Bevel, James, 5
B. G., 87
Beyoncé, 70, 79n11
Bible, 43, 44, 50, 81, 108, 118, 119, 121,
    122, 123, 126, 128, 153, 172
"Bible Break", 108, 111n2
Big Daddy Kane, 36
Biggie Smalls, 8, 21, 39, 40, 81, 107
Birdman, 69
Biz Markie, 55
Black Arts Movement, 132
"Black Belt", 3
Black/Blackness, xii
"Black, Brown and Beige". *See* Ellington,
    Duke
The Black Church, xi, xv, xvi–xiii, 21, 22,
    23, 28n9, 33, 41, 43, 45, 47, 49, 50, 53,
    55–56, 59, 67, 73–76, 77–78, 95, 108,
    109, 110, 112, 138, 154, 155, 159, 161,
    162, 189; Afro-European Church, 95,
    96–99; Denominations of, xi; Dialogue
    with Hip Hop Culture, xvii; Economic
    Influence, xi, 19, 15; History of, xi, xii,
    xiii; In Denial, 15–20; Mission of, xi,
    xv, 22; Political Power, xi, 16;
    Prophetic Role of, xv; Prosperity
    Preaching, 15, 19; Spiritual Influence,
    xi, 16, 22
The Black Community, xi, xii, xiv, 9, 10,
    11, 15, 16, 16–17, 19, 20, 22, 23, 180,
    182
The Black Eyed Peas, 21

Black Freedom Struggle, xvi, 3, 21, 22, 24
Black Is, Black Ain't. See Riggs, Marlon
Black Liberation Army, 6
Black Panther Party, 6, 9, 48
The Black Panther Party for Self Defense.
    See Black Panther Party
Black Popular Music, 55, 57
Black Power, 6, 7, 8
Black Sacred Music, 78
Black Studies, 7
Black Women's Liberation Committee, 6
Black Women's United Front, 6
"Blasphemy", 49, 50, 51, 52, 54n24
Blige, Mary J., 8
"Bling Bling", xvii, 55, 86–93
Blow, Kurtis, 10
Blues, 3, 25, 61, 108
Bone Thugs-n-Harmony, 47, 111n1
Boogie Down Productions, 42n7, 107, 110,
    111n8, 112n31
"Booty Work", 71, 79n14
Boston, MA, 125
Boyd, Todd, 13n9
Brand Nubian, 10, 55
Bronx (South), 109, 110
Brooks, Gwendolyn, 7
Brown, Chris, 69, 72
Brown, Elaine, 6
Brown, James, 7
Brown vs. Topeka Board of Education, xiv,
    23, 158n4
Bryant, Jamal-Harrison, xv
Buddhism, xiv, 36
Bullins, Ed, 7
Butts, Rev. Calvin, 107, 108, 109

Cantrell, Blu, 87, 93n3
Carey, Mariah, 71, 80n18
Carmichael, Stokely, 6
Carter-Hilliard, Francis, 6
Catholicism (Catholic), xvii, 95, 96,
    98–100, 103n7
"A Change Is Gonna Come", 189, 191n5
Chicago, IL, 125, 132
Christ Tabernacle, 121
Christian Methodist Episcopal, xi
Christian Rap, 35–36, 36, 37, 38, 38, 40,
    41, 108–109, 116, 119, 120, 120, 121,
    122, 125–127

Christianity (Christian), 22, 28n12, 33, 34,
    35–36, 37, 38, 39, 40, 41, 49, 85, 86,
    107, 110, 118, 119, 116, 123, 124, 127,
    135, 138, 146, 165, 169, 180
Chuck D., 8, 107
Church of Christ (Holiness), xi. *See also*
    The Black Church, Denominations of
Church of God in Christ, xi, 155. *See also*
    The Black Church, Denominations of
Civil Rights Generation, xiv, xv, xvi, 9, 16,
    17, 19, 22, 23, 154
Civil Rights Movement, 5, 7, 9, 10, 16, 18,
    19, 21–22, 23
Clark, Septima, 6
Clarke, John Henrik, 7
Cleaver, Eldridge, 6
CMCs, 116
Collins, Patricia Hill, 8, 13n10, 70, 79n12
Coltrane, John, 7
Common, 8, 71
Cone, James, 46, 50, 54n9
Contemporary Missions, 131
Cook, Susan Johnson, 76
Cosby, Bill, xiv, 56, 57, 59, 155, 158n4
"Cradle to the Grave", 49, 52, 54n21
Criminal Minded, 107, 111n8
Cross Movement, 36, 41, 109, 115, 128n1
Crossover Community Church, 109,
    112n24
"Tha Crossroads", 111n1, 116
Cultural Awareness, xiv
Cunningham, Shaundra, xvii, 205
Curtis, William H., xv

Dallas, TX, 109
Daniel, Ron, 154
Dash, Damon, 40
Davis, Angela, 6
De La Soul, 8, 107
Dead Prez, 8
Dean, Minister David, 110, 112n30
Delany, Martin, 23
Destiny's Child, 8, 10
Detroit, MI, 116, 132
Detroit Revolutionary Union Movement, 6
"Diamonds and Girls", 160, 163n5
Diop, Cheik Anta, 7
DJ Lady Grace, 158n3
DMX, 108

Dollar, Rev. Creflo, 108
Dorsey Thomas, 55, 60, 61n1, 108
Down with the King, 109
Drake, St. Clair, 157
DuBois, W. E. B., xiii, 175, 184n10
Dunbar, Paul Laurence, xii
Dupri, Jermaine, 10
Dynamic Twins, 13.5
Dyson, Michael Eric, xiv, 13n6, 45, 54n7, 57, 61n7, 74, 154, 158n4

El-Shabazz, El-Hajj Malik. *See* Malcolm X
Elligan, Don, 125, 129n15
Elliott, Missy, 8
Ellington, Duke, xii
Episcopal, xiii, xvii, 95, 96, 97
Eric B., 36
"Ethiopia Awakening". *See* Fuller, Meta Warrick
Ethnic Studies, 7
Evangelism, 36, 109
Evans, Faith, 10
Evans, Mari, 7
Eve, 8
Evers, Medgar, 6
Evers, Myrlie, 6
EX Ministries. *See* Lewis, Elder G. Craige

Fanon, Franz, 7
February 1st Movement, 6
Fiasco, Lupe, 71
"fight the power", 6
Finley, Stephen C., xvii, 205
Fitzgerald, Ella, 170
Five Percent Nations of Gods and Earths, xi, xiv, 28n9, 33, 36, 107, 111n5
Flavor Alliance, 117
Flavor Fest, 109
"For My People". *See* Walker, Margaret
Franklin, Aretha, 7
Free African Society, xi, xiii
Fuller, Meta Warrick, xii

The Game, 160, 163n4
Garvey, Marcus, 23
Gates, Henry Louis, Jr., 25, 29n14
Gaye, Marvin, 7
Generation X, 49

Generational Divide, xiii–xiv, 16, 17, 18, 19, 21; Dilemma of, xv, xvi, 22, 23
Get Real, 108
"getting rich or die trying", 19, 20n2
Gilroy, Paul, 107, 111n4
Giovanni, Nikki, 7
god, 67–78, 161
God, xi, 4, 19, 23, 34, 40, 41, 43, 43–44, 49, 50, 51, 52, 53, 64, 66, 67, 73–74, 85–86, 88, 89–92, 115, 116, 118, 119, 120, 121, 122, 123, 125, 126, 126–128, 134, 141, 153, 165, 167, 169, 170, 171, 172
Good News, 36
"Gold Digger", 11
Gordon, Sherman A., xvii, 205
The Gospel, 115, 123, 124, 131, 134, 135, 136, 137, 143–144, 145, 146, 165, 171, 172
Gospel Gangstaz, 116
Gospel Hip Hop, xiv, 108, 109, 110
Gospel Music, 3, 55, 108, 124
Gospel Rap, xviii, xiv, 33, 36, 37
Grandmaster Flash and the Furious Five, 58, 61n11
"Great Day", 189
Green, Al, 10
Grits, 37

Hamer, Fannie Lou, 6
Hamilton, Anthony, 8, 11
Hampton Ministers' Conference, 76
Hansberry, Lorraine, 21, 26, 28n2, 29n15
Harding, Vincent, 3, 13n3
Harlem Renaissance, 21
Harvard Divinity School, 155, 156
Hawkins, Tremaine, 108
HCBUs. *See* Historically Black Colleges and Universities
"Heartless", 71
Herring, Bobby, 124
Hill, Lauryn, 8, 72, 107
Hilliard, David, 6
Hip Hop Action Network, 11
Hip Hop Christology, 109
Hip Hop Church, 109
The Hip Hop Church, 109, 112n26
Hip Hop Community, xiv, xv, 108, 121, 161

Hip Hop Culture, xi, xiv, xv, xvi, xvii, xv,
    xvi, xviii, 8, 8–13, 21, 24, 33, 36, 37,
    38, 40, 40–41, 43, 44, 55, 56–61, 68,
    77–78, 81, 87, 95, 102, 107–108, 109,
    110, 115, 118, 121, 122, 125, 132, 154,
    155, 156, 157, 189, 159, 160, 161, 165,
    166; Aesthetics of, 108; Breakdancers/
    B-Boys & B-Girls, xiv, 8, 33;
    Conscious Rappers, 35; As a Cultural
    Movement, 25–26, 33; Dialogue with
    the Black Church, xvii; DJs, xiv, 8;
    Gangsta Rappers, 35, 37, 46, 109, 132;
    Graffiti, xiv; History of, xiv, 38;
    International Phenomenon, xv; Mission
    of, xv; Music of, 107, 131, 132, 159,
    165; Rappers/ MCs, xiv, 8, 33, 35, 36,
    36–37, 38, 39, 40, 82; Spirituality
    within, xiv, xv, 9
Hip Hop Generation, ix, xiv, xv, xvi, 3, 9,
    16, 23, 24, 59, 95, 102, 154, 155, 161,
    162, 170; Interaction with Civil Rights
    Generation, 17–18
Hip Hop Matrix, xviii, 132, 165
Hip Hop Prophecies, 161
Hip Hop "Straw Man", 56, 61
The Hip Hop Wars, 69, 79n7
Historically Black Colleges and
    Universities, xiv, 3
Holy Hip Hop, 115–116, 117, 118, 119,
    120, 122, 125–126, 165, 169
Hollywood, CA, 133
Holy Hip Hop Movement, xviii, xiv, 35,
    116
"Holy Horsepower", 121
Holy Rollerz Christian Car Club, 121,
    128n7
Holy Scripture, 36
Holy Spirit, 44, 123, 125, 145, 171
Homophobia, 12, 55, 58, 59, 60, 61, 74–75,
    77
Hopkins, Dwight N., 141, 149n22
Howard, Charles L., xvii, 206
Hughes, Langston, 21, 28n1
Huggins, Erika, 6
Hurston, Zora Neal, xii, 78, 80n30
Hutchinson, Joshua, xvi, 206
"I am that I am", 115, 128n1
"I Get Money", 69

Ice Cube, 107, 153, 157n1
I.D.O.L. King, 116, 117, 128n2
"I'm spiritual but I'm not religious", 9
Impressions, 7
In Dedication of Curtis King. *See* I.D.O.L
    King; Dyson, Michael Eric
Islam, xiv, 10, 33, 36, 41, 107, 135,
    140–141
Isley Brothers, 6

Jackson, Mahalia, 13n6
Jadakiss, 11, 13n13
James, Rick, 38
Jay, B. B., 37, 41
Jay Z, 10, 11, 58, 71, 79n13
Jazz, 3, 25
J. D., 87, 93n4
Jesus Christ, xvii, 23, 36–37, 38–39, 40,
    45, 47, 49–50, 53, 55, 91, 115, 116,
    117, 118, 119, 120, 121, 123, 126–128,
    144, 161, 167, 168, 169, 170, 171
"Jesus Walks", 10, 40, 41, 42n14, 108, 123
Johnson, Kenneth D., xviii, 206
Jones, Bishop Absalom, xiii, 103n6
Jones, Sarah, 8
Jordan, June, 7
Jordan, Montell, 87, 93n2
Judaism, xiv, 36, 167, 169
"Juicy", 21, 28n6

Kardinal Offishall, 8
Ken, Thomas, ix, xn1
Kenyatta, Jomo, 6
Kerygma, 131, 134, 144
Keys, Alicia, 8, 40
Kid 'n Play, 39
King, Coretta Scott, 6
King, Rev. Dr. Martin Luther, Jr., xiii, 5, 6,
    13n4, 21, 28n4, 41, 47, 52
Kitwana, Bakari, 10, 13n9
Knight, Carolyn Ann, 75
KRS-One, 8, 36, 39, 107, 110
Kweli, Talib, 8, 71
Kyllonen, Pastor Tommy, 109, 112n25,
    116

Lamp Mode Recordings, 117
Latifah, Queen, 8, 10
Lawrence, Donal, 10

Lawrence, Jacob, xii
Lawson, James, 5
Last Poets, 7
League of Revolutionary Black Workers, 6
Lee, Jarena, 75
Legend, John, 8
Lesesne, Kathleen, 6
Lewis, Elder G. Craige, xv, 41, 42n16,
    61n6, 110, 117, 118, 118–123, 128n4,
    129n11
Lewis, John, 5
Lil' Kim, 68
LL Cool J, 10, 109
"Look at Me Now", 69
"Lord Live within My Heart", 107
Los Angeles, CA, 132
LPG, 116
Lumumba, Patrice, 6
Luthern, xvii, 95, 96, 97, 103n5

Maafa, 4
Madhubuti, Haki, 7
Malcolm X, xiii, 6, 47, 52
Mark J, 116

Bob Marley and the Wailers, 7

Martin, Lerone A., xvii, 206
Mary, Mary, 10
Mashego, Shana, xvii, 206
Master P, 10, 11
Maxwell, 8
MC Hammer, 38, 42n10, 69, 79n6, 108,
    111n9
MC Lyte, 8
MC Shan, 110
McDaniels, Darryl, 109
McKenzie, Vashti, 75
Memphis, TN, 132
"The Message", 189
Methodism (Methodist), xvii, 95, 96, 101,
    102
"Migration Series". *See* Lawrence, Jacob
Million Man March, 8
Minneaoplis, MN, 132
misogyny, 12, 14n17, 55, 58, 60, 61, 133
"Money, Power & Respect", 68
Moody, Anne, 5
Moore, Jessica Care, 8

Moore, Queen Mother Audley, 6
Morgan, Joan, 13n10
Mos Def, 8, 107
Moses, Bob, 5
Moss, Otis, III, xv, 80n25
Mt. Zion Baptist Church, 154
Much Luv Records, 117, 124

NAACP. *See* National Association for the
    Advancement of Colored People
Nas, 8, 107
Nash, Diane, 5
Nation of Islam, xi, xiii, 28n9, 33, 107
National Association for the Advancement
    of Colored People (NAACP), xiv
National Baptist Convention of America,
    Inc., xi
National Baptist Convention of America,
    Inc. (USA), xi, xiii
National Black Catholic Congress, xi
National Hip Hop Political Convention,
    156, 157n2
NBA/WNBA, 10, 13n11
NdegéOcello, Me'Shell, 8
Neal, Mark Anthony, 13n9, 61n14
Nelly, 10, 12
Never Scared, 69
New Breed, 116
New York, NY, 133
Newark, NJ, 154
Newton, Huey, 6
Nkrumah, Kwame, 6
Nopi Nationals, 121, 129n9
Notorious BIG. *See* Biggie Smalls
NWA, 55, 132
Nyerere, Julius 6

O' Jays, 7
"Once Upon A Time", 87, 93n2
Organization for African Unity, xiii
Outkast, 108
"Over Here Hustling", 160, 163n3

P. Diddy, 10, 11, 71
Parks, Rosa, 6
Peace, Michael, 109, 116
Pentecostal Assemblies, xi. *See also* The
    Black Church, Denominations of
Perry, Imani, 10, 13n8, 108, 111n11

Philadelphia, PA, 40, 109, 132
PID. *See* Preachers in Disguise
Pinn, Anthony, xv, 37, 38, 42n8, 183n5
Pollard, Alton B., III, xvi, 207
Poor Righteous Teachers, 10
Popular Music, 55
"Praise God from Whom All Blessings
    Flow", ix, xn1
"Pray", 42n10
Prayer, 126
Preachers in Disguise, 109, 116
Presbyterian, xvii, 95, 96, 97, 101, 102
Price, Emmett G., III, xvi, xviii, 205,
    158n3, 172n1
Prime Minister, 116
Progressive National Baptist Convention,
    Inc., xi, xiii. *See also* The Black
    Church, Denominations of
Public Enemy, 6, 55, 83
Pugh, Gwendolyn, 13n10
"Put You on the Game, 160, 163n4

Queens, NY, 121

R&B, 3, 25, 40, 108, 120, 124, 132, 159
Ra, Sun, 7
Racism, 8, 159
Rakim, 107
A Raisin in the Sun, 21, 22, 28n2, 29n15
Rap Fest, 109
Rap Music, 45, 46, 47, 108, 115, 119, 122,
    132, 159, 160
"Rapper's Delight", 108, 111n14
The Rapsures, 109
Rastafarian, xiv
Reach Records, 117
Reganomics, 23, 28n13
Religion, 51, 82, 173, 182, 183n5; Black
    Religion, 15
Remnant Militia, 116
The Republic of New Africa, 6
Rev. Run, 10, 39, 41, 109
"Revelations", 189, 191n5
Rhymes, Busta, 107
Riggs, Marlon, xii
Rivers, Eugene F., III, 138, 149n26
Robinson, Jo Ann, 6
Robinson, Sylvia, 34
Roc, Elle, 116

Roc-a-Fella, 40
Rochester, René, xviii, 207
Rock, Chris, 69, 79n8
Rock Music, 35
Rodney, Walter, 7
Rodriguez, Danny "D-Boy", 109, 112n21,
    116
Rogers, Carolyn, 7
Roots, 8
Rose, Tricia, 13n10, 69, 79n7
Run DMC, 10, 39, 109, 111n19

Salaam, Kalamu ya, 7
Salt-n-Pepa, 8, 124, 125
The Salt-n-Pepa Show, 124, 125, 129n13
Sanchez, Sonia, 7
SANE. *See* Saving a Nation Endangered
    Church International
Saving a Nation Endangered Church
    International, 9
Scarface, 107
Scott, Jill, 8
Scott, Paul, xvii, 207
Scott-Heron, Gill, 7
Sekou, Osagyefo Uhuru, xviii, 207
"Self-Destruction", 21, 28n5
Sexist, 12
S.F.C., 116
Shabazz, Betty, 6
Shakur, Assata, 6
Shakur, Tupac, 8, 43, 46, 47–48, 49–53,
    107, 133, 147n6
Sharrieff, Maryam, 158n3
Shrine of the Black Madonna, 6
Simmons, Russell, 11
Simone, Nina, 7
"Single Ladies", 70
Sister Souljah, 8
Slavery, xi, 4, 82, 173
Smith, Ruby Doris, 5
Smith, Will, 35
SNCC. *See* Student Non-Violent
    Coordinating Committee
Snoop Dogg, 38, 87, 93n4
"So Blue", 87
"So Many Tears", 49, 50, 51, 52
Soldiers for Christ. *See* SFC
"Son of the King", 108
"Song Cry", 71, 79n13

Sorett, Josef, xvii, 208, 158n3
Soul, 25, 132
Soul Generation, 3
Spelman College, 3, 13n1
"spiritual but not religious", 154, 155
Spiritually Minded, 107, 111n8
Spirituals, 3, 25, 48, 54n5
St. George's Methodist Church, xiii
St. Louis, MO, 153
Straight Outta Compton, 132
"Steal Away", 189, 191n2
Stephens, Benjamin, III, xv
Stewart, Gina Marcia, 76
Student Non-Violent Coordinating
    Committee, 6, 28n4
Sunni (Islam), 107
"Super Stars", 115, 128n1
Sweet Honey in the Rock, 7

T. Bone, 37, 116
T. Pain, 71, 79n14
Temple of Hip Hop, 107
Texas Holy Hip hop Awards, 124, 129n12
Tharpe, Rosetta, 55
"Their Eyes Were Watching God". *See*
    Hurston, Zora Neal
Thornton, Cassandra, xviii, 208. *See also*
    DJ Lady Grace
Thug Life, 131, 133–146, 147n3, 148n11
Thug Nation, 50
"Tip Drill", 12
"To Be So Black and Blue", 189, 191n4
"Today was a good day", 153, 157n1
Tongues, Native, 107
Touré, Askia Muhammad, 7
Touré, Sékou, 6
Tre9. *See* Herring, Bobby
A Tribe Called Qwest, 8, 107
Trick Daddy, 107
Trina, 35
Trinitarian Protestant Thought, xiv
Truth, Sojourner, 23, 75, 190, 191n9
The Truth behind Hip-Hop, xv
Tubman, Harriet, 23
Tucker, C. Delores, 56
Turner, Nat, 23

United Holy Church, xi. *See also* The
    Black Church, Denominations of

United House of Prayer for All People, xi.
    See also The Black Church,
    Denominations of
Urban Gospel Alliance, 116
Urban Disciple. *See* Kyllonen, Pastor
    Tommy
Usher, 10

Vessey, Denmark, 23

"Wade in the Water", 189, 191n2
Walker, Margaret, xii, 7
Washington, Booker T., xiii
Watkins, Ralph C., xv, 80n25
Wayne, Lil, 160, 163n3
"We Wear the Mask". *See* Dunbar, Paul
    Laurence
Weems, Renita, 75
Wesley, Charles, 189, 190n1
West, Cornell, 46, 54n4, 61n2, 76, 139,
    141, 148n17
West, Kanye, 8, 10, 11, 14n15, 38, 40,
    42n13, 71, 108, 111n10, 122, 123
"Where Is the Love?", 21, 28n7
White-Hammond, Mariama, 158n3
"Why", 11, 13n13
Why the Caged Bird Sings, 189, 191n6
Wiley, Stephen, 108, 109, 111n2, 116
Williams, Chancellor, 7
Williams, Michelle, 10
"The Wobble", 72, 80n21
Women's Studies, 7
Wonder, Stevie, 7
Woodbine, Onaje X. Offley, xviii, 208
"Words of Wisdom", 49, 52, 54n23
Wynn, Prathia Hall, 5, 21, 28n4, 75

X-Clan, 107, 111n7

Younger, Beneatha, 22, 22–23, 24–25,
    28n3
Younger, Lena, 22, 23, 25, 28n3
Younger, Travis, 26, 28n3
Younger, Walter Lee, 22, 24–25, 26–27,
    28n3
Youth Culture, 136–140
Yuinon, 116, 117, 125

About the Editor and Contributors

Emmett G. Price III, PhD, is chair of the Department of African American Studies and associate professor of music and African American studies at Northeastern University in Boston. He is author of *Hip Hop Culture* (2006) and executive editor of the *Encyclopedia of African American Music* (2011). A widely sought-after lecturer, consultant, and preacher, he is one of the leading authorities on music of the African Diaspora, the Black Church, and bridging the generational divide. The acclaimed musician and ordained minister is president and founder of the Black Church Music Ministry Project.

Cynthia B. Belt, DMin, is pastor of Centennial Caroline Street United Methodist Church, Baltimore, Maryland. She is adjunct professor of preaching and worship at Wesley Theological Seminary and a member of the board of directors for *Precious Times* magazine. Her writings can be found in *Sister to Sister* (volume 2), *God's Promises for Women of Color*, and *The Women of Color Study Bible*.

Shaundra Cunningham is an ordained National Baptist Minister who grew up as a military kid and lived all over, but South Carolina is home. She received a BS from the University of South Carolina and an MDiv from Harvard Divinity School.

Stephen C. Finley, MDiv, PhD, is assistant professor of African American religion at Louisiana State University. Jointly appointed in the departments of philosophy and religious studies and African and African American studies, Dr. Finley researches the Black Church, the Nation of Islam, and issues such as embodiment, gender, and sexuality. He is the associate editor of the *Encyclopedia of African American Religious Cultures* (2009), associate editor of *Journal of Men, Masculinities and Spiritualities*, and author of numerous journal articles, book chapters, encyclopedia essays, and book reviews.

Sherman A. Gordon, DMin, is the founding senior pastor of the Family of Faith Christian Center on the campus of California State University, Dominguez Hills. Dr. Gordon is the former pastor and founder of the New Philadelphia A.M.E. Church in Rancho Dominguez, California. Under his dynamic leadership, New Philadelphia grew exponentially and became one of the fastest-growing churches nationally. Dr. Gordon was recognized in *The African American Pulpit* as one of "20 to watch," and *Ebony* magazine referred to Dr. Gordon as one of the "young leaders of the future."

Charles L. Howard, MDiv, PhD, is the university chaplain at the University of Pennsylvania, his alma mater. He is the author of several articles and chapters, and his writings have been featured in such publications as *Black Arts Quarterly*, *Black Theology: An International Journal*, and *The Huffington Post*, where he is a regular contributor. He is also the editor of *The Souls of Poor Folk* (2007), an essay collection and multimedia project raising awareness about poverty. Dr. Howard has spoken and preached in houses of worship and schools around the country on topics such as poverty, spirituality, Hip Hop, and Black history.

Joshua Hutchinson is a freelance writer and native of Atlanta, Georgia.

Kenneth D. Johnson is an independent scholar and consultant to nonprofits, having previously served as a field education supervisor at Harvard Divinity School and as executive director of the Ella J. Baker House in Boston. He has worked with churches and community groups supporting restorative justice, the improved status of disadvantaged African American youths, ex-prisoner reentry, and the relief of AIDS orphans in sub-Saharan Africa. He currently works in the Environmental Division of the City of Sunnyvale, California, for the protection of urban water resources.

Patricia Lesesne is a former high school social sciences instructor and an ordained minister. She is the program manager of Mentoring Tomorrow's Leaders, a dropout prevention, educational re-engagement, and student leadership project of the Student Services Department, Broward County Public Schools. Mentoring Tomorrow's Leaders is funded by a five-year, $4.5-million US Department of Education High School Graduation Initiative Grant. Reverend Lesesne received her bachelor's degree from Harvard University, where she concentrated in social science, and a master of arts in teaching from Tufts University, where her concentration was secondary social studies education. She lives in Ft. Lauderdale with her daughter.

Lerone A. Martin, MDiv, PhD, is assistant professor of American religious history and culture at Eden Theological Seminary. His research interests include history of nineteenth- and twentieth-century American religion and culture and African American cultural practices. He is a licensed minister with the Church of God, Anderson, Indiana, and sits on the National Circle of Ministry Council for the Church of God. Dr. Martin's commentary and writing have appeared in such popular media outlets as *CNN*, the *Atlanta Journal Constitution*, *Religious Dispatches*, and *Charisma*.

Shana Mashego, DMA, is a faculty member in the Department of Music at her alma mater Texas Southern University, where she received her master's and bachelor of arts in music. She earned her doctor of musical arts in ethnomusicology and vocal performance at the University of Arizona. Dr.

Mashego's research contributions include the music of the African American church, the African American female classical composer, and the music traditions of historically Black colleges and universities.

Alton B. Pollard III, PhD, is dean of the Howard University School of Divinity. His research spans the areas of African American religion and culture, sociology of the Black Church, southern African studies, pan-Africanist religious thought, American religious cultures, and sociology of religion. He is the author of *Mysticism and Social Change* and a new introduction to W. E. B. DuBois's *The Negro Church*; editor of *Black Church Studies: An Interdisciplinary Anthology* (forthcoming) and *How Long This Road: Race, Religion and the Legacy of C. Eric Lincoln*, with L. Henry Whelchel; consulting editor of the multivolume Howard Thurman Papers Project *The Sound of the Genuine*; coauthor of the Balm in Gilead's Helpers for a Healing Community: A Pastoral Care Manual for HIV/AIDS (online); and former associate editor of the *Black Sacred Music* journal.

René Rochester, EdD, is the CEO and founder of Urban SET and PHAT STAR Learning. She is a former national advisor of community collaboration to the president of Youth for Christ USA. As a published author, speaker, trainer, and workshop facilitator, she is a child adolescent health specialist, and her primary topics include cultural diversity in education, community collaboration, and partnerships in education and ministry to the whole person: spirit, body, and soul.

Paul Scott (aka "Truth Minista") is the founder of the Messianic Afrikan Nation, based in Durham, North Carolina, and a prolific writer, well-known activist, lecturer, and media expert on rap, race, religion, and revolution. The former ordained Baptist minister has been a guest on *Hannity and Colmes* (FOX News), *Nachman* (MSNBC), *Hot 97* (New York), *Newstalk 1010* (Toronto), *SAfm* (South Africa), *Mo in the Midday* (WVON, Chicago), and many other national and international media outlets.

Osagyefo Uhuru Sekou is considered one of the foremost religious leaders of his generation. Reverend Sekou is the founding national coordinator for Clergy and Laity Concerned about Iraq and founded the Interfaith Worker Justice Center for New Orleans. Recognizing his distinguished work as a public scholar, the Institute for Policy Studies—the United States' oldest multi-issue progressive think tank in Washington, DC—appointed Reverend Sekou as the first associate fellow in religion and justice in July 2006. He authored the critically acclaimed *urbansouls*, which takes a refreshing approach to the spiritual crisis in America. Reverend Sekou was awarded a writing fellowship by Catholics for Free Choice and spent time in Paris writing his forthcoming book, *Gods, Gays, and Guns: Essays on Religion and the Crisis in American Democracy*.

Josef Sorett, PhD, is an assistant professor of religion and African American studies at Columbia University and an elder in the African Methodist Episcopal Church. He is an interdisciplinary historian of religion in America, with a focus on Black communities and cultures in the United States. His research and teaching interests include American religious history, African American religions, Hip Hop, popular culture and the arts, gender and sexuality, and the role of religion in public life. His work has been published in *The African American Pulpit, Callaloo, Culture and Religion, Journal of Scientific Study of Religion, PNEUMA: Journal of Society for Pentecostal Studies*, and *Religious Studies Review*.

Cassandra "DJ Lady Grace" Thornton is a mobile DJ, promoter, freelance writer, and evangelist deeply steeped within Hip Hop culture. She is a member of the Yuinon and a chapter representative of the Urban Gospel Alliance. She frequently speaks on the validity of Holy Hip Hop and raising awareness on its potential as a tool for evangelism.

Onaje X. Offley Woodbine is a doctoral candidate in psychology of religion, specializing in African and African American religious thought. He received his BA in philosophy from Yale University and his MA in theological studies from Boston University's School of Theology. Recently, he served as African Diaspora Scholar in Residence for the Project on African American Religious Research and Education at the School of Theology and was awarded a Fulbright-Hays Scholarship Abroad to study language, religion, and culture in Nigeria, West Africa. Currently, his research interests center on the role of religion in historically disenfranchised African American communities severely impacted by cultural trauma.